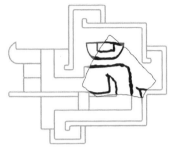

Prehistoric Settlement Patterns in the Upper Huallaga Basin, Peru

Distributed by Yale University Press
NEW HAVEN AND LONDON

For quantity purchases or a complete list of available titles in this series visit
www.yalebooks.com or yalebooks.co.uk

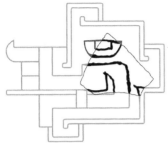

Prehistoric Settlement Patterns in the Upper Huallaga Basin, Peru

Yuichi Matsumoto

NUMBER 95

Published by
the Yale University Department of Anthropology
and the Yale Peabody Museum of Natural History

Distributed by
Yale University Press
NEW HAVEN AND LONDON

Yale

YALE UNIVERSITY PUBLICATIONS IN ANTHROPOLOGY
NUMBER 95

Rosemary Volpe
Publications Manager

Sally H. Pallatto
Graphic Designer
Cover Design

Index by Judy A. Hunt

Front cover: Architectural features at the archaeological site of Waira-jirca in Peru's Upper Huallaga Basin. Photograph by Yuichi Matsumoto.

Back cover: The Kotosh Chavín Phase stone wall at the archaeological site of Piquimina in Peru's Upper Huallaga Basin. Photograph by Yuichi Matsumoto.

Peabody Museum of Natural History, Yale University
P. O. Box 208118, New Haven CT 06520-8118 USA
peabody.yale.edu

Distributed by Yale University Press | NEW HAVEN AND LONDON
www.yalebooks.com | yalebooks.co.uk

ISBN 978-0-913516-31-7
ISSN 1535-7082

Printed in the United States of America

Library of Congress Control Number: 2020941290

∞ This paper meets the requirements of ANSI/NISO Z39.48-1992 (Permanence of Paper).
10   9   8   7   6   5   4   3   2   1

CONTENTS

Figures

CHAPTER FIVE

APPENDIX A

APPENDIX B

APPENDIX C

Appendix D

TABLES

Preface

This book originated with a manuscript that I wrote when I was a Ph.D. candidate at Yale University. My first idea was to write a description of Initial Period and Early Horizon settlement patterns of the Upper Huallaga Basin, Peru, based on the settlement research that was undertaken in 2001. However, all the useful data from my bibliographic research and follow-up material analysis was difficult to publish as a journal article. After conversations with Yale's Richard Burger, and Katharina Schreiber, then the editor of Ñawpa Pacha, I decided to transform my article into a monograph and include the data from follow-up research in the region. This book owes much to both of them for their wise advice and encouragement.

However, the writing process has never been straightforward. When I began this work I was also engaged in my doctoral research in Peru at the site of Campanayuq Rumi, Ayacucho, from 2007 until 2010. With the completion of my dissertation in 2010, I rededicated my time to this project on my return to Japan in 2011. On a visit to the University of Tokyo Museum I had the chance to speak with colleagues that had participated in the Upper Huallaga Valley Archaeological Project. While in Tokyo, I realized that that there was a large amount of unpublished, but useful, information not only from our research in 2001–2002, but also from the investigations carried out in the 1960s by the University of Tokyo Scientific Expedition. These unpublished data, deeply connected to the theme of this book, are quite useful additions, and thus I thought to organize and include them as appendices. Input from the original researcher, Yoshio Onuki, was essential to contextualizing these data. When I asked my colleagues for their help with this, they were all kind and generous with their time and insights. These productive collaborations forced me to rethink my original conclusions, which aided in the successful completion of this book.

I owe many people for their generous help in the long process from field research to the final revision of this manuscript.

I am extremely grateful to Yoshio Onuki of the Little World Museum, Kinya Inokuchi at the University of Saitama, Eisei Tsurumi at the University of Tokyo, Nelly Elvira Martell Castillo, and Alvaro Arturo Ruiz Rubio, all of whom worked on the Upper Huallaga Valley Archaeological Project in 2001–2002. Inokuchi, the director of the project, generously allowed me to use the project data and provided several suggestions for data interpretation. It is a great honor to have appendices written by Onuki, who is one of the original members of the University of Tokyo Scientific Expedition and one of the pioneers of Japanese research in the Andes. As in the closing retrospective by Onuki (Appendix E), and explained in the first chapter, we have different perspectives on the terminology of chronological frameworks, which reflect differences between scholars trained in North America and those trained in Japan. Despite these minor differences, Onuki's appendix is a valuable contribution that connects my recent research with the pioneering work of the original Japanese investigations in the Upper Huallaga Basin in the 1960s.

Permission to carry out field research in the Upper Huallaga Basin was generously granted by Peru's Instituto Nacional de Cultura (INC, now the Ministry of Culture). Furthermore, its branch office in Huánuco kindly provided a great deal of support not only during the field seasons, but in follow-up research in 2005–2006. I express my deep gratitude to the directors of the INC Huánuco, Samuel Armando Cárdich Ampudia and Carlos Lucio Ortega y Obregón. César Luis Sara Repetto, the current director of the Dirección Desconcentrada de Cultura de Huánuco, accompanied me on research in 2005 and permitted me to use his site photographs for this publication. Luis Eduardo Salcedo Camacho and Nadeshna Morina gave us several useful suggestions during the field seasons and facilitated access to several publications related to this project. Denesy Palacios kindly provided useful information from her long experience in the area.

Discussions with several friends and colleagues played a critical role in developing my ideas and shaping the arguments expressed in this book. In particular, I would like to thank Richard Burger, Yoshio Onuki, Kinya Inokuchi, Eisei Tsurumi, Jason Nesbitt, Lucy Salazar, Yuji Seki, Tatsuhiko Fujii, Jeffrey Quilter, Yoshifumi Sato, Gabriel Prieto, Atsushi Yamamoto, Shinya Watanabe, Koichiro Shibata, Yasutake Kato, Masato Sakai, César Luis Sara Repetto, Ryan Clasby, and Chris Milan. Richard Burger especially always encouraged me to keep working on the manuscript and recommended that it be submitted to the Yale University Publications in Anthropology series. Although my first idea was to describe the changing settlement patterns from the Initial Period to the Early Horizon, he suggested that I expand the work significantly to include the entirety of the prehispanic cultural sequence of the Upper Huallaga Basin. Yuji Seki shared his wonderful research experience in Cajamarca, which helped me to consider how the Upper Huallaga Basin fits into the wider pan-Andean context through comparative perspectives. Lucy Salazar provided several useful comments regarding the structure of this book. A special thanks goes to Jason Nesbitt, friend and colleague. He assisted me in survey research in 2006 and gave me several productive suggestions that inspired me during the entire writing process. This collaboration began during our "pre-dissertation trip" during the time we were "growing up together" archaeologically at Yale. His sharp observations in the field and deep knowledge in Andean ethnohistory helped me shape the arguments expressed in the concluding chapter. It was a great pleasure to have several chances to hear about the researches during the 1960s from Yoshio Onuki and Tatsuhiko Fujii, and I hope I could inherit and expand the legacy of that great project, which continues to this day.

The Huánuco Archaeological Project (Kinya Inokuchi, Director) was supported by the Mitsubishi Foundation. My follow-up research in Huánuco in 2005–2006 was funded by Joseph Albers Fellowships and the Michael Coe Fieldwork Fund from the Yale University Council on Archaeological Studies. I also thank anonymous reviewers for providing constructive comments and suggestions. Finally, I wish to acknowledge the patient and careful assistance of Rosemary Volpe in the preparation of this manuscript for this publication.

Yuichi Matsumoto
Faculty of Literature and Social Sciences,
Yamagata University

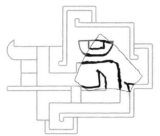 RESEARCH IN THE
UPPER HUALLAGA BASIN
AND ITS BACKGROUND

This work explores the prehistoric settlement patterns of the Upper Huallaga Basin in the central highlands of Peru (Figure 1). Many prehispanic sites dating from the Archaic Period to the Late Horizon had already been identified in the 1960s around the modern city of Huánuco, near the confluence of the Huallaga and Higueras Rivers (Izumi and Sono 1963:2–3; Onuki 1993). Most importantly, in that decade a team from the University of Tokyo conducted three archaeological expeditions there (e.g., Izumi and Sono 1963; Izumi and Terada 1972; Onuki 1993; see also Appendices B–E). The site of Kotosh, a large mound located about 4 km to the west of the center of the modern city of Huánuco, was the most important focus of this research and intensive excavations carried out there produced several new perspectives. Although this pioneering research influenced much of the study of the Late Preceramic Period (3000–1800 BC), Initial Period (1800–800 BC), and Early Horizon (800–200 BC), little archaeological research has been done there since because of widespread violence in this area during the 1970s and 1980s.

However, in other parts of Peru, archaeologists began to emphasize the importance of settlement pattern and its diachronic change and, as a result, the corpus of regional settlement pattern data keeps growing (e.g., Willey 1953; Daggett 1984; Wilson 1988; Billman 1996, 1999; Silva 1996; Parsons, Hastings, and Matos Mendieta 2000, 2013; Silverman 2002). Although the Upper Huallaga Basin had a well-established relative chronology through the excavations at Kotosh, the lack of published settlement data has hindered archaeologists from contextualizing this region in interregional perspectives. For the purpose of reconsidering the prehistory of the Upper Huallaga Basin using contemporary perspectives, I conducted a settlement pattern study in September 2001 together with Kinya Inokuchi of the University of Saitama, Yoshio Onuki of the University of Tokyo and the Little World Museum of Man, Eisei Tsurumi of the University of Tokyo, and Alvaro Ruiz of the Universidad Nacional Mayor de San Marcos. This survey produced a data set that constitutes the main part of this monograph. I was in charge of the data processing and revisited this region in June 2005 and August 2006 for material analysis.

The survey in 2001 aimed at evaluating a promising site to be excavated in the following year. Sajara-patac and Piquimina were selected for excavation in 2002 (Matsumoto

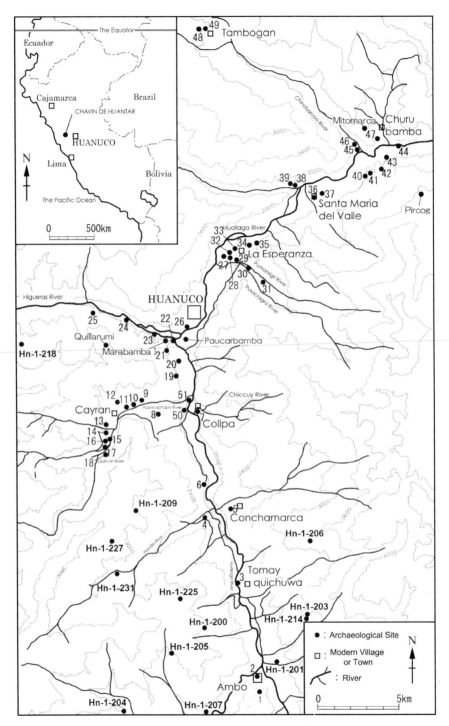

Figure 1. Distribution of archaeological sites in the Upper Huallaga Basin, Peru. Numbers are keyed to the fifty-one sites surveyed in 2001 and described in Chapter 4. Site numbers with the prefix Hn were registered by Grosboll (1988).

2010a; Matsumoto and Tsurumi 2011; see also Appendix D). However, despite huge time constraints, the survey produced a data set valuable enough for a study of diachronic changes in settlement patterns in the Upper Huallaga Basin.

Environmental Setting
of the Upper Huallaga Basin

The environmental setting of the Upper Huallaga Basin has been described in detail (e.g., Maekawa 1963; Bird 1970) and the relationships between environmental zonation and ethnic boundaries have also been discussed (Bird 1970, 1984; Grosboll 1988, 1993). In this section, I provide a general overview of the physical environmental characteristics of the Upper Huallaga Basin, focusing on the area surveyed in 2001 (see Figure 1).

The Upper Huallaga Basin is located on the eastern slopes of the Andes and is characterized by mountainous highlands that are cut by the Huallaga River valley. The modern city of Huánuco is near the confluence of the Huallaga River and Higueras River. For this study, I define the Upper Huallaga Basin as the floodplain and adjacent mountainous slope of the Huallaga and Higueras Rivers, and their tributaries. Ambo can be regarded as its southern limit, with the modern city of Huánuco as the northern limit. The western limit is the confluence of the Mito and Cozo Rivers where these two unite as the Higueras River. The eastern limit will be set at the village of Chullqui on the road from Huánuco to the provincial capital of Tingo Maria, where the valley becomes narrower and slopes on both sides become steeper. Therefore, this definition is not arbitrary, but rather legitimated by the geological setting of the region.

As Iwatsuka described, the Huallaga River rises about 4,000 masl near the town of Cerro de Pasco (Iwatsuka 1963:15; Onuki 1993:71), which is the *puna* natural eco-zone in the terminology of Javier Pulgar Vidal (1987). Here heavy frost makes it difficult to carry out agricultural activities and the land can be used basically for pastureland. The river begins with a U-shaped glacial trough that "gets deeper as it goes down stream" (Iwatsuka 1963:15) to the Huánuco Region. Although the combination of alluvial lowlands and river terraces begins from San Rafael, approximately 50 km to the south of the city of Huánuco, it is from Ambo downstream that the valley becomes broader and large alluvial lowlands and terraces appear (Iwatsuka 1963:18). The extent of these lowlands and terraces is basically the border that I have defined above. Modern settlements are much denser in this area compared with adjacent areas.

According to the environmental zonation established by Pulgar Vidal (1987), the Upper Huallaga Basin includes the *yunga* natural zone (1,800–2,300 masl), *quechua* natural zone (2,300–3,500 masl), and partially *suni* zone (3,500–4000 masl). Although the focus of this study is the *yunga*, as Grosboll (1988:57) described, this can be divided into two areas. Alluvial floodplain, fan, and low terraces extend below an elevation of 2,000 masl, where commercial crops such as sugar cane are intensively cultivated through irrigation. This area is appropriate for cultivation of several crops, tubers, and fruits, such as maize, sweet potato, and cherimoya. The area above 2,100 masl.is composed of steeper slopes and thus is less intensively cultivated, although it can be used for grazing.

In addition to the zonation by Pulgar Vidal, the environmental characteristics of the Upper Huallaga Basin are described using different terminology. For example, Robert Bird (1970:88–94) classified this area as "warm and mild zones" and Fumio Maekawa

(1963:25–26) categorized it as "the tropical–subtropical thorn forest zone." Generally, the environment of the Upper Huallaga Basin is characterized by subtropical dry climate with relatively low annual precipitation (less than 500 mm), where cactus, agave, willow, and acacia are notable.

In the first reports of the excavations at Kotosh (Izumi and Sono 1963; Maekawa 1963), Maekawa summarized the vegetation near the site. It seems appropriate to apply his description to the entire research area of this settlement study. He classified vegetation of this region into the following three categories:

—"a) the sparse woods of cactus and huarango on the slope and terraces,"

—"b) the vegetation in the cultivated lands and villages between a) and c)," and

—"c) the forest of *Baccaris* and *Salix Humboldiana* [*sic*] on the river bed" (Maekawa 1963:30).

In these three categories, archaeological sites are generally found in the cactus and huarango woods (a) and cultivated vegetation areas (b). According to Maekawa (1963:30–31), although the sparse woods vegetation (a) is represented by colonies of large cactus (*Espotoa lamata*), acacia or huarango (*Acacia macracantha*), and thorny shrub (*Porlieria*), the cultivated vegetation (b) is characterized by sparse forest composed of trees such as tara (*Caesalpinia tinctoria*), jacaranda, molle (*Schinus molle*), cactus (*Opuntia ficus-indica*), and agave (*Agave vivipara*), because of the availability of richer water resources through irrigation. In my field observations, although these three vegetation categories all correspond to a *yunga* environment, their distribution is not necessarily separated by elevation. Both woods (a) and cultivated (b) zones are also distributed in the area near the border of the *yunga* and *quechua* above 2,000 masl and might extend to the *quechua* in the Upper Huallaga Basin as well. Although land use in the area has changed radically since 1960, when Maekawa carried out his botanical research, the same variations are generally confirmed through the 2001 survey.

Archaeological Research in the Upper Huallaga Basin

The excavations at Kotosh during the 1960s produced important results, and provided new research topics and approaches in the study of Andean civilization. Here I provide an overview of the excavations at Kotosh and related archaeological investigations.

In the 1960s, Julio C. Tello's idea of the Chavín culture as the cultural matrix of Andean civilization was quite influential not only as an interpretive framework, but with an inherently nationalistic nature against the diffusionist perspective provided mainly by Max Uhle (Tello 1943, 1960; see also Kaulicke 2008, 2010; Burger 2009b). Although many early art styles were regarded as "derivative" of the Chavín culture, the preceding societies had not been well discussed. In fact, it was Tello himself who noticed the importance of the Kotosh site in relation to Chavín culture. Tello visited Kotosh in 1935 and found "an abundance of Chavín potsherds mixed with other types closely resembling, on one hand, incised and painted pottery of the Paracas Cavernas, and, on the other, incised and carved Amazonian pottery" (Tello 1943:152). This description suggests that Tello had noticed that early pottery styles other than that of Chavín existed at Kotosh and that some of them were related to the Amazonian region, from which he assumed close ties with the Chavín culture. With this attractive suggestion by Tello and the results of an extensive survey in 1958

(Ishida et al. 1960), the University of Tokyo Scientific Expedition to the Andes excavated Kotosh for three field seasons, in 1960, 1963, and 1966.

Two volumes of detailed reports for the excavations at Kotosh were published (Izumi and Sono 1963; Izumi and Terada 1972) and the results are frequently discussed in the context of early social organization and monumental architecture in the Andes (e.g., Burger 1992; Onuki 1993, 1998, 2014; Bonnier 1997b; Moore 2005; Matsumoto and Tsurumi 2011). I will simply summarize four focal points of these excavations.

Establishment of Detailed Site Chronology through Intensive Excavations

During the 1960s, large-scale excavation focusing on one site using large trenches was quite uncommon. This technique was applied to the excavations at Kotosh. Because Kotosh is a multi-component site, this methodology was quite appropriate to establish a high-resolution site chronology. As a result, the excavations produced an extended site chronology, from the Late Preceramic to the Early Intermediate Period, with radiocarbon dates. I will come back to this chronological framework later.

Early Horizon Public Architecture and Clear Association with Chavín-related Pottery

Tello's theory of Chavín as the "cultural matrix of Andean Civilization" was influential during the 1950s and 1960s (e.g., Tello 1943, 1960; Carrión Cachot 1948), yet the stratigraphic associations between public architecture and Chavín-style pottery were not firmly confirmed at many sites. The excavations at Kotosh produced one of the rare examples that clarified that public architecture was constructed in association with Chavín-style pottery.

Pre-Chavín Pottery Assemblages Associated with Architecture

As Onuki (1998:58–59) pointed out, one of the important contributions of the excavations at Kotosh to Andean archaeology was the discovery of pre-Chavín pottery assemblages from the layers below the public architecture and Chavín-style pottery. These phases are named the Kotosh Kotosh Phase and Kotosh Waira-jirca Phase, after the archaeological sites in the area. Each assemblage was quite unique and stylistically related to the early pottery of the eastern lowlands, such as Tutishcainyo and Shakimu (e.g., Lathrap 1962, 1970; see also Lathrap and Roys 1963). Because these assemblages were recognized in association with simple stone masonry construction, it became clear that sedentary settlements existed in the central Andes before the emergence of the Chavín culture.

Discovery of Public Architecture of the Late Preceramic Period

Considering the effect on later studies of early Andean cultures, the most important discovery at Kotosh seems to be the public architecture of the Late Preceramic Period (Izumi and Sono 1963; Izumi 1971; Izumi and Terada 1972). Unique architectural complexes were unearthed under the stratum of the Kotosh Waira-jirca Phase. Several constructions were recognized, but these were not associated with pottery sherds. First found was the now well-known "Temple of the Crossed Hands" (*Templo de las Manos Cruzadas*). This was a square chamber that measured 9.5 by 9.5 m and 2 m in height. The building was well made and characterized by split-level floors, niches, and a fire pit at the center that had a ventilation canal associated with it. It is quite plausible that this building was used for public ceremonial purposes for the following reasons.

Both the interior and exterior were nicely plastered. The interior was decorated with niches and a pair of clay reliefs, the well-known crossed hands (e.g., Izumi and Terada 1972, pl. 26). In addition, the architectural features represent dualistic notions (e.g., Burger and Salazar-Burger 1993), exemplified most clearly by the crossed-hand reliefs. These decorated the interior of the chamber and were placed symmetrically along the central axis of the building below the niches for offerings. The sculpture located to the left of the large niche placed along the central axis is smaller than the one to the right. Moreover, whereas the relief on the right shows the right arm over the left, the left relief's right arm is placed under the left. The symmetrical arrangement of the reliefs and the contrasting positions of the arms express the concept of dualism or complementarity, including that of male and female (e.g., Burger and Salazar-Burger 1993; Onuki 1993, 1998). Moreover, the same dualistic concept also seems to have been expressed in the contrasting colors of the building: the exterior was plastered with red and the interior was plastered with white. Here the dualism of red–white and exterior–interior are notable.

The Role of Ceremonial Public Architecture

The Temple of the Crossed Hands was not the only building found at Kotosh. It was actually below the same style of building known as the "Temple of Small Niches" (*Templo de los Nichitos*). The excavations of these structures show that both the construction and abandonment of these chamber buildings were elaborate ritual activities (e.g., Bonnier 1997b; Onuki 1999).

Large-scale excavations at Kotosh convincingly indicate that this architectural process of abandonment of public buildings and construction of new ones signifies important periodic ritual events. Some buildings, such as the Temple of the Crossed Hands, were carefully cleaned and buried through a process of "temple entombment" (Izumi and Terada 1972:304) at the time of abandonment. As for the new construction, the Temple of Small Niches enabled archaeologists to reconstruct how it was built. First, on the top of the flat area created by burying the Temple of the Crossed Hands, the lower level of the split-level floors was delimited with a fire pit associated with a ventilation canal at the center. Second, organic materials were burned in the fire pit, producing a large amount of ash that was dispersed on the square floor. Another floor was placed on this ash layer and then began the building of the upper portion of the split-level floor and the chamber walls (Onuki 1998:66). Onuki linked this process to the slash-and-burn agriculture of the tropical lowlands and indicated the possibility that manioc and possibly other tubers were cultivated in the Late Preceramic Period (Onuki 1998:68–69, 2000:332). It is highly probable that another Kotosh Mito Phase temple exists in the unexcavated levels below the Temple of the Crossed Hands. Both the Temple of Small Niches and Temple of the Crossed Hands are constructed on stone masonry platforms with stepped terraces. A white-plastered Mito temple called the "White Temple" (*Templo Blanco*) was identified, though not directly below the two temples, in association with a platform terrace that is earlier than the one on which the Temple of the Crossed Hands is located, suggesting the presence of another Mito temple in the unexcavated area. Therefore, there seems to have been at least three subphases during the Kotosh Mito Phase.

The public character of these temples is expressed in the monumentality of their architecture. Although these temples were freestanding chambers, they were also part of larger architectural complexes. As mentioned above, both the Temple of the Crossed Hands and the Temple of Small Niches were associated with stone masonry platforms of at least three levels and Mito-style temples were probably located on each level of the platforms. Therefore, the architectural complexes of the Kotosh Mito Phase were large enough to have a monumental, and thus public, character (Onuki 1999:327) and would have needed a relatively large investment of labor.

Certainly, the discovery of public architecture of the Late Preceramic Period provided a new research focus for Andean archaeology. After the investigations at Kotosh, archaeologists began to pay more attention to Preceramic public architecture. Several discoveries occurred on both the coast and in the highlands. For example, public architecture similar to that of the Kotosh Mito Phase was found in the broad area of the central highlands (e.g., Burger and Salazar-Burger 1980, 1985, 1986; Grieder et al. 1988; Bonnier 1997b), which Burger and Salazar named the Kotosh Religious Tradition (Burger and Salazar-Burger 1980).

Cultural Context beyond Kotosh

In parallel with excavations at Kotosh, a survey of the Upper Huallaga Basin and small excavations at the Shillacoto, Waira-jirca, Sajara-patac, Paucarbamba, and Piquimina sites were conducted by Onuki in 1966 (Izumi and Sono 1963; Onuki 1993, 1998, 2000; Matsumoto 2010a; Matsumoto and Tsurumi 2011; see also Appendices B–E). Onuki's objective at that time was to obtain data to test the chronology established at Kotosh and compare the regional cultural context of Kotosh beyond the site itself. However, he found several sites that were earlier or later than Kotosh and confirmed the cultural history of the region from the Archaic to the Late Intermediate Period and Late Horizon. About a quarter of century ago, Onuki described a cultural history and social changes in this region by synthesizing the data of this survey and the results of the excavations at Kotosh (Onuki 1993). His work made it clear that additional data would be needed to study the diachronic transitions of settlement patterns, because of the lack of a systematic survey of the region.

The site of Shillacoto was re-excavated in 1969 and 1970 by the team led by Chiaki Kano (Izumi, Cuculiza, and Kano 1972; Kano 1979). Although the scale of excavation was restricted, two Mito-style temples were discovered, one above the other. The size of the top building is supposedly much larger than the Temple of the Crossed Hands. Its chamber was reused as a funerary facility during the subsequent Kotosh Waira-jirca Phase. At Shillacoto three unique funeral contexts were recovered from its early cultural sequence. During the first excavation at Shillacoto, in 1966, Onuki found a unique head burial of the Kotosh Kotosh Phase (see Appendix C for a detailed description). In addition, Kano (Izumi, Cuculiza, and Kano 1972; Kano 1979) reported two funerary contexts, both associated with rich offerings. One is a Waira-jirca Phase burial, which is an altar-like stone construction placed on the top of the hearth of the Mito Period temple. Osteological remains of seven humans were found in association with finely decorated vessels. The other burial was under the floor of the Kotosh Kotosh Phase level, probably placed with the flooring at the beginning of the phase. Rich offerings, including fine decorated vessels, a lithic figurine, jet mirrors, chipped projectile points, and bone artifacts, were associated with osteological remains of a human body. Among the offerings, two curved bone artifacts are worth noting, as their iconographies are said to be similar to that of the Lanzon monolith at Chavín de Huántar (e.g., Bischof 2008:112).

Although all the investigations during the 1960s shed light on several important topics in the study of the early development of Andean civilization, such as Preceramic monuments and the relationship between Chavín de Huántar and other contemporary centers, the subsequent stagnation of archaeological research in the Upper Huallaga Basin has isolated this region from the important advances made in the north and central coasts, and the north and central highlands of the central Andes (e.g., Burger and Salazar-Burger 1980, 1991; Terada and Onuki 1982, 1985; Burger 1987; S. Pozorski and T. Pozorski 1987, 2002; Elera 1993, 1997, 1998; Onuki 1995; Rick 2005, 2008).

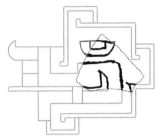

CHAPTER TWO

RESEARCH DESIGN
AND METHODS

Although a full-coverage survey is an ideal way to obtain a data set large enough to consider diachronic changes of settlement patterns in a region, it was not practical for our survey in 2001 for a few reasons, including time and budget constraints. More serious obstacles that made this approach difficult included the characteristic geography of the upper Huallaga River region. The Upper Huallaga Basin consists of narrow valleys and gorges that cut down a high mountainous region from above 3,000 masl. This topography creates radical differences in elevation near the bottomland of the basin and thus the higher section is quite difficult to access. Therefore, we decided to focus on the area near the bottomlands of the Huallaga and Higueras Rivers, since the survey was primarily designed to reexamine the data of the original 1966 survey (Onuki 1993). Moreover, the original idea for this research was heavily influenced by the excavations at Kotosh, which mainly dealt with the earlier period of the sequence, so we wanted to better understand the settlement patterns of the Initial Period and Early Horizon. For these reasons, the following points derived from the previous investigations guided our research strategies.

1. Initial Period and Early Horizon sites tend to cluster on the alluvial bottomlands where rivers unite. For example, many sites, such as Wilcupata, Tingo, Paucarbamba, and Shillacoto, are clustered near the confluence of the Huallaga and Higueras Rivers.

2. The temples of the Kotosh Mito Phase seem to have been located along the Huallaga River at a distance of 5 km from each other (Onuki 1993, 1998). However, the Esperanza District, which is about 5 km from the Shillacoto site, had not been studied, and there is a confluence of rivers there. Thus, a detailed survey was needed in that area.

3. Only the Pircaycoto site had been recognized in the area from the center of Huánuco to the modern city of Ambo (Onuki 1993:77). However, since the Upper Huallaga Basin was closely related to the Junín region at least during the Early Horizon (Izumi and Sono 1963:3; Morales 1998), it is highly probable that this area was a route between them and thus needs to be surveyed intensively.

4. The early sites from the Late Preceramic to the Early Horizon are mainly distributed in the *yunga* (1,800–2,300 masl) in the Upper Huallaga Basin. Considering the importance of the *yunga* in Andean prehistory (e.g., Onuki 1982), this environmental zone should be thoroughly studied.

According to the data from Onuki's past survey and other research in the 1960s, we chose to concentrate on the area from the bottomlands in the vicinity of the Huallaga and Higueras Rivers to the upper limit of the *yunga*, where early sites had been recognized. This research has its own limitations; systematic survey at the higher elevation of the *quechua* and *suni* zones remains to be completed. However, as discussed in later chapters, the exception to this was encountering several post-Early Horizon sites during this survey and occasionally visiting a few early sites in high-altitude areas, using information obtained during the survey. A good example is Jircanera (Site No. 41; see Chapter 4), discovered during the 2001 survey on a visit to an area at an elevation of 3,112 masl. The ceramics collected there indicate a long history of human occupation at that location. The existence of this site signifies that the people of the Upper Huallaga Basin directly used this environment, in addition to the *yunga*, throughout the Late Preceramic Period, Initial Period, and the Early Horizon (see Chapters 4 and 5).

Thus, although I have to admit that our knowledge of post-Early Horizon sites and the higher elevation zones is far from sufficient, it is also true that the survey produced new data in an area where the nature of the post-Early Horizon regional sequence is not well studied. Because of this, I decided to include the data from the later and high-altitude sites that we visited during the survey, and incorporated available data from the Upper Huallaga Basin and the adjacent regions as much as possible (see Chapter 5) to better interpret the survey data presented here.

Considering the available resources from past research in this region that can complement these weaknesses of our survey, it is particularly important to revisit the data of another significant project in the Upper Huallaga Basin during the 1960s, which was led by John V. Murra. This was a rare example of an interdisciplinary project for that time and included ethnohistory (Murra 1967), botany (Bird 1970), and archaeology (Thompson 1967; Grosboll 1988, 1993). Among the many works derived from this project, Sue Grosboll's study is especially important in relation to our survey. By reconstructing the ethnic boundaries and villages described in a type of colonial document known as a *visita*, Grosboll located many archaeological sites at higher elevations above 3,000 masl. These sites in general belong to the post-Early Horizon Period and Grosboll's research includes a rich corpus of data that complement our survey (Grosboll 1988, 1993).

Despite the limitations described here, I believe it is worth trying to reconstruct the entire sequence of prehistoric settlement patterns in the Upper Huallaga Basin by combining our data with other available resources, which will make it possible to compare the archaeological data of this region in an interregional context.

Material Analysis

Surface materials were collected at every site to date the sites by identifying cultural phases. In general, basing chronology on survey data is challenging, because surface materials do not have stratigraphic information. However, because a fine-grained relative chronology had been established at a regional level through the excavations at Kotosh and other sites (e.g., Onuki 1972, 1993), chronological identification of the surface material was not difficult and phase identifications are reliable compared with surveys without much excavation data.

Pottery sherds were the most common surface finds during the survey. Only diagnostic sherds, such as rims and decorated sherds, were collected for analysis. We did not use a systematic sampling strategy, because this would not have been productive in the Upper Huallaga Basin, where most of the sites are mounds in which archaeological remains are buried and do not frequently appear on the surface. In the cultivated areas, we sometimes barely found any diagnostic sherds that could date a site. These would not be useful to understand the spatial organization of the site and could even be misleading, because it was highly probable that the sherds had moved from their original locations.

In most cases, we found only pottery sherds on the surface, though sometimes lithic artifacts were also found. Lithics are also useful for dating a site, because of the detailed stylistic analysis that has been done at Kotosh (Fujii 1972). In our survey, collected surface materials, mainly pottery sherds, were analyzed using the typology from the 1963 and 1966 excavations at Kotosh (Izumi and Terada 1972). In general, rim and decorated sherds were mainly used for chronological identifications, because of their sensitivity in dividing the phases, as shown at Kotosh and Shillacoto (Izumi, Cuculiza, and Kano 1972; Onuki 1972; Kano 1979).

Once chronological identifications were done, site distribution maps for each phase were created using global positioning system (GPS) data. Although we made detailed surface observations and collected information at each site about size, architectural features visible on the surface, and the condition of preservation, such information was not necessarily reflected in the site distribution maps, and so here are provided separately in the site descriptions (see Chapter 4). Even though sometimes this type of information is useful for understanding socioeconomic organization through site hierarchy and functional variability (e.g., Isbell and Schreiber 1978; Wilson 1988; Schreiber 1999; Parsons, Hastings, and Matos Mendieta 2000), I had to refrain from integrating this data into the maps, because of the nature of archaeological sites in the Upper Huallaga Basin. As mentioned earlier, many of the sites are mounds, with most of their architectural remains invisible or obscure, at best. The destruction of sites caused by modern urban and agricultural expansion sometimes partially exposes them and allows us to add descriptive information about architectural technique and site stratigraphy, but this is far from enough to define site size, function, and chronology. In addition, many of the sites have multiple components and had been used repeatedly in prehistoric times, although not always continuously. For example, a few sites were occupied from the Initial Period to Early Intermediate Period for five cultural phases, but others were only used during part of the Early Horizon. These uneven periods of occupation at each site prevented us from establishing a rigid site hierarchy and categorizing sites with functional terminology such as "small village" or "town." On the other hand, it is also true that just simply plotting the sites on a map does not help describe intersite relationships. Therefore, I would interpret the possible site hierarchy and function in relation to the data of earlier investigations, rather than through the survey data alone. This synthetic interpretation of the whole sequence of the prehistory of the Upper Huallaga Basin is presented in Chapter 5.

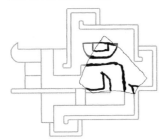

CHAPTER THREE

CHRONOLOGICAL FRAMEWORK

The cultural sequence of the Upper Huallaga Basin established by the excavations at Kotosh is placed here in the broader chronological framework set up by John Rowe to describe the long-term diachronic process with a neutral terminology (e.g., Rowe 1957, 1962). The earlier part of Rowe's chronological framework of the central Andes, the Initial Period (1800–800 BC) and Early Horizon (800–200 BC), seems to be an issue of recent debate and thus needs some clarification. The use of the Initial Period–Early Horizon division for the first and second millennia BC is being critiqued and some archaeologists prefer the term Formative Period instead (see Kato and Seki 1998; Kaulicke 2008, 2010; Rick 2008; Rick et al. 2009). One criticism seems to be whether the Early Horizon was really a horizon as a cultural phenomenon. The implication is that "Horizon" is defined as cultural homogeneity over a short period in a wide geographical area (e.g., Willey 1945; Phillips and Willey 1953; Willey and Phillips 1958). However, Rowe's intention was to create a framework free from evolutionary thought and regional cultural diversity (see Burger 1988, 1993). Despite Rowe's original formulation of a neutral chronological block, the preceding implications for the terms "Initial Period" and "Horizon" keep some archaeologists away from adopting this framework (e.g., Kaulicke 2010:17). The other critique seems to reside in the confusion between Rowe's Early Horizon as a chronological block and "Chavín Horizon" as a cultural phenomenon or an interpretative model (Burger 1988, 1993, 2008). These might lead to the criticism that the Initial Period–Early Horizon division does not fit the reality of recent advances in chronological studies and is too coarse to describe the dynamism and variability of a period covering almost two thousand years.

On the other hand, the use of the term Formative Period in recent literature also varies considerably. Although some who use this term remove its evolutionary implications, some intentionally revive it on the basis of the redefinitions of the character of this time period as the formation of socioeconomic complexity, including marked hierarchical organizations (Rick 2006:203; Rick et al. 2009). Some even change the indicator of the Formative Period from pottery to monumental architecture and thus include Late Preceramic in the Formative Period (e.g., Kato and Seki 1998; Onuki 1999; see also Appendix E).

Considering recent debates over the merit and demerit of these two terminologies, which should be used is ultimately a matter of intellectual taste and the appropriateness of needs to be judged in a regional review of the available archaeological data. I adopt

Rowe's framework of his original intention of creating a chronological block without any cultural implications, because this kind of neutrality seems preferable to situate less well known regional cultural sequences, such as that of the Upper Huallaga Basin. However, here I am pleased to admit there are various preferences derived from different academic traditions to be respected. One of the important alternatives to the chronological framework adopted in this volume is described here by Yoshio Onuki (see Appendix E; see also Onuki 1999).

The excavations at Kotosh during the 1960s produced a fine-grained but relative chronology of the region by using pottery analysis in combination with an architectural sequence. The radiocarbon dates from Kotosh were difficult to interpret, partially because of the technical difficulties at that time, and thus correlating relative chronology with absolute dates was difficult (e.g., Onuki 1993). In 2002, the year after the survey, an Early Horizon site of the Upper Huallaga Basin, Sajara-patac, was excavated by the team led by Kinya Inokuchi and Onuki. I also participated in this project and was in charge of material analysis (Matsumoto 2009; Matsumoto and Tsurumi 2011). New accelerator mass spectrometry (AMS) dates obtained in this project made it possible to reconsider the regional absolute chronology of the Upper Huallaga Basin through the calibration of the old dates from the 1960s research with new dates from Sajara-patac. (See Appendix A for a reexamination of all the available radiocarbon dates in the Upper Huallaga Basin.) The correspondence between Rowe's chronological framework and the regional chronology is as follows.

Note that I have made a change in the terminology of the site chronology at Kotosh. Although the original terminology presented by Izumi and Terada (1972) adopted the term "period" instead of "phase" for the chronological divisions at Kotosh, period is actually used to indicate a distinct cultural unit representing a stratigraphic group for architecture and associated archaeological remains (Izumi and Sono 1963; Izumi and Terada 1972). Thus, designations such as the "Kotosh Mito Period" can be better understood by replacing Period with Phase, a term generally used to indicate a regional or site level chronological division under a broader framework such as Formative Period, Early Horizon, Late Intermediate Period, and so forth (e.g., Willey 1953; Burger 1984; Wilson 1988; Onuki 1995).

Therefore, here in this volume Phase is used instead of Period for the chronology originally used for Kotosh and the Upper Huallaga Basin sites, as follows:
—before the Late Preceramic Period (c. 2500 BC);
—the Late Preceramic Period is the Kotosh Mito Phase (2500–1600 BC);
—the early Initial Period is the Kotosh Waira-jirca Phase (1600–1200 BC);
—the late Initial Period is the Kotosh Kotosh Phase (1200–700 BC);
—the early and middle Early Horizon is the Kotosh Chavín Phase (700–250 BC);
—the late Early Horizon is the Kotosh Sajara-patac Phase (250–50 BC);
—the Early Intermediate Period is the Kotosh Higueras Phase (50 BC–?);
—after the Early Intermediate Period and until the Late Horizon (?–16th century AD).

The cultural sequence recognized at Kotosh is restricted to the time from the Late Preceramic Period to the Early Intermediate Period. Therefore, the chronology before the Late Preceramic Period and after the Early Intermediate Period is much less detailed, because the regional cultural history and associated changes of material styles in these periods are not well studied (but see Cardich [1964] and Grosboll [1988] for exceptions).

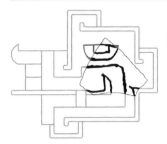 SITE DESCRIPTIONS

This chapter provides descriptions of the fifty-one sites surveyed in the Upper Huallaga Basin in 2001 (sites are numbered for cross referencing; see Figure 1). Bibliographic sources are given for sites that were previously surveyed or excavated. Five additional sites that were not surveyed in 2001 (Quillarumi, Marabamba 1, Paucarbamba, Pircog, and Mitomarca) are described separately. Information about them comes from occasional and short visits made after this survey was completed. Although it is difficult to provide full descriptions for these, it is still worth including these sites to complement the data set from the 2001 survey.

In each description, site location coordinates (Table 1) are given in DMS (degrees-minutes-seconds) format from GPS field data taken with a hand-held Garmin eTrex (Garmin, Ltd.; garmin.com). Pulgar Vidal's (1987) environmental zones are used to classify the natural setting of each site. Diagnostic pottery sherds on the surface were collected and analyzed using the pottery typology at Kotosh (Onuki 1972; Table 2). The chronological position of each site is provided in its description (Table 3).

Surveyed Sites

Site No. 1: Cueva de Jatun Uchco

FIGURE 2

Location: Ambo District, Ambo Province, Department of Huánuco, Peru (10°07′58.3″S, 76°12′08.0″W).

Natural Setting: At an elevation of 2,144 masl in the *yunga* zone, this site is on the natural rocky hill called Cerro de Ishco on the western bank of the Huallaga River.

Modern Land Use: Not applicable.

Site Description: This site is a deep vertical cave in the center of a rocky hill. The entrance is a narrow triangle with a base of 2 m and height of 1.5 m. The cave entrance is horizontal for about 1 m and then falls off vertically. Although Ravines, Ossio, and Núñez described this site as "Jatun Ushcu," this cave is locally known as "Jatun Uchco."

Figure 2. The deep cave site of Cueva de Jatun Uchco (Site No. 1).

Artifacts: None.

Chronological Position: Lauricocha II (Cardich 1964).

Antecedents: Ravines, Ossio, and Núñez (1964:33) described this cave as a Preceramic component of the Lauricocha II Phase in the Preceramic chronology by Cardich (1958, 1964), which has two radiocarbon dates (Ziółkowski et al. 1994:279–280), 4629 ± 350 BP (uncalibrated) and 4660 ± 90 BP (uncalibrated), from the Lauricocha Cave.

Site No. 2: Tambopata

Location: Village of Ambo, Ambo District, Ambo Province, Department of Huánuco, Peru (10°07'46.7"S, 76°12'17.6"W).

Natural Setting: At an elevation of 2,068 masl in the *yunga* zone, this site is on the alluvial floodplain on the western bank of the Huallaga River.

Modern Land Use: Private residential property.

Site Description: An artificial mound. This site was heavily damaged by the expansion of private residential construction. Although a few walls can be seen in the many cuts made by construction activities, the form and size of the mound is difficult to estimate because of modern houses on the mound.

Artifacts: Although surface materials were relatively scarce, eleven diagnostic pottery sherds were collected on the surface. Among them are: Higueras Red (7); Sajara-patac Chocolate Brown Plain (3); Sajara-patac Chocolate Brown Decorated (1).

FIGURE 3. El Morro (Site No. 3), an artificial mound damaged by construction activities.

Chronological Position: Kotosh Sajara-patac Phase, Kotosh Higueras Phase.

Antecedents: None.

Site No. 3: El Morro

FIGURE 3

Location: Village of Tomay Kichwa, Tomay Kichwa District, Ambo Province, Department of Huánuco, Peru (10°04′39.0″S, 76°13′02.2″W).

Natural Setting: At an elevation of 2,037 masl in the *yunga* zone, this site is on the alluvial land on the western bank of the Huallaga River.

Modern Land Use: Private residential property.

Site Description: An artificial mound that extends 150 m north–south by 60 m east–west. Archaeological remains have been heavily damaged by urban expansion. Part of a stone wall made of river cobbles was recognizable in the southern part of the mound where modern construction activities have destroyed the mound.

Artifacts: Three diagnostic pottery sherds were collected: Higueras Red (1); Sajara-patac Chocolate Brown Plain (1); Sajara-patac Chocolate Brown Decorated (1).

Chronological Position: Kotosh Sajara-patac Phase, Kotosh Higueras Phase.

Antecedents: Ravines, Ossio and Núñez (1964); Onuki (1993). Ravines and colleagues (1964) report a neckless jar similar to San Blas Red. Onuki registered this site with the

TABLE 1. Location of the fifty-one Upper Huallaga Basin archaeological sites surveyed in 2001 (see Figure 1), with GPS data. Elevation is given in meters above sea level (masl).

Site no.	Site	Latitude	Longitude	Elevation (masl)
1	Cueva de Jatun Uchco	10°07'58.3"S	76°12'08.0"W	2,144
2	Tambopata	10°07'46.7"S	76°12'17.6"W	2,068
3	El Morro	10°04'39.0"S	76°13'02.2"W	2,037
4	Pariapata	10°02'34.9"S	76°14'02.5"W	2,083
5	Shupra	10°02'07.6"S	76°13'12.7"W	2,205
6	Vichaycoto	10°01'18.5"S	76°14'04.2"W	2,047
7	Izucupata	09°58'55.7"S	76°14'20.5"W	2,031
8	El Hito	09°59'02.6"S	76°15'40.1"W	2,200
9	Fundo Pampa	09°58'14.8"S	76°16'37.9"W	2,283
10	Shongoymaran	09°58'45.4"S	76°16'33.2"W	2,194
11	Capillapata	09°58'50.0"S	76°16'50.5"W	2,238
12	Cotoshpata	09°58'36.8"S	76°17'05.8"W	2,312
13	Chonocotosh	09°59'21.5"S	76°17'30.4"W	2,404
14	Coima 2	09°59'36.0"S	76°17'27.9"W	2,452
15	Mochepata	09°59'50.2"S	76°17'25.8"W	2,410
16	Cotoshloma	09°59'54.5"S	76°17'32.2"W	2,461
17	Tarapata	10°00'07.4"S	76°17'31.0"W	2,486
18	Coima 1	10°00'12.1"S	76°17'37.0"W	2,539
19	Cayhuayna Alta	09°57'47.6"S	76°15'05.1"W	1,991
20	Cayhuayna Baja	09°57'10.6"S	76°14'58.4"W	1,967
21	Marabamba 2	09°57'00.5"S	76°15'24.0"W	2,039
22	Wilcupata	09°56'35.5"S	76°15'14.3"W	2,037
23	Patahuasi	09°56'21.2"S	76°15'47.8"W	2,037
24	Kotosh	09°55'52.2"S	76°16'46.1"W	1,930
25	Cruzpata	09°55'39.9"S	76°17'52.6"W	2,064
26	Shillacoto	09°56'11.3"S	76°14'56.8"W	1,840
27	Jancao	09°53'54.7"S	76°13'22.0"W	1,925
28	La Esperanza 2	09°53'54.0"S	76°13'07.9"W	1,941
29	Cotopata	09°53'59.9"S	76°12'59.5"W	1,955
30	Chupayllia	09°54'15.9"S	76°12'33.8"W	2,117
31	Matamarca	09°54'41.7"S	76°12'05.8"W	2,197
32	La Esperanza 1	09°53'51.4"S	76°13'04.4"W	1,918

Continued

TABLE 1 CONTINUED.

Site no.	Site	Latitude	Longitude	Elevation (masl)
33	Pucarumi	09°53'38.5"S	76°13'00.7"W	1,986
34	Mollepata	09°53'35.9"S	76°12'39.3"W	1,991
35	Huayrana	09°53'33.7"S	76°12'30.3"W	2,005
36	Warampayloma	09°51'55.2"S	76°10'20.9"W	1,900
37	San Cristóbal	09°51'45.8"S	76°10'04.8"W	1,963
38	Armoncalloq	09°51'29.5"S	76°11'02.4"W	1,875
39	Huarampay	09°51'22.6"S	76°11'17.0"W	1,986
40	Tarucopata	09°51'14.5"S	76°08'29.7"W	2,053
41	Puitoc	09°51'11.1"S	76°08'23.8"W	2,085
42	Papayo	09°51'05.0"S	76°08'02.7"W	2,114
43	Waira-jirca	09°50'40.6"S	76°07'55.1"W	1,970
44	Piquimina	09°50'16.9"S	76°07'28.9"W	1,779
45	Tunacirca	09°50'23.5"S	76°08'44.0"W	1,893
46	Chacuas-pampa	09°50'12.5"S	76°08'57.7"W	1,905
47	Sajara-patac	09°50'03.4"S	76°08'09.2"W	1,898
48	Jircanera	09°46'19.3"S	76°14'15.5"W	3,112
49	Huanojpa	09°46'13.9"S	76°13'45.8"W	2,982
50	Huancachupa	09°58'49.6"S	76°14'50.0"W	2,048
51	Vilcamiraflores	09°58'34.4"S	76°14'40.4"W	1,998

name of Pircaycoto and collected pottery sherds of the Kotosh Sajara-patac Phase in 1966 (Onuki 1993). We instead registered this site with the name El Morro, because Pircaycoto is the local name of the natural hill nearby and this site is known locally as El Morro.

Site No. 4: Pariapata

Location: Village of Ñausa, Conchamarca District, Ambo Province, Department of Huánuco, Peru (10°02'34.9"S, 76°14'02.5"W).

Natural Setting: At an elevation of 2,083 masl in the *yunga* zone, this site is on the alluvial land between the western bank of the Huallaga River and the south bank of the Ñausilla River.

Modern Land Use: Agricultural field.

Site Description: No structures were found. Pottery fragments were dispersed on the surface. According to the local residents, there was a low mound with stone walls that was completely destroyed during the 1980s. A few large quarried stones that could have been used for a wall could be seen on the surface.

Figure 4. Shupra (Site No. 5) consists of two artificial mounds covered with thorny vegetation.

Artifacts: There is a small amount of pottery sherds on the surface and four diagnostic sherds were collected: Higueras Red (3); Sajara-patac Chocolate Brown Plain (1).

Chronological Position: Kotosh Sajara-patac Phase, Kotosh Higueras Phase.

Antecedents: None.

Site No. 5: Shupra

Figure 4

Location: Village of Conchamarca, Conchamarca District, Ambo Province, Department of Huánuco, Peru (10°02'07.6"S, 76°13'12.7"W).

Natural Setting: At an elevation of 2,205 masl in the *yunga* zone, this site is on the middle of a large natural hill on the eastern bank of the Huallaga River.

Modern Land Use: The lands around the mounds are used for agriculture. The mounds were covered by natural vegetation and not used for a specific purpose.

Site Description: Two artificial mounds are located at a distance of 10 m from each other. One is 40 m in diameter and 3 to 4 m in height, and the other is 20 m in diameter and about 3 m in height. Thorny plants covered two artificial mounds. Small looters' pits can be seen on the surface and stone walls were visible in those pits. Except for these, the two mounds are well-covered by thorny vegetation and thus architectural remains cannot be seen. Pottery sherds were dispersed mainly on the fields around the mounds.

FIGURE 5. The Initial Period–Early Horizon artificial mound at Vichaycoto (Site No. 6).

FIGURE 6. Early Intermediate Period wall at Vichaycoto (Site No. 6).

FIGURE 7. Examples of Kotosh Waira-jirca Phase pottery from Vichaycoto (Site No. 6).

Artifacts: Ten diagnostic pottery fragments were collected: Higueras Red (7); Sajara-patac Chocolate Brown Plain (2); Sajara-patac Chocolate Brown Decorated (1).

Chronological Position: Kotosh Sajara-patac Phase, Kotosh Higueras Phase.

Antecedents: None

Site No. 6: Vichaycoto

FIGURES 5 and 6

Location: Village of Conchamarca, Conchamarca District, Ambo Province, Department of Huánuco, Peru (10°01′18.5″S, 76°14′04.2″W).

Natural Setting: At an elevation of 2,047 masl in the *yunga* zone, this site is on the top of a large natural hill on the western bank of the Huallaga River. The road between the cities of Huánuco and Ambo passes at the foot of the hill. The hill is rocky with sparse vegetation of maguey and cactus on the slope.

Modern Land Use: A water pump for agricultural use is on the top of the hill. There is a wooden cross at the top of the mound near the water pump. These modern modifications have partially destroyed this archaeological site.

Site Description: An artificial low mound approximately 10 m in diameter and 2 m in height on a natural hilltop (see Figure 5). A few aligned stones can be seen beyond the mound (see Figure 6). Pottery fragments were dispersed in a large area approximately 200 m north–south by 100 m east–west. When I visited the site again in 2005, the installation of a water pump for agricultural use had destroyed the eastern part of the site. A room structure and large amount of Kotosh Higueras Phase pottery and human bones were identified. According to one of the workers, human remains were uncovered during these modern activities.

Artifacts: Sixty-five diagnostic pottery fragments were collected: Kotosh Plain (9); Waira-jirca Red Line-burnished (2); Waira-jirca Fine-line Incised (1); Waira-jirca Red Plain (4); Waira-jirca Zoned Hachure (1); Sajara-patac Chocolate Brown Plain (6); Higueras Red (42); (Figure 7). A spindle whorl made from a body sherd of Sajara-patac Chocolate Brown Plain was found on the surface. Pottery sherds of the Kotosh Waira-jirca Phase tended to

FIGURE 8. The eastern mound at Izucupata (Site No. 7) seen from the southwest.

be found in the central and western part of the site, whereas those of the Kotosh Sajara-patac Phase were mainly seen in the western and eastern areas of the site.

Chronological Position: Kotosh Waira-jirca Phase, Kotosh Sajara-patac Phase, Kotosh Higueras Phase.

Antecedents: None.

Site No. 7: Izucupata
FIGURE 8

Location: Village of Colpa, Huánuco District, Huánuco Province, Department of Huánuco, Peru (09°58′55.7″S, 76°14′20.5″W).

Natural Setting: At an elevation of 2,031 masl in the *yunga* zone, this site is on a natural hilltop near the confluence of the Huallaga River and Chiccuy River.

Modern Land Use: Agricultural field.

Site Description: Three artificial mounds on a natural hill. All the mounds are relatively well preserved, although a small portion near the edge of each mound was destroyed by modern cultivation. Segments of stone walls can be observed on the surface of all the mounds. Large amounts of pottery fragments were dispersed on the surface of each mound.

Artifacts: Seventy-six diagnostic pottery fragments were collected: Sajara-patac Chocolate Brown Plain (22); Sajara-patac Chocolate Brown Decorated (13); Sajara-patac Red (12);

FIGURE 9. Examples of Kotosh Sajara-patac Phase pottery from Izucupata (Site No. 7).

FIGURE 10. Examples of Kotosh Higueras Phase pottery from Izucupata (Site No. 7).

FIGURE 11. Terrace wall at El Hito (Site No. 8) seen from the southwest.

San Blas Red Polished (8); Higueras Red (19); Higueras Brown (2); (Figures 9 and 10). Fine pottery sherds of the Kotosh Sajara-patac Phase, such as Sajara-patac Chocolate Brown Decorated or San Blas Red Polished, were abundant on the surface.

Chronological Position: Kotosh Sajara-patac Phase, Kotosh Higueras Phase.

Antecedents: None.

Site No. 8: El Hito

FIGURES 11 and 12

Location: Village of San Cristóbal de Huayllabamba, San Francisco de Cayrán District, Huánuco Province, Department of Huánuco, Peru (09°59′02.6″S, 76°15′40.1″W).

Natural Setting: At an elevation of 2,200 masl in the *yunga* zone, this site is on the southern bank of the Huancachupa River, a tributary of the Huallaga River, near the border of the Huayllabamba and Huancachupa villages.

Modern Land Use: The land around this artificial mound is used for agriculture. A cross was placed on the top of the mound by a local community and the construction activities for it destroyed a small part of this site.

Site Description: An artificial mound approximately 30 m in diameter and 3 m in height on a natural hilltop. There were a few walls and pottery sherds were dispersed on the surface. Thorny vegetation composed of maguey and algarrobo covered the lower half of the artificial mound.

FIGURE 12. Terrace walls at El Hito (Site No. 8) seen from the northwest.

FIGURE 13. Examples of Kotosh Higueras Phase pottery from El Hito (Site No. 8).

FIGURE 14. Fundo Pampa (Site No. 9), a small natural hill with artificial terracing.

Artifacts: Twelve diagnostic pottery sherds were collected on the surface: Sajara-patac Chocolate Brown Plain (3); Sajara-patac Chocolate Brown Decorated (1); Sajara-patac Red (1); Higueras Red (7); (Figure 13).

Chronological Position: Kotosh Sajara-patac Phase, Kotosh Higueras Phase.

Antecedents: None.

Site No. 9: Fundo Pampa

FIGURE 14

Location: Village of Acombabilla, San Francisco de Cayrán District, Huánuco Province, Department of Huánuco, Peru (09°58′14.8″S, 76°16′37.9″W).

Natural Setting: At an elevation of 2,283 masl in the *yunga* zone, this site is on the southern slope of a natural hill called Cerro Pillcomoso on the north of the Huancachupa River.

Modern Land Use: Not applicable.

Site Description: This site is a small natural hill with an approximate height of 5 m, but it is artificially terraced. A few possible retaining walls for terraces were visible on the surface.

Artifacts: Archaeological materials were scarce on the surface. A few nondiagnostic pottery fragments were collected. None fit the pottery typology of Kotosh (Onuki 1972). This site might belong to the period after the Kotosh Higueras Phase.

Chronological Position: Unknown. Post-Early Intermediate Period?

Antecedents: None.

TABLE 2. Distribution of pottery types by site, from all sherds collected in the 2001 surface survey of fifty-one Upper Huallaga Basin archaeological sites (see Figure 1). Diagnostic sherds were analyzed using the pottery typology at Kotosh (Onuki 1972).

Pottery type	\multicolumn{25}{c}{Site number}
	1	2	3	4	5	6	7	8	9	10	11	12	13	14	15	16	17	18	19	20	21	22	23	24	25
Higueras Red		7	1	3	7	42	19	7		21	2	14	7	9	4	3	14	4				15			16
Higueras Brown							2											2				12			
San Blas Red Decorated																									
San Blas Red Polished							8												2	1					
Sajara-patac Red		3		1			12	1		5							1		4	2			5		1
Sajara-patac Chocolate Brown Plain			1		2	6	22	3		9			4		7		4		3	2		8	7		1
Sajara-patac Chocolate Brown Decorated		1	1		1		13	1		7			2		1		4		1	4		1			
Paucarbamba Brilliant Plain																									
Paucarbamba Brilliant Decorated																									
Paucarbamba Gray																									
Kotosh Plain						9				7										1		1			
Kotosh Coarse Grooved																									
Kotosh Grooved A																									
Kotosh Grooved B																									
Kotosh Red Grooved																									
Kotosh Graphited																									
Kotosh Red Modeled																									

Continued

TABLE 2 CONTINUED.

Pottery type													Site number												
	1	2	3	4	5	6	7	8	9	10	11	12	13	14	15	16	17	18	19	20	21	22	23	24	25
Waira-jirca Red Plain						4														1					
Waira-jirca Fine-line Incised						1																			
Waira-jirca Broad-line Incised																									
Waira-jirca Zoned Hachure						1																2			
Waira-jirca Shallow Incised																									
Waira-jirca Black Line-burnished										1															
Waira-jirca Red Line-burnished						2															2				
Unclassified																									
Total	n/a	11	3	4	10	65	76	12	n/a	50	2	14	13	9	12	3	23	6	10	11	2	39	12	n/a	18

Continued

TABLE 2 CONTINUED.

	Site number																									
Pottery type	26	27	28	29	30	31	32	33	34	35	36	37	38	39	40	41	42	43	44	45	46	47	48	49	50	51
Higueras Red		38	3	8	5		2	6	11	7	6	1					2		3				15			13
Higueras Brown		4							4														11	6		2
San Blas Red Decorated																										
San Blas Red Polished		2						2									3									
Sajara-patac Red		18						2				1					5									
Sajara-patac Chocolate Brown Plain					3			3				1				3	23	2	3	5						5
Sajara-patac Chocolate Brown Decorated		1			3			1								7	8	1		1						1
Paucarbamba Brilliant Plain		16			13	1													1				2			
Paucarbamba Brilliant Decorated		7			3	1																				
Paucarbamba Gray					5																					
Kotosh Plain		25		18	9	4					11						1	2	5	2			15			3
Kotosh Grooved A		3		8							1								4							
Kotosh Grooved B				1																						
Kotosh Red Grooved				2														1					1			
Kotosh Graphited											1															
Kotosh Red Modeled		2		1																						

Continued

TABLE 2 CONTINUED.

Pottery type	Site number																									
	26	27	28	29	30	31	32	33	34	35	36	37	38	39	40	41	42	43	44	45	46	47	48	49	50	51
Waira-jirca Red Plain		14		9		2					9												1			1
Waira-jirca Fine-line Incised		9				1					3							3		1						
Waira-jirca Broad-line Incised											1															
Waira-jirca Zoned Hachure		3									4							1	1				1			
Waira-jirca Shallow Incised		10		1																			1			1
Waira-jirca Black Line-burnished		4																	2				1			1
Waira-jirca Red Line-burnished		8									1									2						1
Unclassified						2														2			1	3		
Total	n/a	164	3	48	41	11	2	14	15	7	37	3	n/a	n/a	n/a	10	42	10	19	13	n/a	n/a	49	9	n/a	28

TABLE 3. Chronological relationships among the archaeological sites in the Upper Huallaga Basin, Peru. *Abbreviations:* BKMT, Before the Kotosh Mito Phase; KMT, Kotosh Mito Phase; KWJ, Kotosh Waira-jirca Phase; KK, Kotosh Kotosh Phase; KCH, Kotosh Chavín Phase; KSP, Kotosh Sajara-patac Phase; KH, Kotosh Higueras Phase; PKH, Post-Kotosh Higueras Phase. Dots are identified phases; dashes indicate phases that have not been identified at a site.

Site no.	Site	BKMT	KMT	KWJ	KK	KCH	KSP	KH	PKH
1	Cueva de Jatun Uchco	•	—	—	—	—	—	—	—
2	Tambopata	—	—	—	—	—	•	•	—
3	El Morro	—	—	—	—	—	•	•	—
4	Pariapata	—	—	—	—	—	•	•	—
5	Shupra	—	—	—	—	—	•	•	—
6	Vichaycoto	—	•?	•	—	—	•	•	—
7	Izucupata	—	—	—	—	—	•	•	—
8	El Hito	—	—	—	—	—	•	•	—
9	Fundo Pampa	—	—	—	—	—	—	—	•
10	Shongoymaran	—	•?	•	—	—	•	•	—
11	Capillapata	—	—	—	—	—	—	•	—
12	Cotoshpata	—	—	—	—	—	—	•	—
13	Chonocotosh	—	—	—	—	—	•	•	—
14	Coima 2	—	—	—	—	—	—	•	—
15	Mochepata	—	—	—	—	—	•	•	—
16	Cotoshloma	—	—	—	—	—	—	•	—
17	Tarapata	—	—	—	—	—	•	•	—
18	Coima 1	—	—	—	—	—	—	•	—
19	Cayhuayna Alta	—	—	—	—	—	•	—	—
20	Cayhuayna Baja	—	•?	•	—	—	•	•	—
21	Marabamba 2	—	•?	•	—	—	—	—	—
22	Wilcupata	—	•?	•	—	—	•	•	—
23	Patahuasi	—	—	—	—	—	•	—	—
24	Kotosh	—	•?	•	•	•	•	•	—
25	Cruzpata	—	—	—	—	—	•	•	—
26	Shillacoto	—	•?	•	—	—	—	•	—
27	Jancao	—	•?	•	•	•	•	•	—
28	La Esperanza 2	—	—	—	—	—	—	•	—

Continued

Site No. 10: Shongoymaran

FIGURES 15 and 16

Location: Shabintopampa, San Francisco de Cayrán District, Huánuco Province, Department of Huánuco, Peru (09°58′45.4″S, 76°16′33.2″W).

Natural Setting: At an elevation of 2,194 masl in the *yunga* zone, this site is on the north bank of the Huancachupa River.

Modern Land Use: Private property. The northern and eastern parts of the site are used for agriculture.

Site Description: An artificial mound that extends 20 m north–south by 50 m east–west. The top of the mound was covered by thorny vegetation, such as maguey, cactus, cabuya azul, and molle. Room structures and stone masonry walls could be seen on the surface

TABLE 3 CONTINUED.

Site no.	Site	BKMT	KMT	KWJ	KK	KCH	KSP	KH	PKH
29	Cotopata	—	●?	●	●	—	—	●	—
30	Chupayllia	—	—	—	—	●	●	●	—
31	Matamarca	—	●?	●	—	●	—	●	..
32	La Esperanza 1	—	—	—	—	—	—	●	—
33	Pucarumi	—	—	—	—	—	●	●	—
34	Mollepata	—	—	—	—	—	—	●	—
35	Huayrana	—	—	—	—	—	—	●	—
36	Warampayloma	—	●?	●	●	—	—	—	—
37	San Cristóbal	—	—	—	—	—	●	●	—
38	Armoncalloq	—	—	—	—	—	—	—	●
39	Huarampay	—	—	—	—	—	—	—	●
40	Tarucopata	—	—	—	—	—	—	—	●
41	Puitoc	—	—	—	—	—	●	—	—
42	Papayo	—	—	—	—	—	●	●	—
43	Waira-jirca	—	●?	●	●	—	—	●	—
44	Piquimina	—	●?	●	●	●	●	●	—
45	Tunacirca	—	● ?	●	—	—	●	●	—
.46	Chacuas-pampa	—	—	—	—	—	—	—	●
47	Sajara-patac	—	—	—	—	●	●	—	—
48	Jircanera	—	●?	●	●	●	—	●	●
49	Huanojpa	—	—	—	—	—	—	●?	●
50	Huancachupa	—	—	—	—	—	—	—	●
51	Vilcamiraflores	—	●?	●	—	—	●	●	—
—	Quillarumi*	●	—	—	—	—	—	—	—
—	Marabamba 1*	●	—	—	—	—	—	—	—
—	Paucarbamba*	—	—	—	—	●	●	—	—
—	Pircog*	—	—	—	—	—	—	—	●
—	Mitomarca*	—	—	—	—	—	●	●	●

* Archaeological sites that were not part of the 2001 Upper Huallaga Basin survey.

and in looters' pits. The walls were constructed with quarried stones and river cobbles. Use of mud mortar was confirmed in some of the walls. Superposition of walls observed in a looters' pit suggests that this could be a multi-component site. The southern limit of the site is a natural cliff facing the Huancachupa River. According to the landowner, the original southern part of the site was destroyed by a landslide that occurred in the early 1990s.

Artifacts: Fifty diagnostic pottery sherds were collected on the surface and from looters' pits: Kotosh Plain (7); Waira-jirca Black Line-burnished (1); Sajara-patac Chocolate Brown Plain (9); Sajara-patac Chocolate Brown Decorated (7); Sajara-patac Red (5); Higueras Red (21); (Figures 17 and 18). There was one unique body sherd with a line of red paint on a smoothed unslipped surface. This sherd cannot be classified using the Kotosh typology.

Figure 15. Shongoymaran (Site No. 10) seen from the southeast.

Figure 16. The main mound at Shongoymaran (Site No. 10).

FIGURE 17. Examples of Kotosh Waira-jirca Phase and Kotosh Sajara-patac Phase pottery from Shongoymaran (Site No. 10).

FIGURE 18. Examples of Kotosh Higueras Phase pottery from Shongoymaran (Site No. 10).

Figure 19. Capillapata (Site No. 11), a small artificial mound mostly destroyed by modern road construction.

Figure 20. Examples of Kotosh Higueras Phase pottery from Cotoshpata (Site No. 12).

Chronological Position: Kotosh Waira-jirca Phase, Kotosh Sajara-patac Phase, Kotosh Higueras Phase.

Antecedents: None.

Site No. 11: Capillapata

FIGURE 19

Location: Village of San Francisco de Cayrán, San Francisco de Cayrán District, Huánuco Province, Department of Huánuco, Peru (09°58'50.0"S, 76°16'50.5"W).

Natural Setting: At an elevation of 2,238 masl in the *yunga* zone, this site is on the northern bank of the Huancachupa River.

Modern Land Use: Urban area of the village of San Francisco de Cayrán.

Site Description: Small artificial mound. Original size is unknown because probably more than 80% of the original mound has been destroyed by modern road construction (see Figure 19). A low stone wall approximately 40 cm in height could be seen from the cut made by the road construction. Pottery fragments were visible on the surface.

Artifacts: Although many undecorated body sherds were abundant on the surface, only two diagnostic sherds were collected: Higueras Red (2).

Chronological Position: Kotosh Higueras Phase.

Antecedents: None.

Site No. 12: Cotoshpata

Location: East of the village of San Francisco de Cayrán, San Francisco de Cayrán District, Huánuco Province, Department of Huánuco, Peru (09°58'36.8"S, 76°17'05.8"W).

Natural Setting: At an elevation of 2,312 masl in the *yunga* zone, this site is 1 km to the west of the Plaza de Armas in the village of San Francisco de Cayran on the top of the natural rocky hill called El Cerro de Trigopunta. Thorny vegetation such as maguey and cactus are sparsely distributed near the site.

Modern Land Use: Not applicable.

Site Description: Small artificial mound approximately 20 m in diameter and 1 to 2 m in height. Architectural features were clearly visible on the surface. A room structure and stone walls were recognized.

Artifacts: Fourteen diagnostic pottery sherds were collected on the surface: Higueras Red (14); (Figure 20).

Chronological Position: Kotosh Higueras Phase.

Antecedents: None.

Site No. 13: Chonocotosh

FIGURE 21

Location: Warangoucuro, San Francisco de Cayrán District, Huánuco Province, Department of Huánuc, Peru, located approximately 1.5 km to the southeast of the center of the village of San Francisco de Cayran (09°59'21.5"S, 76°17'30.4"W).

Natural Setting: At an elevation of 2,404 masl in the *yunga* zone, this site is on the southern bank of the Parara River.

Figure 21. The platform wall at Chonocotosh (Site No. 13).

Figure 22. Examples of Kotosh Sajara-patac Phase pottery from Chonocotosh (Site No. 13).

Modern Land Use: The land around the mound is used for agriculture.

Site Description: An artificial circular mound approximately 20 m in diameter and 3 to 4 m in height. Thorny vegetation composed of maguey, cactus, algarrobo, and molle covered the mound. Retaining walls around the mound suggest that an artificial platform exists near the edge of the site. In addition, a looters' pit on the margin of the site revealed artificial fill for the platform. There was a room complex of at least three small rooms on the top of the mound. Pottery sherds were dispersed not only on the mound, but also in the area around the mound, which is now used as an agricultural field.

Artifacts: Thirteen diagnostic pottery sherds were collected from the surface of the mound: Sajara-patac Chocolate Brown Plain (4); Sajara-patac Chocolate Brown Decorated (2); Higueras Red (7); (Figure 22).

Chronological Position: Kotosh Sajara-patac Phase, Kotosh Higueras Phase.

Antecedents: None.

Site No. 14: Coima 2

Location: Village of San Francisco de Cayrán, San Francisco de Cayrán District, Huánuco Province, Department of Huánuco, Peru (09°59′36.0″S, 76°17′27.9″W). This site is located approximately 2 km to south of the village of San Francisco de Cayrán.

Natural Setting: At an elevation of 2,452 masl in the *yunga* zone, this site is on the southern bank of the Parapara River.

Modern Land Use: Agricultural field.

Site Description: A small, low artificial mound approximately 10 by 6 m and 1 to 2 m in height. Some pottery sherds were distributed beyond the area of the mound. A few square room structures could be seen on the surface. Quarried stone and mud mortar were used for wall construction.

Artifacts: Nine diagnostic pottery sherds were collected on the surface: Higueras Red (9).

Chronological Position: Kotosh Higueras Phase.

Antecedents: None.

Site No. 15: Mochepata

FIGURE 23

Location: Coima, San Francisco de Cayrán District, Huánuco Province, Department of Huánuco, Peru (09°59′50.2″S, 76°17′25.8″W). Cotoshloma (Site No. 16) is located approximately 200 m to the east of this site.

Natural Setting: At an elevation of 2,410 masl in the *yunga* zone, this site is on the western bank of the Quircan River.

Modern Land Use: Agricultural field.

Site Description: A low artificial mound with a long and narrow shape. Alluvial deposition makes it difficult to define the border between the mound and the natural hill. The area where pottery sherds are dispersed extends 300 m north–south by 50 m east–west. A few double-faced walls and revetments made of quarried stones and mud mortar are exposed on the surface. An abandoned modern house is on the western edge of the site. Its construction materials include pottery sherds.

FIGURE 23. Overview of Mochepata (Site No. 15) from the south.

Artifacts: Twelve diagnostic pottery sherds were collected: Sajara-patac Chocolate Brown Plain (7); Sajara-patac Chocolate Brown Decorated (1); Higueras Red or Sajara-patac Red (4).

Chronological Position: Kotosh Sajara-patac Phase, Kotosh Higueras Phase.

Antecedents: None.

Site No. 16: Cotoshloma

Location: Coima, San Francisco de Cayrán District, Huánuco Province, Department of Huánuco, Peru (09°59′54.5″S, 76°17′32.2″W). This site is located approximately 200 m to the west of Mochepata (Site No. 15).

Natural Setting: At an elevation of 2,461 masl in the *yunga* zone, this site is in the area between the Parara River and the Quircan River.

Modern Land Use: The area outside of the mound is used for agriculture.

Site Description: This site is an artificial mound 25 by 25 m. It is covered by algarrobo, maguey, and cactus. Dense vegetation prevented detailed surface observations. The original size could have been much larger, because the marginal area of this site is being destroyed by the expansion of agricultural land. Many looters' pits have damaged the mound and exposed stone walls built of quarried and field stones, and mud mortar. It seems that both rooms and platforms originally existed at this site. Pottery sherds were scarce on the surface.

Artifacts: Dense vegetation at the site did not allow us to conduct a systematic surface collection. Only three diagnostic sherds were collected: Higueras Red (3).

FIGURE 24. The platform wall at Tarapata (Site No. 17).

Chronological Position: Kotosh Higueras Phase.

Antecedents: None.

Site No. 17: Tarapata

FIGURE 24

Location: Coima, San Francisco de Cayrán District, Huánuco Province, Department of Huánuco, Peru (10°00'07.4"S, 76°17'31.0"W). A road to the village of Huancayacu passes nearby.

Natural Setting: At an elevation of 2,486 masl in the *yunga* zone, this site is on the western bank of the Quircan River.

Modern Land Use: Residential area.

Site Description: An artificial mound that extends 60 m north–south by 30 m east–west. This site is covered by thorny vegetation, including maguey, cabuya, and molle. A few room-like structures could be seen on the surface. A large revetment 12 m in length was exposed at the northern edge of the mound. In general, this site is badly damaged by the construction of modern houses and the expansion of agricultural land.

Artifacts: Twenty-three diagnostic sherds were collected from the surface and from looters' pits: Sajara-patac Chocolate Brown Plain (4); Sajara-patac Chocolate Brown Decorated (4); Sajara-patac Red (1); Higueras Red (14); (Figures 25 and 26).

Chronological Position: Kotosh Sajara-patac Phase, Kotosh Higueras Phase.

Antecedents: None.

FIGURE 25. Examples of Kotosh Sajara-patac Phase pottery from Tarapata (Site No. 17).

FIGURE 26. Examples of Kotosh Higueras Phase pottery from Tarapata (Site No. 17).

Site No. 18: Coima 1

Location: Coima, San Francisco de Cayrán District, Huánuco Province, Department of Huánuco, Peru (10°00′12.1″S, 76°17′37.0″W).

Natural Setting: At an elevation of 2,539 masl in the *yunga* zone, this site is on the slope of a natural hill called Cerro Misión.

Modern Land Use: Agricultural field.

Site Description: On the hillside of Cerro Misión. There are a series of aligned stones made to delineate modern agricultural fields. However, there were many pottery sherds of the Kotosh Higueras Phase in the cultivated fields. It is difficult to know whether the modern stone alignments were built using the archaeological materials.

Artifacts: Six diagnostic sherds were collected from the surface: Higueras Red (4); Higueras Brown (2).

Chronological Position: Kotosh Higueras Phase.

Antecedents: None.

Site No. 19: Cayhuayna Alta

Location: Cayhuayna, Pilcomarca District, Huánuco Province, Department of Huánuco, Peru (09°57′47.6″S, 76°15′05.1″W). This site is located approximately 2 km from the center of the city of Huánuco. A modern cemetery is to the east of the site.

Natural Setting: At an elevation of 1,991 masl in the *yunga* zone, this site is on a low natural hill on the western bank of the Huallaga River. This rocky hill does not have a name, but is considered part of a much larger hill to the northwest called Cerro Pillcomoso.

Modern Land Use: Not applicable.

Site Description: A low artificial mound approximately 10 by 15 m and 1 m in height. Archaeological remains, such as parts of stone walls, could be seen on the surface beyond the area of the mound.

Artifacts: Ten diagnostic pottery sherds were collected on the surface: Sajara-patac Chocolate Brown Plain (3); Sajara-patac Chocolate Brown Decorated (1); Sajara-patac Red (4); San Blas Red Polished (2); (Figure 27).

Chronological Position: Kotosh Sajara-patac Phase.

Antecedents: None.

Site No. 20: Cayhuayna Baja

Location: Cayhuayna, Pilcomarca District, Huánuco Province, Department of Huánuco, Peru (09°57′10.6″S, 76°14′58.4″W). This site is located in a margin of the modern city of Huánuco and approximately 400 m to southwest of the Universidad Nacional de Hermillio Valdizán de Huánuco.

Natural Setting: At an elevation of 1,967 masl in the *yunga* zone, this site is on the alluvial land on the western bank of the Huallaga River.

Modern Land Use: Urban area.

Site Description: No trace of archaeological remains could be seen on the surface. However, major construction activities in 2001 to replace water pipes uncovered archaeological remains. Some early pottery sherds were mixed in piles of soil that were removed to make

FIGURE 27. Examples of Kotosh Sajara-patac Phase pottery from Cayhuayna Alta (Site No. 19).

FIGURE 28. Examples of Kotosh Waira-jirca Phase and Kotosh Sajara-patac Phase pottery from Cayhuayna Baja (Site No. 20).

a long, deep trench for the pipes. A corner of stone masonry architecture was exposed at the bottom of the trench. From the profile of the trench, the following stratigraphy was observed:

—First layer. Surface layer. This layer composed of sandy, brown soil is 60 cm thick with a loose texture. A few nondiagnostic pottery sherds were visible.

—Second layer. Sandy, grayish soil with semi-compact texture. A few nondiagnostic pottery sherds were visible.

—Third layer. Sandy, compact reddish brown soil. A Kotosh Waira-jirca Period pottery sherd (Waira-jirca Red Plain) was identified. The top of a stone wall was seen in this layer.

—Fourth layer. Compact, black soil. No archaeological materials were recognized.

Because this fourth layer, which contains the buried stone structure, did not produce any archaeological remains, this structure might belong to the Kotosh Mito Phase.

According to local residents, before the urban expansion to this area there were a few mounds that had pottery sherds on the surface.

Artifacts: Eleven diagnostic pottery sherds were collected from the soil removed from the trench to place a water pipe: Kotosh Plain (1); Waira-jirca Red Plain (1); Sajara-patac Chocolate Brown Plain (2); Sajara-patac Chocolate Brown Decorated (4); Sajara-patac Red (2); San Blas Red Polished (1); (Figure 28).

Chronological Position: Kotosh Mito Phase (?), Kotosh Waira-jirca Phase, Kotosh Sajara-patac Phase, Kotosh Higueras Phase.

Antecedents: Denesy Palacios (1988) referred to a possible Formative (Initial Period or Early Horizon, or both) site in Cayhuayna that had been destroyed several years ago. This site could be the same site as Cayhuayna Baja.

Site No. 21: *Marabamba 2*

Location: Marabamba, Pircomarca District, Huánuco Province, Department of Huánuco, Peru (09°57'00.5"S, 76°15'24.0"W).

Natural Setting: At an elevation of 2,039 masl in the *yunga* zone, this site is on a natural hill on the western bank of the Huallaga River to the east of Cerro Pillcomoso.

Modern Land Use: Private residential property and agricultural land.

Site Description: Two small artificial mounds on a natural hilltop. They are 10 m distant from each other and both are 30 m in diameter. Because this site is on residential property and surrounded by modern agricultural fields, both mounds were badly damaged. Stone walls have been exposed by the destruction and a small amount of pottery sherds were dispersed around the mound, although most of these were nondiagnostic.

Artifacts: Only two diagnostic pottery sherds were collected from the surface: Waira-jirca Red Line-burnished (2); (Figure 29).

Chronological Position: Kotosh Waira-jirca Phase.

Antecedents: None. However, note that this site is different from the site of Marabamba that Onuki registered in 1966 (Onuki 1993:72). For convenience, I have tentatively named this site Marabamba 2, and the site registered by Onuki as Marabamba 1 (see "Reported Sites Not in the 2001 Survey" below).

FIGURE 29. Examples of Kotosh Waira-jirca Phase pottery from Marabamba 2 (Site No. 21).

Site No. 22: Wilcupata

FIGURE 30

Location: Huánuco, Huánuco District, Huánuco Province, Department of Huánuco, Peru (09°56′35.5″S, 76°15′14.3″W). This site is located approximately 3 km from the modern city of Huánuco and close to the village of Marabamba.

Natural Setting: At an elevation of 2,037 masl in the *yunga* zone, this site is on a hill near the confluence of the Huallaga and Higueras Rivers.

Modern Land Use: Agricultural field.

Site Description: Two flat mounds on a large natural hill. One measures 30 by 35 m and the other 40 by 45 m. Both could be low platforms and are less than 1 m in height. An unusual amount of river cobbles and boulders were dispersed around the site. Both mounds had a few looters' pits and stone walls could be seen inside these.

Artifacts: Thirty-nine diagnostic pottery sherds were collected on the surface: Waira-jirca Zoned Hachure (2); Kotosh Plain (1); Sajara-patac Chocolate Brown Plain (8); Sajara-patac Chocolate Brown Decorated (1); Higueras Red (15); Higueras Brown (12); (Figures 31 and 32).

Chronological Position: Kotosh Waira-jirca Phase, Kotosh Sajara-patac Phase, Kotosh Higueras Phase.

Antecedents: Onuki (1993).

Site No. 23: Patahuasi

FIGURE 33

Location: Huánuco, Huánuco District, Huánuco Province, Department of Huánuco, Peru (09°56′21.2″S, 76°15′47.8″W).

FIGURE 30. Wilcupata (Site No. 22) consists of two flat mounds on a natural hill.

Natural Setting: At an elevation of 2,037 masl in the *yunga* zone, this site is on the alluvial floodplain on the southern bank of the Higueras River.

Modern Land Use: None.

Site Description: A large flat mound. Although many pottery sherds were dispersed on the surface, no structures have been recognized. The extent of the site is unknown because of the alluvial deposition that covers the mound. Certain parts of the site were covered by maguey. Because it is close to the Higueras River, the site could have been damaged by seasonal flooding.

Artifacts: Twelve diagnostic pottery sherds were collected on the surface: Sajara-patac Chocolate Brown Plain (7); Sajara-patac Red (5).

Chronological Position: Kotosh Sajara-patac Phase.

Antecedents: Onuki registered this site as "Tingo" in 1966 (Onuki 1993:73).

Site No. 24: Kotosh

Location: Huánuco, Huánuco District, Huánuco Province, Department of Huánuco, Peru (09°55'52.2"S, 76°16'46.1"W).

Natural Setting: At an elevation of 1,930 masl in the *yunga* zone, this site is on the alluvial land on the southern bank of the Higueras River.

Modern Land Use: Archaeological park.

FIGURE 31. Examples of Kotosh Waira-jirca Phase and Kotosh Sajara-patac Phase pottery from Wilcupata (Site No. 22).

FIGURE 32. Examples of Kotosh Higueras Phase pottery from Wilcupata (Site No. 22).

FIGURE 33. Patahuasi (Site No. 23) is a large flat mound covered by alluvial deposits.

Site Description: See Izumi and Sono (1963) and Izumi and Terada (1972). See Chapter 1 for the excavations done in the 1960s.

Artifacts: Not applicable.

Chronological Position: Kotosh Mito Phase, Kotosh Waira-jirca Phase, Kotosh Kotosh Phase, Kotosh Chavín Phase, Kotosh Sajara-patac Phase, Kotosh Higueras Phase.

Antecedents: The University of Tokyo team conducted intensive archaeological investigations at this site in 1960, 1963, and 1966 (e.g., Izumi and Sono 1963; Izumi and Terada 1972; see Chapter 1).

Site No. 25: Cruzpata

FIGURES 34 and 35

Location: Huánuco, Huánuco District, Huánuco Province, Department of Huánuco, Peru (09°55′39.9″S, 76°17′52.6″W). This site is located approximately 1 km to the west of Kotosh.

Natural Setting: At an elevation of 2,064 masl in the *yunga* zone, this site is on a natural hill on the southern bank of Higueras River.

Modern Land Use: None.

Site Description: The site is composed of two artificial mounds arranged in an east–west direction. The smaller one, referred to as Mound 1, is on the eastern area of the hilltop. Mound 1 is a flat-topped, low artificial mound. Stone masonry walls with light brown

FIGURE 34. The larger mound, Mound 2 at Cruzpata (Site No. 25), with possible Early Intermediate Period architecture.

FIGURE 35. Another view of Mound 2 at Cruzpata, showing possible Early Intermediate Period stone masonry.

mud plaster were visible in looters' pits. Mound 2 is larger than Mound 1 and consists of two superimposed platforms made by stone masonry revetments (see Figures 34 and 35). Huge quarried stones were used for the platform revetments. Room-like constructions are recognizable on the surface. The stone masonry architecture of Mound 2 is large and elaborated enough to be compared with that of Kotosh. Though main architectural features were visible on the hilltop, coarsely made stone walls surround the hillside. The site was densely covered by thorny vegetation such as maguey, cactus, algarrobo, and cabuya.

Artifacts: Eighteen diagnostic sherds were collected on the surface: Sajara-patac Chocolate Brown Plain (1); Sajara-patac Red (1); Higueras Red (16). The sherds of Sajara-patac Chocolate Brown Plain and Sajara-patac Red were found on Mound 1, whereas all the Higueras Red sherds were collected on Mound 2. This may imply different time periods for Mound 1 and Mound 2.

Chronological Position: Kotosh Sajara-patac Phase, Kotosh Higueras Phase. Because the pottery of the Kotosh Sajara-patac Phase tended to be found on Mound 1 and that of the Kotosh Higueras Phase on Mound 2, it may be possible that this site can be divided into two sites, with Mound 1 assigned to the Kotosh Sajara-patac Phase and Mound 2 to the Kotosh Higueras Phase.

Antecedents: Ravines, Ossio, and Núñez (1964); Onuki (1993).

Site No. 26: Shillacoto

Figures 36 and 37

Location: Huánuco, Huánuco District, Huánuco Province, Department of Huánuco, Peru (09°56'11.3"S, 76°14'56.8"W). This site is located in the floodplain near the confluence of the Huallaga and Higueras Rivers, where currently there is an urban area near the center of the modern city of Huánuco on the Cuadra 4 of Jirón Seiichi Izumi.

Natural Setting: At an elevation of 1,840 masl in the *yunga* zone, this site is in the urban area of Huánuco near the confluence of the Huallaga and Higueras Rivers.

Modern Land Use: Urban area.

Site Description: Although this site is composed of a few large mounds and extends more than 200 by 200 m in area (Izumi, Cuculiza, and Kano 1972; Kano 1979), most of it had been destroyed before 1966. Expansion of the urban residential area continued to destroy the site and almost the entire site has been lost. Building and road construction exposed the revetments of a large platform that extends at least 30 by 30 m (see Figures 36 and 37). For detailed information of the excavations done in the 1960s, see Izumi, Cuculiza, and Kano (1972), Kano (1979), and Onuki (1993); see also Appendix C.

Artifacts: Not applicable. Although the investigators did not do any surface collection, some of the materials from Kano's excavations were deposited in the Ministerio de Cultura of Huánuco.

Chronological Position: Kotosh Mito Phase, Kotosh Waira-jirca Phase, Kotosh Kotosh Phase, Kotosh Higueras Phase.

Antecedents: Izumi, Cuculiza, and Kano (1972); Kano (1979); Onuki (1993).

FIGURE 36. A possible Initial Period platform wall at Shillacoto (Site No. 26).

FIGURE 37. A platform wall at Shillacoto (Site No. 26) visible under a modern house.

FIGURE 38. A road through cut divides the large mound at Jancao (Site No. 27).

Site No. 27: Jancao

FIGURES 38 and 39

Location: Village of Amarilis, Amarilis District, Huánuco Province, Department of Huánuco, Peru (09°53'54.7"S, 76°13'22.0"W). A road to Tingo Maria divides the site into two.

Natural Setting: At an elevation of 1,925 masl in the *yunga* zone, this site is on the alluvial land on the southern bank of the Huallaga River.

Modern Land Use: Road and residential area.

Site Description: A large artificial mound. The building of a road to the city of Tingo Maria in the 1960s split the mound into two and subsequent expansion of the urban area destroyed most of the site (see Figure 38). More than 80% has been lost. The original size of the mound could have been 120 m in diameter and 9 m in height, and thus comparable to Kotosh. Walls and floors could be seen in the profile made by the road and house construction.

Artifacts: One hundred sixty-four diagnostic sherds were collected on the surface and from the soil removed by construction activities: Kotosh Plain (25); Waira-jirca Red Plain (14); Waira-jirca Red Line-burnished (8); Waira-jirca Zoned Hachure (3); Waira-jirca Fine-line Incised (9); Waira-jirca Shallow Incised (10); Waira-jirca Black Line-burnished (4); Kotosh Red Modeled (2); Kotosh Grooved A (3); Paucarbamba Brilliant Plain (16); Paucarbamba Brilliant Decorated (7); Sajara-patac Chocolate Brown Plain (18); Sajara-patac Chocolate Brown Decorated (1); San Blas Red Polished (2); Higueras Red (38); Hi-

Figure 39. Jancao (Site No. 27) seen from the southwest.

gueras Brown (4); (Figures 40 to 55). Pottery sherds from all phases known from Kotosh were collected.

Chronological Position: Kotosh Waira-jirca Phase, Kotosh Kotosh Phase, Kotosh Chavín Phase, Kotosh Sajara-patac Phase, Kotosh Higueras Phase.

Antecedents: None.

Site No. 28: *La Esperanza 2*

Location: Village of Amarilis, Amarilis District, Huánuco Province, Department of Huánuco, Peru (09°53′54.0″S, 76°13′07.9″W). This site is located in an agricultural field 400 m to the south of the Plaza de Armas in the village of Amarilis.

Natural Setting: At an elevation of 1,941 masl in the *yunga* zone, this site is on the alluvial land on the southern bank of the Huallaga River.

Modern Land Use: Agricultural field.

Site Description: A low artificial mound that extends approximately 50 by 50 m and is 0.5 m in height. No architectural features were observed on the surface. The cement base of a modern structure was dug into the mound and has destroyed many of the archaeological remains. A small number of pottery sherds were visible on the surface.

Artifacts: Three diagnostic pottery sherds were collected on the surface: Higueras Red (3).

Chronological Position: Kotosh Higueras Phase.

Antecedents: None.

Figure 40. Examples of Kotosh Waira-jirca Phase pottery from Jancao (Site No. 27).

Figure 41. Examples of Kotosh Waira-jirca Phase pottery from Jancao (Site No. 27).

Figure 42. Examples of Kotosh Waira-jirca Phase pottery from Jancao (Site No. 27).

Figure 43. Examples of Kotosh Waira-jirca Phase pottery from Jancao (Site No. 27).

FIGURE 44. Examples of Kotosh Waira-jirca Phase pottery from Jancao (Site No. 27).

FIGURE 45. Examples of Kotosh Waira-jirca Phase pottery from Jancao (Site No. 27).

FIGURE 46. Examples of Kotosh Waira-jirca Phase pottery from Jancao (Site No. 27).

FIGURE 47. Examples of Kotosh Waira-jirca Phase and Kotosh Kotosh Phase pottery from Jancao (Site No. 27).

FIGURE 48. Examples of Kotosh Kotosh Phase pottery from Jancao (Site No. 27).

FIGURE 49. Examples of Kotosh Chavín Phase pottery from Jancao (Site No. 27).

FIGURE 50. Examples of Kotosh Chavín Phase pottery from Jancao (Site No. 27).

FIGURE 51. Examples of Kotosh Chavín Phase pottery from Jancao (Site No. 27).

Site No. 29: Cotopata

FIGURES 56 and 57

Location: Village of Amarilis, Amarilis District, Huánuco Province, Department of Huánuco, Peru (09°53′59.9″S, 76°12′59.5″W).

Natural Setting: At an elevation of 1,955 masl in the *yunga* zone, this site is on the alluvial land on the southern bank of Huallaga River and to the east of its tributary, the Pumarinri River.

Modern Land Use: Private property, agricultural field.

FIGURE 52. Examples of Kotosh Sajara-patac Phase pottery from Jancao (Site No. 27).

FIGURE 53. Examples of Kotosh Sajara-patac Phase pottery from Jancao (Site No. 27).

Site Description: A large artificial mound. Although a considerable part has been destroyed by continuous cultivation and looting, this mound would originally have been at least 80 m in diameter and 6 m in height. According to the local residents, the central part of the mound was badly destroyed by heavy machinery in the 1960s or 1970s. White-plastered walls and stone masonry architecture with niches could be seen in the profile of the cut made by the machinery (see Figure 57). Pottery sherds were dispersed around the looters' pits. The entire mound was covered by dense thorny vegetation composed of

FIGURE 54. Examples of Kotosh Higueras Phase pottery from Jancao (Site No. 27).

FIGURE 55. Examples of rims and handles of Kotosh Higueras Phase pottery from Jancao (Site No. 27).

FIGURE 56. Cotopata (Site No. 29) seen from the west.

FIGURE 57. Section of wall, 1.2 m in height, seen in a cut made into the mound at Cotopata (Site No. 29).

Figure 58. Examples of Kotosh Kotosh Phase pottery from Cotopata (Site No. 29).

maguey, cactus, cabuya, and molle. When I visited the site again in 2006, the eastern edge of the mound had been newly damaged by the landlord to expand his private residence. According to the construction workers, square rooms were uncovered along with many human bones, including skulls. I had the opportunity to check the materials from this destructive episode and recognized that all pieces were finely made Kotosh Kotosh Phase pottery, such as Kotosh Red Modeled, Kotosh Graphited, and Kotosh Grooved A.

Artifacts: Forty-eight diagnostic sherds were collected on the surface, from looters' pits and the trenches made by house construction: Kotosh Plain (18); Waira-jirca Red Plain (9); Waira-jirca Shallow Incised (1); Kotosh Grooved A (8); Kotosh Grooved B (1); Kotosh Red Grooved (2); Kotosh Red Modeled (1); Higueras Red (8); (Figure 58). A spindle whorl made from a Kotosh Plain body sherd was also found.

Chronological Position: Kotosh Waira-jirca Phase, Kotosh Kotosh Phase, Kotosh Higueras Phase.

Antecedents: Onuki mentioned a site in the village of La Esperanza. Chiaki Kano visited in 1966 and found Kotosh Waira-jirca Phase pottery sherds (Onuki 1993:84). This probably is that site.

Site No. 30: Chupayllia

Figures 59 and 60

Location: Village of Amarilis, Amarilis District, Huánuco Province, Department of Huánuco, Peru (09°54′15.9″S, 76°12′33.8″W).

Natural Setting: At an elevation of 2,117 masl in the *yunga* zone, this site is on the southern bank of the Huallaga River, where two of its tributaries, the Pusacuragra River and the

FIGURE 59. The site surface at Chupayllia (Site No. 30) seen from the south.

FIGURE 60. A looter's pit at Chupayllia (Site No. 30).

FIGURE 61. Examples of Kotosh Chavín Phase pottery from Chupayllia (Site No. 30).

FIGURE 62. Examples of Kotosh Chavín Phase pottery from Chupayllia (Site No. 30).

Pumanrigri River, unite. The site is south of the confluence of these two rivers and on the natural terrace between them.

Modern Land Use: Agricultural field.

Site Description: A flat low mound with a gentle slope. Although it is difficult to define the limit of the site in the natural hill, its mound size is approximately 50 by 50 m and 1 m in height. Stone walls were observed in a large looter's pit where many pottery sherds and bones have been left dispersed (see Figure 60). From observation of the stone walls exposed in the looters' pits, there is probably a platform-like structure on the center of the mound with dimensions approximately 10 by 10 m. Quarried stones and mud mortar were used for construction. In general, this site is badly destroyed by looting and expansion of the agricultural field.

Artifacts: Forty-one diagnostic pottery sherds were collected on the surface and from looters' pits: Kotosh Plain (9); Paucarbamba Gray (5); Paucarbamba Brilliant Plain (13); Paucarbamba Brilliant Decorated (3); Sajara-patac Chocolate Brown Plain (3); Sajara-patac Chocolate Brown Decorated (3); Higueras Red (5); (Figures 61 to 64).

Chronological Position: Kotosh Chavín Phase, Kotosh Sajara-patac Phase, Kotosh Higueras Phase.

Antecedents: None.

Site No. 31: Matamarca

FIGURE 65

Location: Village of Matamarca, Amarilis District, Huánuco Province, Department of Huánuco, Peru (09°54′41.7″S, 76°12′05.8″W). This site is situated in an old hacienda called Matamarca. There is an abandoned colonial church 150 m east of the old house of the hacienda. Early pottery sherds are dispersed around the main church building and in the adobe walls.

Natural Setting: At an elevation of 2,197 masl in the *yunga* zone, this site is on the eastern bank of Pusacuragra River.

Modern Land Use: Agricultural field.

Site Description: A low, flat mound on alluvial land. Although it is difficult to define its size, because of destruction by agriculture and the construction of a colonial church, an area 30 m north–south by 20 m east–west is well preserved. Two large looters' trenches have been placed in the central part of the mound and stone walls could be seen in them. Walls are generally made of quarried stones and mud mortar. Probably many of the stones from the prehispanic walls have been reused in the modern partition walls of the agricultural field around the site. Parts of the site are covered by cabuya, maguey, and cactus.

Artifacts: Eleven diagnostic pottery sherds were collected from the looters' trenches: Kotosh Plain (4); Waira-jirca Red Plain (2); Waira-jirca Fine-line Incised (1); Paucarbamba Brilliant Plain (1); Paucarbamba Brilliant Decorated (1); (Figure 66). Two sherds could not be unambiguously classified using the Kotosh typology. However, the dark-gray paste from reduced firing suggests that these belong to the Kotosh Waira-jirca Phase.

Chronological Position: Kotosh Waira-jirca Phase, Kotosh Chavín Phase, Kotosh Higueras Phase.

Antecedents: None.

Site No. 32: La Esperanza 1

Location: Village of La Esperanza, Amarilis District, Huánuco Province, Department of Huánuco, Peru (09°53′51.4″S, 76°13′04.4″W). This site is located approximately 300 m to the southwest of the Plaza de Armas in the village of Esperanza.

Natural Setting: At an elevation of 1,918 masl, in the *yunga* zone, this site is on the alluvial land on the southern bank of the Huallaga River.

FIGURE 63. Examples of Kotosh Chavín Phase pottery from Chupayllia (Site No. 30).

FIGURE 64. Examples of Kotosh Sajara-patac Phase pottery from Chupayllia (Site No. 30).

FIGURE 65. Matamarca (Site No. 31), a low, flat mound on alluvial land now used for agriculture.

FIGURE 66. Fragment of a possible stirrup-spout bottle with dentate rocker stamping that is an example of Kotosh Chavín Phase pottery from Matamarca (Site No. 31).

Modern Land Use: Agricultural field.

Site Description: This site is in the center of an agricultural field. Pottery sherds are dispersed on the surface. Although no architectural remains are recognized, the many stones piled in the agricultural field could have come from destroyed prehispanic architecture.

Artifacts: Only two diagnostic sherds were collected on the surface: Higueras Red (2).

Chronological Position: Kotosh Higueras Phase.

Antecedents: None.

FIGURE 67. Examples of Kotosh Sajara-patac Phase and Kotosh Higueras Phase pottery from Pucarumi (Site No. 33).

Site No. 33: Pucarumi

Location: Village of Amarilis, Amarilis District, Huánuco Province, Department of Huánuco, Peru (09°53′38.5″S, 76°13′00.7″W).

Natural Setting: At an elevation of 1,986 masl in the *yunga* zone, this site is on the alluvial land on the southern bank of the Huallaga River.

Modern Land Use: Agricultural field.

Site Description: A low, flat mound with a gentle slope on a natural flat hill, although it is difficult to define the border of the site. Pottery sherds are dispersed across an area 200 m north–south by 60 m east–west. Almost the entire mound is used as cultivated land and only a few lines of stone walls can be seen on the surface. This site could be badly damaged by modern agricultural activities.

Artifacts: Fourteen diagnostic sherds were collected on the surface: Sajara-patac Chocolate Brown Plain (3); Sajara-patac Chocolate Brown Decorated (1); Sajara-patac Red (2); San Blas Red Polished(2); Higueras Red (6); (Figure 67).

Chronological Position: Kotosh Sajara-patac Phase, Kotosh Higueras Phase.

Antecedents: None.

Site No. 34: Mollepata

FIGURES 68 and 69

Location: Village of Amarilis, Amarilis District, Huánuco Province, Department of Huánuco, Peru (09°53′35.9″S, 76°12′39.3″W). This site is located approximately 600 m to the northeast of the village of La Esperanza.

Natural Setting: At an elevation of 1,991 masl in the *yunga* zone, this site is on the southern bank of the Huallaga River.

FIGURE 68. Mollepata (Site No. 34) seen from the west.

FIGURE 69. Wall of a room construction at Mollepata (Site No. 34).

Figure 70. Examples of Kotosh Higueras Phase pottery from Mollepata (Site No. 34).

Figure 71. Huayrana (Site No. 35) seen from the south.

Modern Land Use: Although the northern part of the site is used as an agricultural field, most of the site remains intact.

Site Description: A large, artificial mound on a natural hill that is probably artificially terraced. The mound extends approximately 120 m north–south by 65 m east–west, with a height of 4 to 5 m. Stone masonry architecture was visible on its surface. Several room complexes and small platforms were exposed. Most of the architecture seems to share a southeast–northwest axis. The central part of the mound is composed of three superimposed terraces and a large, rectangular 10 by 14 m plaza delineated by a stone masonry wall more than 1 m thick. Although many small looters' pits exposed parts of the architectural remains, overall the site is well preserved.

Artifacts: Fifteen diagnostic pottery sherds were collected from looters' trenches: Higueras Brown (4); Higueras Red (11); (Figure 70).

Chronological Position: Kotosh Higueras Phase.

Antecedents: None.

Site No. 35: Huayrana

FIGURE 71

Location: Village of Amarilis, Amarilis District, Huánuco Province, Department of Huánuco, Peru (09°53'33.7"S, 76°12'30.3"W). This site is located approximately 1 km to the northeast of the village of La Esperanza and 200 m to the southwest of the site of Mollepata (Site No. 34).

Natural Setting: At an elevation of 2,005 masl in the *yunga* zone, this site is on the southern bank of the Huallaga River, in an area between two small, dry quebradas (ravines).

Modern Land Use: Not applicable.

Site Description: An artificially terraced natural hilltop with stone masonry architecture placed on the terrace. In addition to room structures, a long, double-faced wall up to 10 m along the northwest was visible on the surface. A modern irrigation canal destroyed the northwestern part of the site. A few molle (pepper trees) covered the northern edge of the mound.

Artifacts: Seven diagnostic sherds were collected on the surface: Higueras Red (7).

Chronological Position: Kotosh Higueras Phase.

Antecedents: None.

Site No. 36: Warampayloma

FIGURE 72

Location: Santa Maria del Valle, Santa Maria del Valle District, Huánuco Province, Department of Huánuco, Peru (09°51'55.2"S, 76°10'20.9"W). This site is located approximately 200 m to the west of the Plaza de Armas (central square) on private property along a dirt road.

Natural Setting: At an elevation of 1,900 masl in the *yunga* zone, this site is on the alluvial land on the southern bank of the Huallaga River.

Modern Land Use: Private property. A part of the site is used as a garbage dump.

Site Description: A large, artificial mound covered with cactus and agave. The mound is elongated in plan. It has an approximate dimension of 80 m north–south by 50 m east–

FIGURE 72. Possible platform wall and looter's pit at Warampayloma (Site No. 36).

west and is 6 m in height. Large looters' pits are on top of it (see Figure 72) and stone walls with cream-colored plaster were visible in these holes. Pottery sherds were scattered around the pits and dense thorny vegetation composed of maguey, molle, and cactus covered the entire site. The southern part of the site may have been destroyed by the expansion of modern agricultural fields.

Artifacts: Thirty seven diagnostic sherds were collected on the surface and from looters' pits: Kotosh Plain (11); Waira-jirca Red Plain (9); Waira-jirca Red Line-burnished (1); Waira-jirca Zoned Hachure (4); Waira-jirca Fine-line Incised (3); Waira-jirca Broad-line Incised (1); Kotosh Grooved A (1); Kotosh Graphited (1); Higueras Red (6); (Figure 73 and 74).

Chronological Position: Kotosh Waira-jirca Phase, Kotosh Kotosh Phase, Kotosh Higueras Phase.

Antecedents: Ravines, Ossio, and Núñez (1964); Onuki (1993).

Site No. 37: San Cristóbal

Location: Santa Maria del Valle, Santa Maria del Valle District, Huánuco Province, Department of Huánuco, Peru (09°51'45.8"S, 76°10'04.8"W).

Natural Setting: At an elevation of 1,963 masl in the *yunga* zone, this site is on the alluvial land on the southern bank of the Huallaga River.

Modern Land Use: Not applicable.

FIGURE 73. Examples of Kotosh Waira-jirca Phase pottery from Warampayloma (Site No. 36).

FIGURE 74. An example of Kotosh Kotosh Phase pottery with orange slip and graphite painting along a broad line incision, from Warampayloma (Site No. 36).

Site Description: This site was completely destroyed by quarrying for road construction during the late 1970s. Some pottery sherds could be seen around the area where the site once existed. According to Ravines and colleagues, there had been an artificial mound and stone walls on its surface (Ravines, Ossio, and Núñez 1964:36).

Artifacts: Three diagnostic sherds were collected from the area where the site had been located: Sajara-patac Chocolate Brown Plain (1); Sajara-patac Red (1); Higueras Red (1).

FIGURE 75. Exposed room feature at Armoncalloq (Site No. 38).

Chronological Position: Kotosh Sajara-patac Phase, Kotosh Higueras Phase.

Antecedents: Ravines, Ossio, and Núñez (1964).

Site No. 38: Armoncalloq
FIGURE 75

Location: Village of Conchumayo, Santa Maria del Valle District, Huánuco Province, Department of Huánuco, Peru (09°51′29.5″S, 76°11′02.4″W).

Natural Setting: At an elevation of 1,875 masl in the *yunga* zone, this site is on the northern bank of the Huallaga River to the west of a creek called Quebrada Conchumayo.

Modern Land Use: Not applicable.

Site Description: A few small structures of double-faced walls on the slope of the dry natural hill (see Figure 75). There is also an 8 by 9 m square structure on the surface. In this case, simple architecture composed of single stone alignments gives the impression that these structures were unroofed open spaces such as corrals rather than rooms for habitation. The architectural style of this site shows strong similarities with that of Huarampay (Site No. 39) and Tarucopata (Site No. 40).

Artifacts: A small amount of nondecorated body sherds were visible on the surface. All have orange surfaces and paste. They do not fit the typology established at Kotosh and could be of later periods.

Figure 76. Square feature with double-faced walls at Huarampay (Site No. 39).

Chronological Position: Unknown. Late Intermediate Period (?).

Antecedents: None.

Site No. 39: *Huarampay*

Figure 76

Location: Village of Conchumayo, Santa Maria del Valle District, Huánuco Province, Department of Huánuco, Peru (09°51′22.6″S, 76°11′17.0″W).

Natural Setting: At an elevation of 1,986 masl in the *yunga* zone, this site is on the northern bank of the Huallaga River and to the west of Quebrada Conchumayo.

Modern Land Use: Not applicable.

Site Description: A few small structures of double-faced walls on the lower hillside slope of a natural hill. All the architecture seemed to be square with double-faced walls. With its coarse stonework, the architecture of this site shows strong similarities to that of Armoncalloq (Site No. 38) and Tarucopata (Site No. 40).

Artifacts: A small amount of nondecorated body sherds were seen on the surface. All sherds have oxidized paste and an orange surface. They do not fit the typology established at Kotosh and thus could belong to the later period.

Chronological Position: Unknown. Late Intermediate Period (?).

Antecedents: None.

FIGURE 77. Line of unworked natural stones at Tarucopata (Site No. 40).

Site No. 40: Tarucopata

FIGURE 77

Location: Village of Taruca, Santa Maria del Valle District, Huánuco Province, Department of Huánuco, Peru (09°51′14.5″S, 76°08′29.7″W). This site is located approximately 300 m west of Puitoc (Site No. 41).

Natural Setting: At an elevation of 2,053 masl in *yunga* zone, this site is on the southern bank of the Huallaga River.

Modern Land Use: Not applicable.

Site Description: A large, square structure of double-faced walls on top of a dry natural hill. This stone structure has a corral-like shape and extends 25 m north–south by 20 m east–west. All walls consisted of a single line of unworked natural stones, which suggests use as an unroofed space. The architecture of this site shows strong similarities to that of Armoncalloq (Site No. 38) and Huarampay (Site No. 40).

Artifacts: A small amount of nondecorated body sherds were visible on the surface. All sherds have orange surfaces and paste. They do not fit the typology established at Kotosh and could belong to the later period.

Chronological Position: Unknown. Late Intermediate Period (?).

Antecedents: None.

Figure 78. Examples of Kotosh Sajara-patac Phase pottery from Puitoc (Site No. 41).

Site No. 41: Puitoc

Location: Village of Taruca, Santa Maria del Valle District, Huánuco Province, Department of Huánuco, Peru (09°51′11.1″S, 76°08′23.8″W). This site is located west of Papayo (Site No. 42) at the KM 423 marker of the road to Tingo Maria.

Natural Setting: At an elevation of 2,085 masl in the *yunga* zone, this site is on a large natural hill on the southern bank of the Huallaga River.

Modern Land Use: Pastureland.

Site Description: An artificial mound that extends 50 m north–south by 30 m east–west on a large natural hill. Although it is difficult to identify its precise extent, the approximate height of the mound would be less than 3 m. Many stone walls could be seen on the surface and some of them constituted room features. There were a few small looters' pits and pottery fragments were dispersed around them. Except for these looters' pits, the site is relatively well preserved.

Artifacts: Ten diagnostic sherds were collected on the surface and from looters' pits: Sajara-patac Chocolate Brown Plain (3); Sajara-patac Chocolate Brown Decorated (7); (Figure 78).

Chronological Position: Kotosh Sajara-patac Phase.

Antecedents: Onuki (1993:76) reported room constructions of different sizes on the site's surface, which could not be identified in the 2001 survey. According to Onuki, in 1966 the rooms measured 3 by 4 m, 3 by 5 m, 3 by 6 m, and 4 by 12 m.

Site No. 42: Papayo

Figures 79 to 81

Location: Village of Taruca, Santa Maria del Valle District, Huánuco Province, Department of Huánuco, Peru (09°51′05.0″S, 76°08′02.7″W). This site is located almost on the

FIGURE 79. Papayo 3 mound at Papayo (Site No. 42).

FIGURE 80. Canal in the Papayo 3 mound (Site No. 42).

Figure 81. The mounds Papayo 2 (*at left*) and Papayo 1 (*at right*) seen from the Papayo 3 mound (Site No. 42).

border of Taruca and Chullqui, approximately 600 m to the southwest of Waira-jirca (Site No. 43).

Natural Setting: At an elevation of 2,114 masl in the *yunga* zone, this site is on the slope of a large natural hill on the southern bank of the Huallaga River.

Modern Land Use: Agricultural field.

Site Description: Three artificial mounds (Papayo 1, 2, and 3) are on a large natural hill. Papayo 1 and Papayo 2 (see Figure 81) are closer to the Huallaga River than Papayo 3 (see Figures 79 and 80). Papayo 1 and Papayo 2 are arranged east–west and Papayo 3 is to the south of them. The description of each mound is as follows:

—Papayo 1 (09°51′01.6″S, 76°08′04.2″W): Stone walls were visible on the surface of the Papayo 1 mound. A looter's pit near the edge of the mound revealed a stone wall composed of flat stone and gray mud mortar. Kotosh Sajara-patac Phase pottery sherds were seen on the surface and in the looter's pit.

—Papayo 2 (09°51′02.8″S, 76°08′04.6″W): Papayo 2 is the smallest mound at the site. A coarse stone wall made of flat stones and mud mortar was observed on the surface. All the pottery sherds dispersed on the site surface belong to the Kotosh Sajara-patac Phase.

—Papayo 3 (09°51′05.0″S, 76°08′02.7″W): By far the largest mound at the site, Papayo 3 measures 30 m in diameter and 5 m in height. The southern part of the site had been destroyed by the construction of a soccer court. Here walls, superimposed floors, and canals were observed (see Figure 80). Some walls were composed of larger stones than others and had niches with white plaster. A large amount of Kotosh Sajara-patac Phase material was

Figure 82. Examples of Kotosh Sajara-patac Phase pottery from Papayo (Site No. 42).

Figure 83. Examples of Kotosh Sajara-patac Phase pottery from Papayo (Site No. 42).

FIGURE 84. Examples of Kotosh Sajara-patac Phase pottery from Papayo (Site No. 42).

visible on the surface. Papayo 3 is a large mound with high quality architecture, whereas Papayo 1 and Papayo 2 are modest in size with coarsely made architectural features.

Artifacts: Forty-two diagnostic pottery sherds were collected on the surface and looters' pits: Kotosh Plain (1); Sajara-patac Chocolate Brown Plain (23); Sajara-patac Chocolate Brown Decorated (8); Sajara-patac Red (5); San Blas Red Decorated (3); Higueras Red (2); (Figures 82 to 84).

Chronological Position: Kotosh Sajara-patac Phase, Kotosh Higueras Phase.

Antecedents: Onuki (1993).

Site No. 43: Waira-jirca

FIGURES 85 and 86

Location: Village of Chullqui, Churubamba District, Huánuco Province, Department of Huánuco, Peru (09°50'40.6"S, 76°07'55.1"W). This site is located in the area referred to as Waira-jirca, which is approximately 2 km to the south of the road to Tingo Maria.

Natural Setting: At an elevation of 1,970 masl in the *yunga* zone, this site is on a large natural hill on the southern bank of the Huallaga River.

Modern Land Use: The area around the site is used as a field for agriculture.

Site Description: An artificial mound that has an approximate diameter of 20 m and a height of 3 to 4 m. Lines of the trench of Onuki's excavation in 1966 could be seen on the top of the mound and there was a large looter's pit to the south of it. A square stone structure was exposed by the looter's pit. It is a room-like construction of double-faced

FIGURE 85. Waira-jirca (Site No. 43) seen from the south, showing exposed architectural features.

FIGURE 86. Possible Mito-style architecture at Waira-jirca (Site No. 43).

FIGURE 87. Examples of Kotosh Waira-jirca Phase and Kotosh Sajara-patac Phase pottery from Waira-jirca (Site No. 43).

walls made of flat mica schist and mud mortar. In a corner there was a niche in a wall. These architectural features are clearly similar to those of the Mito-style temple at Kotosh (see Figure 86). Moreover, no pottery sherds were observed in the soil over the floor or in a profile of the pit.

Considering that Onuki recognized two Mito-style constructions in the area 3 to 4 m to the south of this feature (see Appendix B), it is highly probable that this stone structure was exposed after 1966 and belongs to the Kotosh Mito Phase. Except for the looter's pit on the top of the mound, this site was relatively well preserved in 2001. However, when I visited the site in 2006, the edge of the mound had been badly destroyed by road construction. A canal and a few revetments were visible in the profile of the damaged area. These architectural features could be tied to the Mito temples on the top of the mound.

Artifacts: Ten diagnostic sherds were collected on the surface and from looters' pits: Kotosh Plain (2); Waira-jirca Zoned Hachure (1); Waira-jirca Fine-line Incised (3); Kotosh Red Grooved (1); Sajara-patac Chocolate Brown Plain (2); Sajara-patac Chocolate Brown Decorated (1); (Figure 87).

Chronological Position: Kotosh Mito Phase, Kotosh Waira-jirca Phase, Kotosh Kotosh Phase, Kotosh Sajara-patac Phase.

Antecedents: Onuki (1993). Onuki excavated this site in 1966 with Hiroyasu Tomoeda, Arturo Ruiz, and Fernando Chaud. He confirmed two Mito-style structures and Kotosh Waira-jirca Phase, Kotosh Kotosh Phase, and Kotosh Sajara-patac Phase occupations (see Appendix B).

FIGURE 88. Piquimina (Site No. 44), showing the small portion of the site remaining after construction of a sports court.

Site No. 44: Piquimina

FIGURE 88

Location: Village of Chullqui, Churubamba District, Huánuco Province, Department of Huánuco, Peru (09°50′16.9″S, 76°07′28.9″W). This site is located 200 m to the north of the highway to Tingo Maria.

Natural Setting: At an elevation of 1,779 masl in *yunga* zone, this site is on the southern bank of the Huallaga River, on the sandy alluvial floodplain close to the river.

Modern Land Use: Sports court.

Site Description: Almost the entire archaeological site has been lost to the construction of a sports court. A small portion was preserved around the edge of the site and pottery sherds were dispersed around the construction cuts. According to a local family, there was a low sand mound with aligned stones on its surface. In addition, they remembered that there were many bones, including human skulls, and a large amount of pottery sherds in the soil moved by construction activities in the early 1990s.

Artifacts: Nineteen diagnostic pottery sherds were collected on the surface and the soil dump made by construction activities: Kotosh Plain (5); Waira-jirca Black Line-burnished (2); Waira-jirca Zoned Hachure (1); Kotosh Grooved A (4); Paucarbamba Brilliant Plain (1); Sajara-patac Chocolate Brown Plain (3); Higueras Red (3); (Figures 89 and 90).

Chronological Position: Kotosh Waira-jirca Phase, Kotosh Kotosh Phase, Kotosh Chavín Phase, Kotosh Sajara-patac Phase, Kotosh Higueras Phase.

FIGURE 89. Examples of Kotosh Waira-jirca Phase and Kotosh Kotosh Phase pottery from Piquimina (Site No. 44).

FIGURE 90. An example of Kotosh Chavín Phase pottery from Piquimina (Site No. 44).

Antecedents: Onuki (1993); Kinya Inokuchi and Nelly Martell Castillo, 2002 unpublished report, "Informe Preliminar del Proyecto de Investigaciones Arqueológicas de Sajarapatac y Piquimina en Huánuco, Perú," Instituto Nacional de Cultura, Lima. This site was first excavated in 1966 by Onuki, Hiroyasu Tomoeda, Carlos Chaud, and Fernando Chaud. Onuki found a burial associated with Kotosh Chavín Phase pottery and suggested that this site could have been a cemetery of the Kotosh Chavín Phase (Onuki 1993:76). In

FIGURE 91. The elongated mound and large potters' pit at Tunacirca (Site No. 45).

2002, Nelly Martell Castillo and I excavated the southern margin of this site as a part of the Huánuco Archaeological Project directed by Kinya Inokuchi and Onuki. A wall associated with Kotosh Chavín Phase materials and diagnostic pottery sherds from the Kotosh Waira-jirca Phase through to the Kotosh Higueras Phase were identified (see Appendix D).

Site No. 45: Tunacirca

FIGURE 91

Location: Village of Cascay, Churubamba District, Huánuco Province, Department of Huánuco, Peru (09°50′23.5″S, 76°08′44.0″W). This site is located approximately 120 m to the south of the Plaza de Armas in the village of Cascay.

Natural Setting: At an elevation of 1,893 masl in the *yunga* zone, this site is in the triangular area where the Huallaga River and the Chinobamba River unite. The edge of the site is a cliff more than 10 m in height.

Modern Land Use: The southern part of the site is used as a clay source by local potters.

Site Description: A flat artificial mound on a low natural hill that is artificially terraced. It is difficult to calculate the area of the site, because the border that divides the site from the natural landscape could not be identified well. However, the mound seems to have an elongated plan and extends at least 30 m north–south by 10 m east–west and is 1 to 2 m in height. On the northern edge of the site there was a huge pit made by local potters for clay procurement. This had plastered walls and a burned floor. There was some vegetation composed of maguey and molle near the edge of the mound and a few small looters' pits could be seen on the surface.

FIGURE 92. Examples of Kotosh Waira-jirca Phase pottery from Tunacirca (Site No. 45).

FIGURE 93. Examples of Kotosh Sajara-patac Phase pottery from Tunacirca (Site No. 45).

Artifacts: Thirteen diagnostic pottery sherds and one spindle whorl were collected on the surface: Kotosh Plain (2); Waira-jirca Red Line-burnished (2); Waira-jirca Fine-line Incised (1); Sajara-patac Chocolate Brown Plain (5); Sajara-patac Chocolate Brown Decorated (1); (Figures 92 and 93). There are two additional sherds that cannot be classified in the Kotosh typology. Both have fine dark-gray paste and a black surface with a metallic

Figure 94. The small circular construction at Chacuas-pampa (Site No. 46).

Figure 95. The large semipentagonal construction at Chacuas-pampa (Site No. 46).

luster. One is decorated with triangles filled in with punctations, a typical design of the Sajara-patac Chocolate Brown Decorated pottery type. One spindle whorl made from a Waira-jirca Red Plain body sherd was also found on the surface.

Chronological Position: Kotosh Waira-jirca Phase, Kotosh Sajara-patac Phase.

Antecedents: None.

Site No. 46: Chacuas-pampa

FIGURES 94 and 95

Location: Village of Cascay, Churubamba District, Huánuco Province, Department of Huánuco, Peru (09°50′12.5″S, 76°08′57.7″W). This site is located behind the Cascay community cemetery.

Natural Setting: At an elevation of 1,905 masl in *yunga* zone, this site is on a flat-topped natural hill on the southern bank of the Huallaga River. The Chinobamba River passes to the north of the site.

Modern Land Use: Pastureland.

Site Description: There were two stone features on the top of the dry, flat hill. One was circular with a diameter of 6 m (see Figure 94). The other was 50 m in diameter with aa semi-pentagonal shape (see Figure 95). Both are composed of double-faced walls. There was only a small amount of pottery sherds near these constructions, but more sherds were collected in the area to the north.

Artifacts: Although no diagnostic sherds were collected on the surface, there seems to be a clear difference between the pottery sherds near the constructions and those from the northern area of the site. Whereas the former are mainly a coarse, orange ware without slip (Figure 96), the latter are characterized by red slip with gray to dark-gray paste and show a strong similarity to Higueras Red. The former probably belong to the later period.

Chronological Position: Kotosh Higueras Phase (?). Late Intermediate Period (?).

Antecedents: Luis E. Salcedo Camacho, 2000 unpublished report, "Informe No. 007-2000-INC/HCO-Pat. Arql.," Instituto Nacional de Cultura, Dirección Departamental de Cultura de Huánuco, Oficina de Patrimonio Arqueológico, Huánuco, Perú.

Site No. 47: Sajara-patac

Location: Village of Pacapucro, Churubamba District, Huánuco Province, Department of Huánuco, Peru (09°50′03.4″S, 76°08′09.2″W). This site is located approximately 1 km to the southwest of the village of Churubamba.

Natural Setting: At an elevation of 1,898 masl in the *yunga* zone, this site is on a natural hill on the northern bank of the Huallaga River.

Modern Land Use: Part of the site (Mound 1 and Mound 2 in Onuki [1993]) is on private property.

Site Description: Three mounds line up from southwest to northeast along the Huallaga River. Mound 1 is a flat-topped mound on the top of the hill and extends 17 m north–south by 30 m east–west; it is partially cut by the road to Churubamba. Mound 2 is on a gentle hillside to the northeast of Mound 1 and extends more than 20 m north–south by 40 m east–west. For more detail see Inokuchi et al. (2003), Matsumoto (2009), and Matsumoto and Tsurumi (2011).

Artifacts: See Matsumoto and Tsurumi (2011).

FIGURE 96. Unclassified body sherds from Chacuas-pampa (Site No. 46).

Chronological Position: Kotosh Chavín Phase, Kotosh Sajara-patac Phase.

Antecedents: In 1966, Yoshio Onuki and Yasushi Miyazaki conducted test excavations on the northwestern edge of Mound 1, placing a trapezoidal trench with base lengths of 3.45 m (northwest side), 2.50 m (southeast side), and 4.52 m (northeast-to-southwest axis) in accordance with the form of the mound edge. One room construction with three superimposed floors was uncovered. The lower two floors probably belong to the Kotosh Chavín Phase and the upper one to the Kotosh Sajara-patac Phase. The earliest floor was associated with a fire pit filled with ash and charcoal (Onuki 1993:75). In 2002, Kinya Inokuchi, Onuki, Eisei Tsurumi, and I excavated this site as part of the Huánuco Archaeological Project (see Inokuchi et al. [2003]; Matsumoto [2007, 2009]; Matsumoto and Tsurumi [2011]).

Site No. 48: Jircanera

FIGURE 97

Location: Village of Tambogan, Churubamba District, Huánuco Province, Department of Huánuco, Peru (09°46'19.3"S, 76°14'15.5"W). This site is located approximately 1 km to the north of the village of Tambogan.

Natural Setting: At an elevation of 3,112 masl in the *quechua* zone, this site is on a large natural hill.

Modern Land Use: Agricultural field.

Site Description: Some room-like constructions and stone walls around the lower part of the hill called Jircanera. Considering the construction technique and style of its looted pottery, this site possibly belongs to the Late Horizon. There are pottery sherds of the

FIGURE 97. View of Jircanera (Site No. 48).

Kotosh Waira-jirca Phase through the Kotosh Chavín Phase on the southern side of Jircanera and its eastern slope, whereas those of the Kotosh Higueras Phase were found throughout the hilltop area.

Artifacts: Forty-nine diagnostic pottery sherds were collected on the surface: Kotosh Plain (15); Waira-jirca Red Plain (1); Waira-jirca Black Line-burnished (1); Waira-jirca Shallow Incised (1); Waira-jirca Zoned Hachure (1); Kotosh Grooved B (1); Paucarbamba Brilliant Plain (2); Higueras Red (15); Higueras Brown (11); (Figures 98 to 102). There is one un-classified sherd with red surface slip and a geometric design with black paint. The paste is oxidized red. This piece could belong to the Late Horizon. One of the landlords showed me a few looted pieces. One was a typical aryballos of the Late Horizon (see Figure 102).

Chronological Position: Kotosh Waira-jirca Phase, Kotosh Kotosh Phase, Kotosh Chavín Phase, Kotosh Higueras Phase, Late Horizon.

Antecedents: None.

Site No. 49: Huanojpa

FIGURE 103

Location: Village of Tambogan, Churubamba District, Huánuco Province, Department of Huánuco, Peru (09°46′13.9″S, 76°13′45.8″W). This site is located approximately 1 km to the north of the village of Tambogan.

Natural Setting: At an elevation of 2,982 masl in the *quechua* zone, this site is an artificially modified hill.

Modern Land Use: None.

FIGURE 98. Examples of Kotosh Waira-jirca Phase pottery from Jircanera (Site No. 48).

FIGURE 99. Examples of Kotosh Kotosh Phase and Kotosh Chavín Phase pottery from Jircanera (Site No. 48).

FIGURE 100. Examples of Kotosh Higueras Phase pottery from Jircanera (Site No. 48).

FIGURE 101. Examples of Kotosh Higueras Phase pottery (*at left*) and possible Late Horizon pottery (*at right*) from Jircanera (Site No. 48).

FIGURE 102. Looted pottery from Jircanera (Site No. 48), including a Late Horizon aryballos.

Site Description: A small natural hill at the foot of the large hill where Jircanera (Site No. 48) is located. This small rocky hill is approximately 10 to 15 m in height. Its slope has been transformed into a series of artificial terraces and its top flattened. With this modification, this site looks like a terraced platform. Pottery sherds were found on the surface.

Artifacts: Nine diagnostic pottery sherds were collected on the surface. None had any decoration. Although six can be classified as Higueras Brown, the other three fragments might belong to the Late Intermediate Period or Late Horizon.

Chronological Position: Kotosh Higueras Phase (?), Late Intermediate Period (?), Late Horizon (?).

Antecedents: None.

Site No. 50: Huancachupa

Location: Village of Huancachupa, San Francisco de Cayrán District, Huánuco Province, Department of Huánuco, Peru (09°58′49.6″S, 76°14′50.0″W). This site is located approximately 4 km to the south of the city of Huánuco.

Natural Setting: At an elevation of 2,048 masl in the *yunga* zone, this site is on the eastern terrace of the Huallaga River.

Modern Land Use: Not applicable.

Site Description: This site is a large artificial mound with an approximate dimension of 60 by 50 m. Two circular structures were located near the edge of the mound. These were deep circular holes with an approximate diameter of 3 m each and constructed with quarried stones and mud mortar. Although quarried stones were used for the revetments and

FIGURE 103. The artificial terraces and flattened top of Huanojpa (Site No. 49).

some surface features, large river cobbles were mainly used as construction fill. The entire site was covered by thorny vegetation, such as cactus and maguey.

Artifacts: Only a small amount of pottery was seen on the surface and no diagnostic sherds were collected. However, a few body sherds collected from this site have orange paste, complete oxidized firing, and a coarse temper. This suggests that this site belongs to the period after the Kotosh Higueras Phase.

Chronological Position: Late Intermediate Period (?), Late Horizon (?).

Antecedents: None.

Site No. 51: Vilcamiraflores

Location: Vilcamiraflores, San Francisco de Cayrán District, Huánuco Province, Department of Huánuco, Peru (09°58′34.4″S, 76°14′40.4″W). This site is located approximately 3 km to the southwest of the city of Huánuco.

Natural Setting: At an elevation of 1,998 masl in the *yunga* zone, this site is on a natural hill on the western terrace of the Huallaga River.

Modern Land Use: None.

Site Description: An artificial mound that extends 40 by 40 m and is 4 to 5 m in height. About 20% of the mound has been destroyed by looters. Plastered stone walls and burned superimposed floors could be seen in the looters' pits. Possible room or platform constructions were made of river cobbles, quarried stones, and mud mortar.

FIGURE 104. Examples of Kotosh Waira-jirca Phase pottery from Vilcamiraflores (Site No. 51).

Artifacts: Twenty-eight diagnostic sherds were collected on the surface and from looters' pits: Waira-jirca Red Plain (1); Waira-jirca Red Line-burnished (1); Waira-jirca Black Line-burnished (1); Waira-jirca Shallow Incised (1); Kotosh Plain (3); Sajara-patac Chocolate Brown Plain (5); Sajara-patac Chocolate Brown Decorated (1); Higueras Red (13); Higueras Brown (2); (Figure 104).

Chronological Position: Kotosh Waira-jirca Phase, Kotosh Sajara-patac Phase, Kotosh Higueras Phase.

Antecedents: None.

Reported Sites Not in the 2001 Survey

The following is a summary of the five sites in the Upper Huallaga Basin that we were unable to visit during our research in 2001.

Quillarumi

According to Onuki's (1993:72) description, Quillarumi is a rock shelter located 2 km to the south of Kotosh (Site No. 24) at an elevation of approximately 2,500 masl. It has many petroglyphs painted with red pigments. Onuki assigns this site to the Early or Middle Preceramic Period (before 2500 BC).

Marabamba 1

This site was registered with the name Marabamba by Onuki (1993:72) during his survey in the 1960s. To differentiate this site from the site registered during the 2001 survey (see Site No. 21), I tentatively name it Marabamba 1. It is a petroglyph site located near the confluence of the Huallaga and Higueras Rivers. It could belong to the Early Preceramic Period (Onuki 1993:72). This site could not be confirmed by the 2001 survey and may have been destroyed.

Figure 105. Exposed architectural features at the Mitomarca site.

Figure 106. View of a portion of the 1.5 m wide perimeter wall at the site of Mitomarca.

Figure 107. Jason Nesbitt at the Mitomarca site in 2006.

Paucarbamba

Paucarbamba was destroyed by the urban expansion of the city of Huánuco. We could not find any trace of architecture nor pottery sherds in 2001. Onuki (1993:74) excavated the site in 1966 and found a Kotosh Chavín Phase ceremonial structure with a staircase made of selected large stones. According to Onuki, the site had three mounds that could have been arranged in a possible U-shaped layout (Y. Onuki, pers. comm. 1999).

Pircog

The site of Pircog is located at an elevation of approximately 3,200 masl in the *quechua* zone. Onuki (1993:75) reported the existence of many stone structures with roofed high stone masonry walls. The walls have niches in several levels, as seen in other Late Intermediate and Late Horizon sites of the region (e.g., Thompson 1967; Morales 1984). Onuki also noticed the similarity in pottery style between this site and the site of Icchu excavated by Donald Thompson (Thompson 1967; Onuki 1982).

Mitomarca

I visited the site of Mitomarca (Figures 105 to 107) with Jason Nesbitt and Denesy Palacios in 2006. Our surface survey confirmed pottery sherds of the Kotosh Sajara-patac and Kotosh Higueras Phases. This site is located on a hilltop near Sajara-patac at an elevation of approximately 2,300 masl. It extends 1.8 ha in area and is surrounded by a massive perimeter wall 1.5 m in width. Inside the wall were a plaza, which measured 22 by 24 m, and many small platform and room complexes. The architectural style is different from that of the Initial Period, Early Horizon, and Early Intermediate Period in this region and seems to share similarities with the Late Intermediate Period architecture at nearby sites, such as Piruru and Garu (Bonnier 1997a; Salcedo Camacho et al. 2000). In addition, the many pottery sherds observed on the surface did not fit the typology of Kotosh. They were characterized by coarse oxidized paste and red paint, and probably belong to the later period after the Kotosh Higueras Phase. The existence of later period pottery suggests that this is a multi-component site and raises the possibility that all the architecture visible on the surface was constructed in the later period. Although the perimeter wall looked like a defensive wall, the large square plaza may suggest communal activities at the site as well. More research is required to reveal the character of this site (see also Matsumoto, Nesbitt, and Palacios 2012).

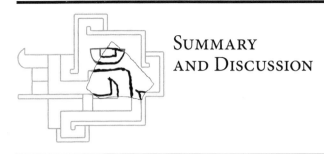

CHAPTER FIVE

Summary
and Discussion

Of the fifty-one sites visited in the 2001 Upper Huallaga Basin survey, thirty-five were newly registered. Again, this study is basically restricted to the *yunga* zone and therefore has certain limitations. Additional surveys are obviously needed to more fully consider the entire settlement pattern in the Upper Huallaga Basin. However, it is worth integrating the 2001 survey data to provide a comprehensive interpretation of the regional cultural sequence and to generate future research questions. Synthesis of settlement pattern data with available archaeological data will make it possible to compare the cultural sequence of the Upper Huallaga Basin to that of other regions.

For these reasons, in addition to interpreting the 2001 survey settlement data, this study will attempt to integrate all the available data up to the present, including the archaeological investigations of the 1960s and those after 2001.

Before the Late Preceramic Period (c. 2500 BC)

No new archaic sites were found by our survey. Although we know of some examples (Figure 108) of Early and Middle Preceramic Period (8000–4000 BC) sites, such as Cueva de Jatun Uchco (Site No. 1) and Quillarumi (Onuki 1993:72), the sites of this period are mainly rock shelters and petroglyphs, and many are in the higher elevations, from the *quechua* to *puna* zones, as the data from the site of Lauricocha suggest (e.g., Cardich 1964). Because the main focus of our survey was the bottomland of the Upper Huallaga Basin, in the future the research area should be expanded to consider locations favored by Early and Middle Preceramic Period people. However, as Onuki (1993:72) indicated, the existence of a few sites, especially petroglyphs such as at Quillarumi and Marabamba, in the *yunga* suggest that the hunter-gatherers of this period organized their subsistence economy using *yunga* resources in addition to resources in the *quechua* or *puna* (MacNeish et al. 1981; Onuki 1982:212–213). An important theme for future study will be the transition from this period to the following Late Preceramic Period.

How did nonsedentary hunter-gatherers in rock shelter and cave sites at higher elevations construct Mito-style monumental architecture in the bottomland of the basin, that

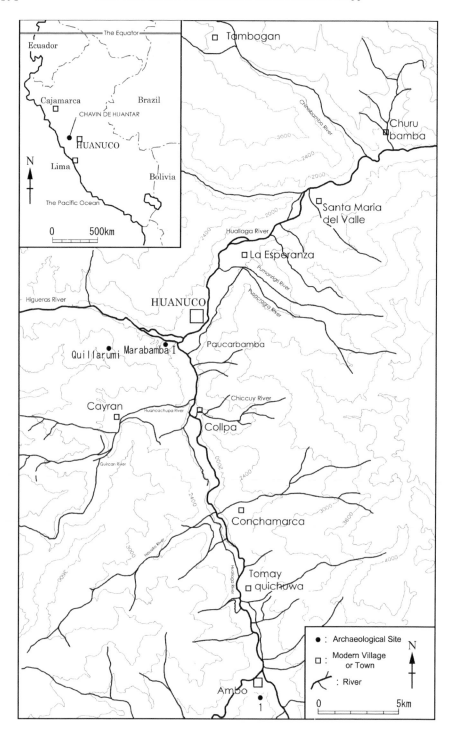

Figure 108. Archaeological sites earlier than the Kotosh Mito Phase (c. 2500 bc).

is, the *yunga* (e.g., Onuki 1999)? All previous studies seem to suggest that the emergence of monumental architecture in the Upper Huallaga Basin was a radical change, because of the architectural sophistication and symbolic complexity of Mito temples (e.g., Burger and Salazar-Burger 1993; Onuki 1999). However, as Elizabeth Bonnier (1997b) noted for the early monumental architecture of Piruru in Tantamayo, located approximately 80 km to the north of the Upper Huallaga Basin, it is difficult to reject the possibility that an architectural tradition preceding the Kotosh Mito Phase existed in the *quechua* or *suni* zones. Only more surveys in these zones will make it possible to evaluate the transition to the Kotosh Mito Phase in this region.

The Late Preceramic Period:
The Kotosh Mito Phase (2500–1600 BC)

In the chronological framework of the Upper Huallaga Basin (see Chapter 3), the Kotosh Mito Phase corresponds to the Late Preceramic Period, well known for the Mito-style temples represented by the Temple of the Crossed Hands (e.g., Izumi and Sono 1963; see Chapter 1). Because in the 2001 survey the dating of each site relied heavily on surface-collected pottery sherds, the settlement pattern of the Preceramic Period cannot be shown from this research. However, investigations at Kotosh (Site No. 24), Shillacoto (Site No. 26), and Waira-jirca (Site No. 43) revealed that all the Mito temples excavated there are under the Kotosh Waira-jirca Phase occupation (Onuki 1993, 1998:72–74; see also Appendix B). Therefore, presumably there were temples of the Kotosh Mito Phase under the occupation level of the Kotosh Waira-jirca Phase (Onuki 1993, 1998:72–74; see also Appendix B). Although this assumption should be tested through excavation at Kotosh Waira-jirca Phase sites, I tentatively treat the settlement pattern of the Kotosh Waira-jirca Phase as that of the Kotosh Mito Phase, and synthesize available archaeological data on the basis of this assumption.

The pottery sherds of the Kotosh Waira-jirca Phase were recognized at sixteen sites. Depending on location and size, the sites of this period can be divided into two types. The sites comparable with Kotosh (see Figure 108) in mound size are: Shillacoto, Jancao (Site No. 27), Cotopata (Site No. 29), and Warampayloma (Site No. 36). These sites tend to be in open space close to, or on, alluvial floodplains near the confluence of rivers. In contrast, a second type (smaller sites like Waira-jirca) tends to be located on the hills that overlook the juncture of two rivers (Inokuchi et al. 2002:83). All are multi-component sites and form mounds, preventing us from estimating the scale of this public architecture. However, the excavation data from Kotosh (Izumi and Terada 1972), Shillacoto (Izumi, Cuculiza, and Kano 1972), and Waira-jirca (see Appendix B) seems to imply that there is a correlation between the site size and number or size of Mito temples at each site (Onuki 1993, 1998). This needs to be tested through excavation.

This pattern might suggest that the location of ceremonial centers was chosen to provide access to river water, perhaps related to some kind of control over it. In addition, it could reflect an ideological importance of the location. As Burger (1992:130) noted in the case of Chavín de Huántar, the juncture of two rivers is referred to by the Quechua term *tinkuy*, which means the harmonious meeting of opposing forces. This ideological aspect of the site location seems to be supported by the data from Kotosh, which indicate that dualism was an important part of the religious belief of the Kotosh Mito Phase. During the excavations at Kotosh two clay wall reliefs from a Mito-style temple were found (Izumi and Sono 1963; Izumi and Terada 1972; Onuki 1993, 1998). These were two sets of crossed hands, for which the Temple of the Crossed Hands was named (see Chapter 1). Though these two sculptures were symmetrically arranged on the temple, they differ in size and show contrasting positioning of the arms. The difference in size of the arms symbolizes male–female opposition, and the contrasting position of the arms and their location on the opposite sides of the architectural axis imply a general dualistic concept (Izumi 1971:89; Burger and Salazar-Burger 1993; see Chapter 1). The dual chambers of Mito-style temples found at Kotosh also represent dualism during the Kotosh Mito Phase (Burger and Salazar-Burger 1993:108–109). With these data from Kotosh, it is possible to interpret that this settlement pattern is a reflection of this dualistic concept that prevailed during this time.

The settlement data also give us a clue to consider the sociopolitical situation of the Upper Huallaga Basin. Although the survey confirmed the pattern of relatively large mounds with Mito-style temples distributed along the Huallaga River at intervals of 5 km, as had been indicated by Onuki (1993:83), it also showed that smaller mound sites that could contain Mito-style temples were located on hilltops near the confluence of rivers. Burger and Salazar presented an interesting discussion to consider this issue on the basis of the data from their excavation at Huaricoto in Callejón de Huaylas (Burger and Salazar-Burger 1980, 1985, 1986). They noted that public architecture stylistically similar to that of the Kotosh Mito Phase is distributed in a wide geographical area covering the central highlands and suggested that these temples derived from the same religious tradition, named the Kotosh Religious Tradition, that shared burning rituals in a closed space. By comparing the public buildings at Huaricoto and Kotosh, they argued that there could have been two different systems of labor investment and associated social organization among the societies of the Kotosh Religious Tradition.

One is corporate labor, which was carried out by the coming together of more than one family (Burger and Salazar-Burger 1986) and needed a social organization with leaders to control the labor required for monumental construction projects. The other is a cargo-like system, in which religious authority rotated among families in a community. According to Burger and Salazar, although corporate labor was necessary for the construction of elaborate temples at Kotosh, such as the Temple of the Crossed Hands, the simpler and smaller-scale buildings found at Huaricoto did not need this kind of hierarchical organization and could have been constructed under a cargo-like system. Although presumably social integration beyond one family developed from corporate labor, the cargo-like system may not have caused this type of change in social organization (Burger and Salazar-Burger 1986:77).

Burger and Salazar applied this difference in labor organization to explain the difference between Kotosh and Huaricoto, that is, a difference at an interregional level between the Upper Huallaga Basin and Callejón de Huaylas. However, this difference could even be seen among the centers in the Upper Huallaga Basin, considering the temple of Waira-jirca (see Appendix B) and small hilltop mounds found in our 2001 survey. As Onuki (1998:74, 2000) discussed, there are differences in size among the Mito-style temples and platforms associated with them in the Upper Huallaga Basin, as seen at Kotosh, Shillacoto, and Waira-jirca. This seems to reconfirm Onuki's interpretation that each center corresponded to a community and their relationships were not only competitive, but also complementary. In this context, note that all the centers belonged to the same religious tradition and were loosely united through it (Onuki 1993:83, 1998:74) as the Kotosh Religious Tradition, or Mito Tradition (Burger and Salazar-Burger 1980, 1985, 1986; Bonnier 1997b). This situation in the Upper Huallaga Basin can be described as "peer polity interaction," as proposed by Colin Renfrew (1982, 1986), because the distribution of Mito-style temples can be interpreted to show the coexistence of autonomous political units despite differences in population size and social organization. A study of relationships among these small peer polities in this region would be a productive path for future research.

The Early Initial Period:
The Kotosh Waira-jirca Phase (1600–1200 BC)

The Kotosh Waira-jirca Phase corresponds to the early Initial Period. Sixteen sites of this phase (Figure 109) were recognized in the 2001 survey. These can be divided in two groups: those located in the open space near the confluence of rivers and the others on the hilltops overlooking the rivers. Although there is not much to add about this period from only the settlement pattern data, it seems useful to integrate the available data on the assumption that peer polity relations continued from the preceding Kotosh Mito Phase.

Although data on the architecture of this phase are scarce, the pottery styles provide new insight on the intraregional relationships of these centers. Several differences between the pottery assemblages at Kotosh and Shillacoto can be analyzed using the typology established with Kotosh samples (e.g., Kano 1979). In the case of the pottery assemblage at Shillacoto in the Kotosh Waira-jirca Phase, some stylistic features that did not appear at Kotosh until the next Kotosh Kotosh Phase already existed. The most representative feature among them is anthropomorphic representation expressed in flaring bowls with grooved lines (e.g., Izumi and Sono 1963, pl. 130; Onuki 1972). For example, elaborate bowls with this stylistic feature were excavated from a unique funeral context of this period (SR-6/Tomb No. 6; see Izumi, Cuculiza, and Kano 1972:30, 45–46). In the contemporary pottery assemblage at Kotosh, this representation did not exist and is restricted to the Kotosh Grooved A and Kotosh Red Modeled styles, both of which mainly appear in the Kotosh Kotosh Phase (Onuki 1972; Kano 1979:18).

In this context, as Kano noted, many examples of these types with anthropomorphic representations were excavated from the early Kotosh Waira-jirca Phase layers at Shillacoto (Kano 1979:18–19, 41–42). This anthropomorphic imagery at Shillacoto stylistically changes from a monkey-like face of the Kotosh Waira-jirca Phase to a more human-like face of the Kotosh Kotosh Phase. This pattern is not recognized at Kotosh and thus it is safe to say that the pottery assemblages of Kotosh and Shillacoto in the Kotosh Waira-jirca Phase were at least partially different, which probably suggests that a stylistic invention at Shillacoto was accepted at Kotosh in the subsequent phase. Moreover, although Shillacoto and Kotosh share the same pottery style, which shows a clear affiliation to that of the eastern slope of the Andes (e.g., Lathrap 1962, 1970), the overall variations of decorative motifs, including possible religious iconographies, are far richer at Shillacoto (Kano 1979).

In addition to pottery style, an important aspect of social organization differentiates Shillacoto from Kotosh. Although an elaborate burial suggesting the presence of an elite class was recognized at Shillacoto, for now no evidence of status differentiation has been found from the Kotosh Waira-jirca Phase context at Kotosh.

In sum, these data seem to suggest that during the Kotosh Waira-jirca Phase the intersite relationships in the Upper Huallaga Basin were similar to that of the Kotosh Mito

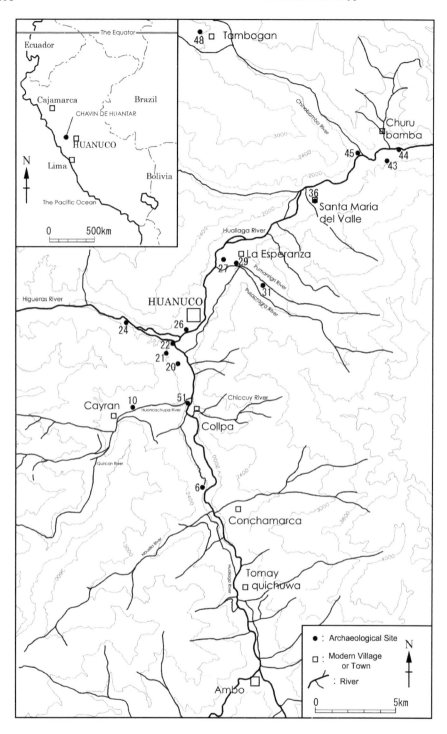

Figure 109. Sites of the Kotosh Mito and Kotosh Waira-jirca Phases (2500–1200 BC). Numbers are keyed to the site descriptions in Chapter 4.

Phase. In other words, autonomous polities different in size and social organization coexisted and interacted with each other. These differences in the overall similarity of pottery styles between Shillacoto and Kotosh may suggest that they were in the same religious tradition, but were politically independent from each other. The presence of a burial with rich offerings at Shillacoto seems to imply that the social hierarchy was more marked at Shillacoto than at Kotosh.

The Late Initial Period:
The Kotosh Kotosh Phase (1200–700 BC)

Pottery sherds of the Kotosh Kotosh Phase, which corresponds to the late Initial Period, were found at seven sites (Figure 110), including three newly registered ones. Although the sites of the Kotosh Waira-jirca Phase continued to be occupied in this period, the number of sites decreased by half. Except for Waira-jirca, almost all the small sites located on hilltops were abandoned and only larger sites, which are in the open spaces near the confluence of rivers, continued to be occupied from the previous phase. Although it is difficult to know the reason for this change, some possibilities can be suggested. The populations that had dispersed in the Kotosh Mito and Kotosh Waira-jirca Phases may have concentrated at the larger sites. This change may have been associated with a change of the political landscape among the centers, or with an increased importance of agriculture as a main part of the subsistence economy, or both. The excavations at Kotosh and Shillacoto in the 1960s provide important data sets with which to consider this question.

These excavation data show that radical changes occurred, at least in the pottery styles of the Upper Huallaga Basin, not only for vessel forms but also in decorative motifs. As stated, the anthropomorphic imagery existed only at Shillacoto in the iconography of the Kotosh Waira-jirca Phase. However, in this phase it appeared at Kotosh and seems to have been established as an important stylistic feature in the pottery assemblage there. If this anthropomorphic representation was important in the religious iconography, as suggested by Kano (1979), it can be hypothesized that the religious tenets that developed at Shillacoto were accepted at Kotosh and probably at other contemporary sites in the Upper Huallaga Basin. Another unique feature of Shillacoto is its contact with Chavín de Huántar, as shown in the important burial (SR-4/Tomb No. 4) associated with bone artifacts with Chavín iconography similar to that of Lazón (Izumi, Cuculiza, and Kano 1972; Kano 1979, pl. xiv; Bischof 2008:12). One of these bone artifacts has a simple anthropomorphic image (Kano 1979:22), which may correspond to those that developed at Shillacoto and were accepted in the Upper Huallaga Basin during the Kotosh Kotosh Phase. In contrast, no evidence of such direct contact with Chavín de Huántar was recognized at Kotosh.

Considering the large site size, burials with rich offerings, and unique evidence of interregional interaction with Chavín de Huántar, presumably Shillacoto became more important and began to have religious influence on other sites, including Kotosh. As a result of this change the Upper Huallaga Basin became more socially integrated. At the same time, the decrease in the number of sites may have occurred because of the concentration of population in the large open space sites after abandonment of small hilltop sites. Social integration through the hegemony of Shillacoto may have caused this population movement. Although this pattern can be explained by the increased importance of agriculture, these two hypotheses are not mutually exclusive and could be complementary.

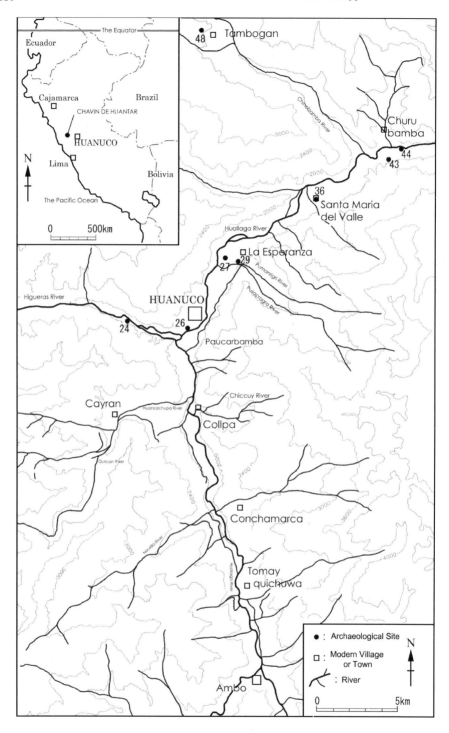

FIGURE 110. Sites of the Kotosh Kotosh Phase (1200–700 BC). Numbers are keyed to the site descriptions in Chapter 4.

Obviously, the intersite political relationships in the Upper Huallaga Basin remain to be studied. In the preceding Kotosh Waira-jirca Phase clear differences were recognized between Kotosh and Shillacoto in the decorative techniques and variations of iconography applied to pottery, yet no marked difference can be seen between pottery styles of these two sites in this period. It is not clear what this change means. In addition, it is difficult to evaluate whether the religious influence from Shillacoto caused political integration at a regional level, or whether the centers remained peer polities maintaining political autonomy. To consider these questions, there should be more excavation projects at other sites that focus on the transition from the Kotosh Waira-jirca Phase to the Kotosh Kotosh Phase.

The Early Early Horizon:
The Kotosh Chavín Phase (700–250 BC)

Pottery sherds of the Kotosh Chavín Phase, which corresponds to the early Early Horizon, were found in six sites (Figure 111), including three newly registered sites. Kotosh and Jancao were the only sites continued to be occupied from the Kotosh Kotosh Phase. Other sites of the Kotosh Kotosh Phase were abandoned, and new locations were selected for building activities. As a result of the 2001 survey, it became clear that there was a pattern for the selection of locations for new buildings activities.

In modern urban areas around the confluence of the Huallaga and Higueras Rivers, the Shillacoto site was abandoned and the Paucarbamba site was constructed on the opposite bank. The same pattern was observed in the villages of Amarilis and Chullqui. In Amarilis, the Cotopata site on the river was abandoned and the Chupaylla site (Site No. 30) was constructed on the opposite bank, 1 km upstream. In Chullqui, the Waira-jirca site was abandoned and the Sajara-patac site was built on the opposite bank of the Huallaga River. These new locations were chosen near the confluence of rivers where the same natural settings were available. However, in the village of Santa Maria del Valle, even though Warampayloma (Site No. 36) was abandoned after the Kotosh Kotosh Phase, the Early Horizon site of the Kotosh Chavín Phase was not found by the 2001 survey. Yet, according to Ravines, Ossio, and Núñez (1964), there was a Formative Period (Initial Period and Early Horizon) site called San Cristobal (Site No. 37) about 800 m northwest of Warampayloma. They reported the existence of a mound with stone walls at the site (Ravines, Ossio, and Núñez 1964:34), which in the 1970s was completely destroyed by heavy machinery digging materials for road construction. Though only a few pottery sherds of the later Sajara-patac phase were recovered from the site in the 2001 survey, presumably it had the same pattern of abandonment in the previous period and a move to a new location.

Clearly, the change of settlement pattern from the Kotosh Kotosh Phase to the Kotosh Chavín Phase reflects radical transformation of religious ideology from the local to a pan-regional Chavín cult (Burger 1988, 1992, 1993). According to the excavation data from Kotosh, Shillacoto, Paucarbamba, and Sajara-patac (Izumi and Sono 1963; Izumi, Cuculiza, and Kano 1972; Izumi and Terada 1972; Kano 1979; Onuki 1993; Inokuchi et al. 2002; Matsumoto and Tsurumi 2011), this transformation corresponds to radical changes in pottery and architectural styles. In addition, this change also might suggest that the Initial Period centers of the Upper Huallaga Basin experienced a change in the style of ritual activity from the restricted activities related to the Kotosh Religious Tradition to more public rituals in open spaces, which reflects the influence from Chavín de Huántar

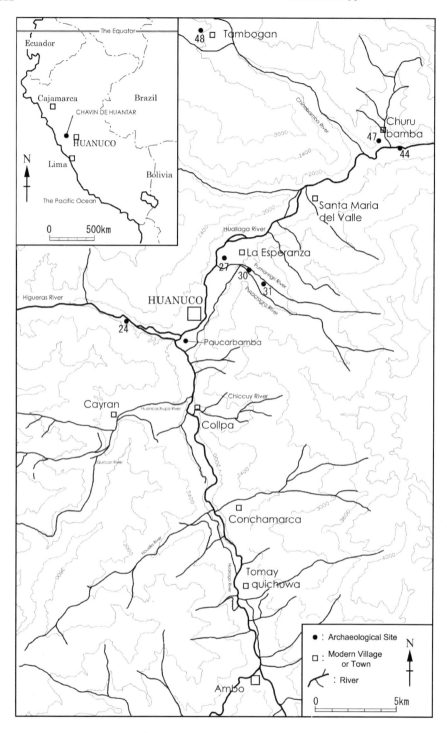

FIGURE 111. Sites of the Kotosh Chavín Phase (700–250 BC). Numbers are keyed to the site descriptions in Chapter 4.

(Matsumoto 2009, 2010a; Matsumoto and Tsurumi 2011). Whereas abandonment and destruction of the sites of the previous phase clearly suggest the rejection of local ideology, the new locations kept the same ecological environment and similar landscape, which may suggest that little change occurred in the subsistence economy.

The Influence of Chavín de Huántar in the Upper Huallaga Basin

Although radical changes occurred in settlement patterns, pottery, and architectural styles, it seems dangerous to conclude that the Upper Huallaga Basin received coercive influence or acculturation from Chavín de Huántar. The excavation data from Kotosh and Sajara-patac imply their political and religious autonomy through their own manipulation of this external influence. For instance, whereas the society of Kotosh intensively emulated not only pottery style, but also the architectural conventions of Chavín de Huántar (Izumi and Terada 1972), the case of Sajara-patac, 20 km to the east of Kotosh, looks quite different. Although some general architectural concepts, such as sunken plazas and platforms, were accepted from Chavín de Huántar, overall architectural technique and layout remained quite local at Sajara-patac (Matsumoto 2009; Matsumoto and Tsurumi 2011). For pottery styles, both the excavation data from Kotosh and Sajara-patac and the surface-collected material of the 2001 survey indicate that the pottery style of the Upper Huallaga Basin during this period was under the strong influence of Janabarriu Phase or "Janabarriu-related" pottery (Burger 1984, 1988), suggesting intensive interactions with Chavín de Huántar.

However, Kotosh and Sajara-patac emulated the Janabarriu Phase pottery style in quite different ways. This stylistic diversity under this overall homogeneity is important in considering intersite relationships in the Upper Huallaga Basin. Whereas the pottery assemblage of Kotosh shows clear intention to emulate or even copy the Janabarriu Phase pottery style, including not only vessel forms but also decorative techniques and iconographies (Izumi and Sono 1963; Izumi and Terada 1972), at the Sajara-patac site the pottery assemblage only partially emulates that of the Janabarriu Phase in these aspects (Matsumoto 2009; Tsurumi and Matsumoto 2011). For example, despite the broad variety of decorative techniques and iconographies seen in both the Kotosh Chavín Phase at Kotosh and the Janabarriu Phase at Chavín de Huántar, at Sajara-patac most of the decorative motifs are geometric designs represented by typical circles-and-dots motifs or concentric circles. Religious iconography is rare and looks local. These differences seem to suggest that Kotosh and Sajara-patac accepted and interpreted the new religious ideology of Chavín de Huántar quite differently. This seems applicable to the intersite relationships in the Upper Huallaga Basin in general during this phase.

Although these data indicate that the influence from Chavín de Huántar was a radical change and caused an abandonment of local religious traditions throughout the Upper Huallaga Basin, they do not necessarily suggest total socioeconomic change or strong political integration in this region. Probably they were in peer-to-peer relationships and thus each center could have negotiated, made their own decisions, and manipulated the external religious beliefs. I would assume that these processes of intersite interactions in the Upper Huallaga Basin functioned to consolidate the political autonomy of each center rather than resulting in regional political integration or unification (Matsumoto 2009, 2010a).

Evaluating the "Chavín Problem" in the Upper Huallaga Basin

It is worth considering how what we have learned about the Upper Huallaga Basin can be used to evaluate the ongoing debate known as the "Chavín Problem." For more than half a century, Chavín de Huántar and its role in the formation of Andean civilization has been debated in Andean archaeology (e.g., Tello 1960; Lumbreras 1989; Burger 1992; Kaulicke 1994; Inokuchi 1998; Rick 2008). Rather than describe the long history of this question, I will focus on the most recent debate, which began in the early 2000s. With his influential 1988 article and its subsequent revisions, Richard Burger (1988, 1992, 1993, 2008) has argued that Chavín de Huántar was founded around 1000 BC and transformed into an influential pan-regional center around 400 BC during the Janabarriu Phase. According to Burger, in this phase an interregional religious network centered on Chavín de Huántar appeared. This network covered a wide geographical area of the central Andes and was associated with the expansion of an influential religious ideology (the Chavín cult). This caused radical socioeconomic transformations in the central Andes, such as the emergence of social hierarchy and the acceleration of long-distance trade (Burger 1988, 1992).

Since 2000, this view has been challenged by John Rick and his colleagues. Their extensive excavations of both monumental cores and the areas surrounding Chavín de Huántar have led them to conclude that Chavín de Huántar was founded between 1500 and 1200 BC and ceased to function as a ceremonial center around 500 BC (e.g., Rick 2005; Kembel 2008; Rick et al. 2009). Their assessment differs from Burger's not only on chronology, but also on the site's relationships with other contemporaneous sites. In their view, Chavín de Huántar was not the only center that influenced other coeval centers distributed in the central Andes, but rather it was *primus inter pares* (Kembel and Rick 2004). The socioeconomic change occurred gradually as a long-term process (Rick 2005, 2008).

I think both excavation and survey data from the Upper Huallaga Basin fit well with Burger's view if the beginning date of Chavín de Huántar's interregional influence can be pushed back about three hundred years. That is, although the radiocarbon evidence indicates the beginning of the Kotosh Chavín Phase at about 700 BC rather than 400 BC (see Appendix A), all the available data suggest that the elements related to Chavín de Huántar appeared as the results of a radical change, which agrees with his recent revision (Burger 2019). Not only emulation of a new material culture style, but also destruction of earlier architecture and a change of settlement pattern, suggest that Chavín de Huántar was an intrusive external influence causing radical changes in the entire Upper Huallaga Basin. Although I do not intend to say that this interpretation is uniformly applicable everywhere in the central Andes, at least these data clearly show the need to evaluate this explanation in other regions, not only at Chavín de Huántar and the nearby area.

The Late Early Horizon:
The Kotosh Sajara-patac Phase (250–50 BC)

Pottery sherds of the Kotosh Sajara-patac Phase, which corresponds to the late Early Horizon, were found at twenty-eight sites (Figure 112), including seventeen newly registered sites. The sites are distributed near the bottomlands, including on alluvial lands near the confluence of rivers, on natural hills overlooking these rivers, and on the slopes between these topographic features. Most of the new sites that appear in this period can be classified into two types: mounds much smaller than the sites of the earlier phase and sites without any mound construction but instead associated with widely dispersed pottery sherds and coarse stone walls. In general, the newly established sites tended to be smaller than the sites that continued to be occupied from the earlier phases.

The number of sites radically increased from the Kotosh Chavín Phase and their distribution expanded to the upper border of the *yunga* zone. Note that many locations that had been used in the early Initial Period, the Kotosh Waira-jirca Phase, were reused in this period.

The sharp increase in the number of sites in the Kotosh Sajara-patac Phase seems to signify not only a simple increase in population, but also its redistribution from the centers that had served as ceremonial and political cores during the previous Kotosh Chavín Phase. The architectural remains of the Kotosh and Sajara-patac sites suggest that the ceremonial architecture of the Kotosh Chavín Phase was unused and both sites were reorganized as residential complexes (Onuki 1998:56; Matsumoto and Tsurumi 2011). Possibly the ceremonial centers lost their centripetal force and failed to function as political cores in the Upper Huallaga Basin. In this context, the population that had belonged to the ceremonial centers splintered into many small groups and dispersed across the Upper Huallaga Basin.

There were radical changes in settlement pattern in the broad area of the central Andes during the late Early Horizon, or the transition period from the Early Horizon to the Early Intermediate Period. However, published settlement pattern data for this period showing the changes in response to the collapse of ceremonial centers have been relatively scarce. The pattern recognized in the Upper Huallaga Basin seems different from those reported for Nepeña, Santa, Casma, Virú, and Huamachuco (Daggett 1984; S. Pozorski and T. Pozorski 1987; J. Topic and T. Topic 1987; Wilson 1988; Ghezzi 2006), where many fortified sites appeared and the population was clustered around them. The pottery style of the Kotosh Sajara-patac Phase was shared beyond the Upper Huallaga Basin, as the data from Salinas de San Blas in Junín suggest (Nomland 1939; Morales 1977, 1998). Therefore, it may be dangerous to assume the existence of increased conflict with the neighboring regions, although possible fortified sites such as Mitomarca may have existed in the higher elevation zone (Matsumoto, Nesbitt, and Palacios 2012). Because the survey in 2001 did not cover the area above the limit of the *yunga* zone, an additional survey that includes the higher elevation area is necessary to test the ideas presented here. This settlement pattern in the Upper Huallaga Basin during the late Early Horizon is also different from the situation in the Lurín Valley, where a complex mosaic of pottery styles indicates interaction between adjacent valleys and highlands (Makowski 2009). In addition to the pottery style collected in our survey, the excavation data from Kotosh and Sajara-patac (Izumi and Terada 1972; Inokuchi et al. 2003) suggest that the pottery of the Kotosh Sajara-patac Phase is fairly uniform among the sites in the Upper Huallaga Basin (Matsumoto and Tsurumi 2011), unlike those of the Lurín Valley.

The radical increase in sites near the interface between the *yunga* and *quechua* zones in the Upper Huallaga Basin could imply the expansion of settlements at the higher elevation. This phenomenon could be related to the establishment of animal domestication and intensification of interaction between the *quechua* and *puna* zones. Because the data from Kotosh suggest that animal domestication was established from the Kotosh Chavín Phase (Wing 1972; Onuki 1982:219; Miller and Burger 1995), the change of settlement pattern in this period may indicate the increased importance of pastoralism in the subsistence economy. In addition, as mentioned above, that the pottery style of this period shows close similarities to that of Junín (Normland 1939; Morales 1977, 1998) suggests a strong tie

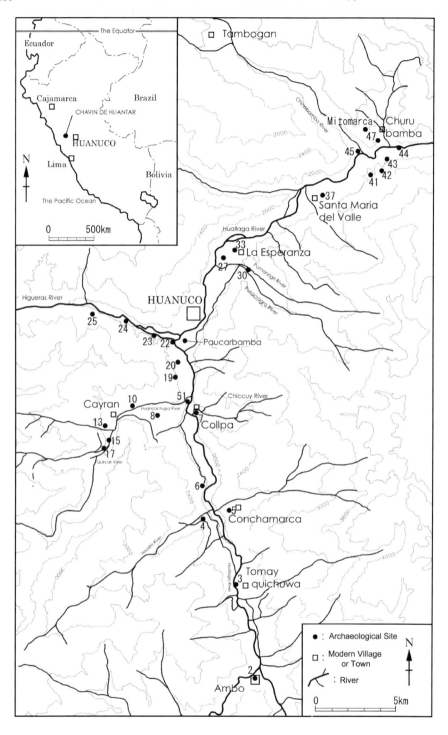

Figure 112. Sites of the Kotosh Sajara-patac Phase (250–50 bc). Numbers are keyed to the site descriptions in Chapter 4.

between the Upper Huallaga Basin and the high *puna* zone to the south, where pastoralism was the most important part of the subsistence economy. This demographic question needs to be considered in light of the Junín data.

Burger observed that the long-term successful adaptation to a pastoral economy in the *puna* zone in Junín began during the Initial Period and continued until the early Early Horizon. He concluded that the low carrying capacity of the *puna* zone hindered population growth in the central highlands (Burger 1992:126–127). A systematic survey of the upper Mantaro and Tarma drainages in Junín by Parsons, Hastings, and Matos Mendieta (2000:104–105) basically supports this view. As Onuki (1982) and Burger (1992:43–45, 124–127) suggested, from the late Preceramic to the late Initial Period, interactions between the *puna* zone of the central highlands and the lower *quechua* and *yunga* ecological zones were relatively sporadic. Scarce excavation data and radiocarbon dates make it difficult to evaluate the interactions between the Upper Huallaga Basin and the Junín *puna* zone during the early and middle Early Horizon. However, as Burger (1980) observed, the scarcity of obsidian from the Early Horizon context at Pachamachay cave (Rick 1980) implies that these *puna* zone pastoralists at Junín did not play an active role in the transport of Quispisisa obsidian from Ayacucho, whereas the Junín plain could have been the route for the movement of obsidian (Burger 1980:261; Contreras 2011).

In contrast, shared pottery styles of the late Early Horizon suggest that these interactions were intensive. The data from the upper Mantaro and Tarma drainages show an increase in sites in the *quechua* zone during the Early Intermediate Period and Middle Horizon (Parsons, Hastings, and Matos Mendieta 2000:134–135), which may mean that the *puna*-centered pastoralism of the Late Preceramic Period changed with the transition from the Early Horizon to the Early Intermediate Period. Though it is difficult to directly compare the data with those of the Upper Huallaga Basin, it seems possible to hypothesize that this shift of the settlement in the upper Mantaro and Tarma drainages corresponded chronologically to the late Early Horizon. An expansion of settlements to the *quechua* zone in Junín could have overcome the drawback of adaptation to the low carrying capacity of the *puna* environment during the Initial Period and Early Horizon, which probably hindered population growth in the Junín area (Burger 1992:127).

The radical increase in the number of sites and the expansion of settlements to the higher elevation in the Upper Huallaga Basin may be linked to this change at Junín. In this case, more sites indicates not only political disintegration, but also a demographic expansion in accordance with the intensive usage of the high altitude pastureland and an integration of agricultural and agropastoral systems. These two different subsistence economies were probably complementary and their integration could have been beneficial to both groups; one focused mainly on agriculture in the *yunga* zone and the other on its agropastoral subsistence base in the high altitude *puna* zone. Ethnographic research in a high altitude *puna* zone in the southern highlands of Peru by R. Brooke Thomas (1973, 1976) presents evidence consistent with this argument. Though Thomas's study focused on the modern energy flow system of the Nuñoa area in Puno, he concluded that the "food energy that can be extracted from the high *puna* flow system is not sufficient to meet consumption requirements of a substantial segment of the Nuñoa population" (Thomas 1976:396). According to Thomas, the exchange of animal resources such as wool, hides, and meat with high calorie foods grown at lower elevations makes it possible to maintain adequate energy levels (Thomas 1976:396). Therefore, in the Nuñoa area, exchange with groups at lower elevations was crucial for maintenance of the population, which seems to be the same in other *puna* communities. In this case, if, as Burger (1992:127) discussed, adaptation to the high *puna* zone from the Preceramic to the Early Horizon suppressed population growth in the region, the radical increase in the number of sites may be a result of the intensified integration of the high *puna* zone and the lower *yunga* and *quechua* zones. That is, an increase in the carrying capacity of the high pastureland through intensive interaction with lower elevation areas and the exchange of high calorie food might have allowed population growth in the *puna* zone during the late Early Horizon. In the Upper Huallaga Basin, such integration of the *yunga* and *puna* zones could have stimulated population growth and an increase of sites near the border of the *yunga* and *quechua* zones, and probably in the *quechua* zone itself.

On the other hand, Parsons and his colleagues provide an important alternative argument to this interpretation. According to them, their survey data of the Tarma–Chinchaycocha region, approximately 150 km to the south of the Upper Huallaga Basin, suggest that the Formative (Initial Period and Early Horizon) and Early Intermediate Period societies flourished in the adjacent Mantaro Valley rather than in their survey area (Parsons, Hastings, and Matos Mendieta 2000:192–193). They consider that continuous negative relationships between *quechua* cultivators and *puna* pastoralists before agricultural productivity developed could have created "an incentive for sustained interregional interaction" (Parsons, Hastings, and Matos Mendieta 2000:193) and that this was partially because of the difference between the narrower *puna* and wider *quechua*, which was better suited for agricultural communities. If this scenario is applied to the Upper Huallaga Basin, the expansion of settlements in this period might be simply interpreted as a result of agricultural development and associated population growth.

Additional survey in the *quechua–puna* zones in the Upper Huallaga Basin and in the Junín area will be crucial to evaluate these hypotheses.

The Early Intermediate Period: The Kotosh Higueras Phase (50 BC–?)

Among the sites surveyed, thirty-eight sites (Figure 113) belong to the Kotosh Higueras Phase, which corresponds to the Early Intermediate Period, including thirty-one newly registered sites. The settlement pattern in this phase is similar to the previous Kotosh Sajara-patac Phase. That is, the sites are distributed near the confluence of rivers, on natural hills that overlook the rivers, and on the slopes between these two areas. About 80% of the Kotosh Sajara-patac Phase sites (*n*=24) continued to be occupied in this phase. Whereas the number of small sites increased, a few large sites such as Mollepata (Site No. 34) and Huayrana (Site No. 35) were newly constructed. Probably similar large stone structures seen at other sites, such as Mound 2 at Cruzpata (Site No. 25) and a part of Mitomarca, were constructed during this period (Matsumoto, Nesbitt, and Palacios 2012). On the other hand, small occupations without any trace of architecture, such as at Coima 2 (Site No. 14) and Esperanza 1 and Esperanza 2 (Sites No. 32 and No. 28, respectively) are known as well. These could have been temporary use sites or small domestic components.

This period is the most enigmatic in the chronological sequence established at Kotosh in both its duration and its socioeconomic organization. As for its relationship within the chronological framework of the Upper Huallaga Basin, stratigraphic excavations have revealed architectural superpositions among the constructions of the Kotosh Sajara-patac

Phase and those of the Kotosh Higueras Phase. However, the only dates obtained from this period suggest that this period simply includes the Early Intermediate Period and do not help to define its beginning and end. The relatively characterless pottery of this period also prevents detailed stylistic comparisons. Although I tentatively correlate this period with the Early Intermediate Period, as discussed below, it could have continued much longer. As for socioeconomic organization, although the settlement pattern shows continuity from the Kotosh Sajara-patac Phase, a few sites seems to suggest possible differences in social organizations among them. Whereas the Kotosh Sajara-patac Phase can be partially interpreted as a period of social disintegration after the collapse of the ceremonial centers that flourished during the Kotosh Chavín Phase, because of its dispersed settlements and lack of monumental construction represented by platforms, there may have been political reintegration at a regional level in the Kotosh Higueras Phase. Although monumental construction projects are less evident during the Kotosh Sajara-patac Phase than in former periods, there seems to have been a revival of such projects during this phase, as represented by a few large sites with platforms, such as at Mollepata and Cruzpata. Possibly, sites with platforms correspond to an autonomous political unit and other small sites pertained to them as domestic components. Only future excavations can clarify socioeconomic and intersite organization during the Kotosh Higueras Phase.

After the Early Intermediate Period through the Late Horizon (?–16th century AD)

The period after the Kotosh Higueras Phase has not been systematically studied. The lack of excavation data especially makes it impossible to establish a basic chronology from pottery styles and absolute dating. Furthermore, the long-term continuity of the pottery styles of the Upper Huallaga Basin as discussed by Onuki (1982) and Grosboll (1988:355) makes attempts at a chronology even more difficult. Although the Kotosh Sajara-patac Phase radiocarbon dates obtained at Sajara-patac (see Appendix A) are helpful for estimating the beginning of the Kotosh Higueras Phase (and dating at Kotosh suggests that this includes the Early Intermediate Period), it is difficult to estimate an end date for the Kotosh Higueras Phase. The possibility that the Kotosh Higueras culture continued until the Middle Horizon or even the Late Intermediate Period cannot be disregarded.

In the central Andes, the Middle Horizon is characterized as a period of new sociopolitical development centered at the site of Wari in Ayacucho. Although this is not the place to discuss the socioeconomic complexity of the Wari polity and its influence on other regions (e.g., Jennings 2010), it is worth mentioning that there was no evidence of Wari trade ware or the typical stylistic features of Wari administrative centers in our 2001 survey in the Upper Huallaga Basin. This is quite similar to investigations in the Tarma–Chinchaycocha and Wanka regions, where no obvious evidence of Wari influence was recognized (Parsons, Hastings, and Matos Mendieta 2000:113, 194, 2013:104–105). However, the investigators describe a possible settlement pattern change in the Tarma–Chinchaycocha region and assume that it was an indirect result of Wari expansion. This case does not seem applicable to the Upper Huallaga Basin, because the settlement pattern of the Kotosh Higueras Phase clearly follows that of the previous Kotosh Sajara-patac Phase. There is therefore less, or even no, evidence of Wari influence in this region, which could be attributable to its farther distance from the Wari heartland than the Tarma–Chinchaycocha

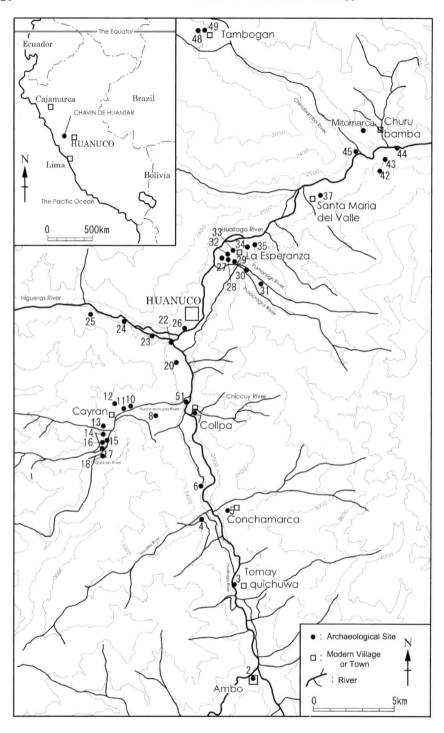

FIGURE 113. Sites of the Kotosh Higueras Phase (later than c. 50 BC). Numbers are keyed to the site descriptions in Chapter 4.

region. Of course, we should be cautious. Except for Kotosh, no systematic excavations have been carried out at the sites corresponding to the Kotosh Higueras Phase. However, I would tentatively argue that the Upper Huallaga Basin could have been a "backwater" of Middle Horizon socioeconomic development related to the Wari polity and located outside of its influence.

Along these lines, I will tentatively treat all post-Kotosh Higueras Phase sites (Figure 114) as a single chronological block, which may correspond to the Late Intermediate Period and Late Horizon (AD 1000–1535) and may or may not include the Middle Horizon. I admit that this division is confusing, especially after indicating the possibility that the Kotosh Higueras Phase covers the Middle Horizon. The dating of Middle Horizon sites is urgent, because here we see two completely different scenarios for the Middle Horizon settlement pattern in this region. If the Kotosh Higueras Phase includes the Middle Horizon (AD 600–1000), many settlements were located in the bottomlands. However, if not, the settlements of the Middle Horizon decreased near the bottomlands and concentrated at higher elevation zones. This coarse and ambiguous chronological framework definitely needs revision through more survey and excavation data.

Seven sites that could belong to the post-Kotosh Higueras Phase were registered in our 2001 survey. Among these, Armoncalloq (Site No. 38), Huarampay (Site No. 39), and Tarucopata (Site No. 40) have strong similarities in architectural and pottery styles. All have coarse stone aligned into square rooms or corrals, or both. The pottery sherds associated with these sites are characterized by coarse orange paste, oxidized firing, and red slip, and tend to show surface cracks probably caused by poor firing. Though they share some similarities with the Higueras Red and Higueras Brown pottery styles of Kotosh, the paste and firing seem to differentiate them and they could be used as chronological markers. Chacuas-pampa (Site No. 46) may fit this category even though its stone alignments are circular.

There were two examples of artificially terraced hills: Fundo Pampa (Site No. 9) and Huanojpa (Site No. 49). Though only a small amount of pottery sherds were recovered from these sites, these sherds share similar characteristics to those of the pottery types of the Kotosh Higueras Phase. The Mitomarca site has a clearly different architectural style. Its high walls of piled flat stones and a massive revetment, or retaining wall, enclosing a hilltop are similar to the Late Intermediate Period and Late Horizon architectural style of the higher zone of the region (e.g., Thompson 1967; Girault 1981; Morales 1984; Grosboll 1988, 1993; Bonnier 1997a; Salcedo Camacho et al. 2000; Mantha 2009). In the 2001 survey data, only Jircanera (Site No. 48) has clear evidence of Late Horizon material.

Although available data are scarce, the architectural style of Mitomarca (Matsumoto, Nesbitt, and Palacios 2012) seems to be affiliated with the building style distributed from *quechua* to *puna* along the Marañon and Huallaga drainages and documented at sites such as Piruru (Girault 1981; Bonnier 1997a), Garu (Sánchez Murrugarra and Palacios Jimenez 1988; Salcedo Camacho et al. 2000), and high altitude sites in the Rapayán Valley (Mantha 2009) and the Province of Dos de Mayo in the Department of Huánuco (Morales 1984). The existence of Kotosh Higueras Phase pottery at Mitomarca may suggest (Matsumoto, Nesbitt, and Palacios 2012), as Grosboll (1988:354–358) discussed, considerable continuity in pottery style from the beginning of the Early Intermediate Period until late prehispanic times. The pottery style similar to that of the Kotosh Higueras Phase was defined as a CB (Cruddy Brown) series by Isbell (1974) and, according to Onuki (1982:219–220), existed until the Late Intermediate Period. Grosboll's (1988) data of the Late Horizon pottery of

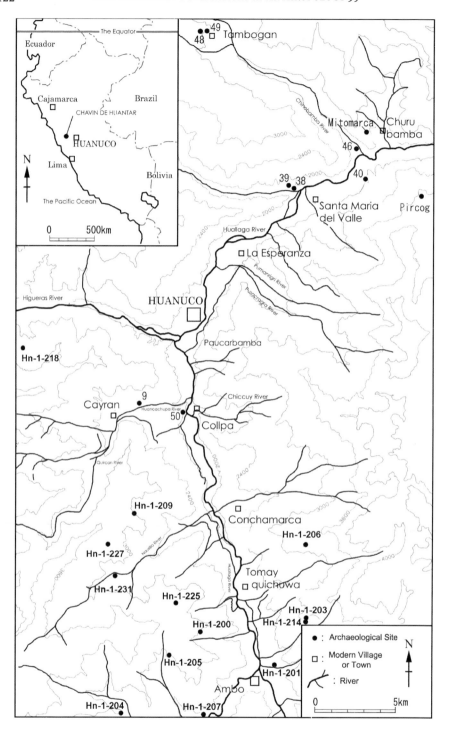

FIGURE 114. Possible post-Kotosh Higueras Phase sites. Numbers are keyed to the site descriptions in Chapter 4. Site numbers with the prefix Hn are from Grosboll (1988).

this region provide supportive evidence for this argument. The local pottery style of the Late Horizon in the Upper Huallaga Basin shares many attributes with those of the Kotosh Higueras Phase, such as horizontal jar handles, short-necked jars with thickened rims, and coarsely smoothed surfaces, which correspond to the traits of the CB series defined by Isbell. Grosboll correctly described this trend in the following way: "Between the Higueras Phase and the Late Horizon, ceramic attributes appear to have changed gradually, as a continuation or elaboration of attributes first seen in the Higueras Phase" (Grosboll 1988:355–356). This corresponds to Terada's (1972:311) earlier observation on the similarities between the pottery style of the Kotosh Higueras Phase and that of Chupachu pottery of the Late Horizon. This argument is also supported by the data from the site of Piruru in the Tamtamayo near the Marañon River, approximately 80 km to the north of the modern city of Huánuco at an elevation of 3,800 masl, near the border of the *quechua* and *suni* zones (Bonnier 1997a). In the pottery typology by Rozenberg (1982), Tantamayo Rouge Estampe (Tantamayo Red Stamped) and Tantamayo Brun Micace (Tantamayo Red Mica) fit in the CB series and share some elements of the Kotosh Higueras Phase style. It is possible that these pottery types at Piruru correspond to the Chupachu group, as Thompson discussed with the data of the Icchu site (Rozenberg 1982:131–135). In this case, these types can be connected to the multi-story stone masonry structures of Piruru 1, which were associated with Churupas (Girault 1981), and thus these types probably belong to the Late Intermediate Period or Late Horizon, or both.

Similarly, these data allow us to accept the continuity of Higueras style into later periods. However, there are obvious differences between the architectural styles of the Kotosh Higueras Phase at Kotosh and these multi-story buildings located at higher elevations along the Marañon and Huallaga Rivers (e.g., Morris and Thompson 1985; Grosboll 1988). Therefore, there may have been a shift of settlement in the Upper Huallaga Basin to higher elevations at some point after the Kotosh Higueras Phase. Grosboll's (1988, 1993) study of Late Horizon settlement provides supportive evidence for this. Her survey of the area where the Chupachu and Quero ethnic groups lived located many of the Late Horizon sites documented in the *visitas* of 1549 and 1562 written by Iñigo Ortiz de Zuñiga (1967, 1972). She mainly focused on the area south of the Higueras River and west of the Huallaga River, especially in the zone between 3,000 and 4,000 masl, which complements our research on the bottomlands of the Upper Huallaga Basin. According to Grosboll (1988:75), the sites that belong to the Middle Period (AD 500–1300) in her terminology tended to be found in the range of 2,400 to 2,900 masl, whereas the Late Horizon or late preconquest period sites are frequently between 3,000 and 4,000 masl. However, it is very probable that the sites she recognizes as Late Horizon sites have Late Intermediate Period components as well (Grosboll 1993:74). Daniel Morales (1984) also reports similar types of sites belonging to the Late Intermediate Period and Late Horizon in Dos de Mayo Province of the Department of Huánuco.

Therefore, it seems reasonable to assume that there was a shift in settlements to higher elevations during the Middle Horizon or the early Late Intermediate Period. However, it is difficult to evaluate whether this shift occurred as radical and abrupt changes, or gradually. Despite these ambiguities, after the Early Intermediate Period later settlement patterns obviously present a sharp contrast with those of the Initial Period and Early Horizon. As discussed above, multiple small polities seem to have interacted in the Upper Huallaga Basin from the Kotosh Mito Phase to the Kotosh Chavín Phase. Probably people gathered at public centers and formed independent political units. Although this pattern seems to have ended at the beginning of the Kotosh Sajara-patac Phase, the Kotosh Higueras Phase shows the revival of monumental construction and thus probably political reintegration, which is similar to the periods before the Kotosh Sajara-patac Phase. It is difficult to say whether this intraregional pattern up until the Kotosh Higueras Phase is completely different from the Late Intermediate Period and Late Horizon, and the later political landscape in the Upper Huallaga Basin should be considered separately. However, at least, multiple polities and ethnic groups such as the Chupachu, Yacha, Quero, Wamali, and Yaros were distributed in the Upper Huallaga Basin before the arrival of the Inca (Morris and Thompson 1985; Grosboll 1988, 1993). Their sites are generally located in high defendable locations, such as on the crests of ridges. In addition, our data suggest that the bottomlands of the Upper Huallaga Basin were not used intensively for settlements during the Late Intermediate Period and Late Horizon. Although it is highly probable that the *yunga* was continuously used for agricultural activities such as maize cultivation, people did not live in the area for some reason. This settlement pattern occurs in the adjacent regions for different ethnic groups, such as in the upper valley of the Marañon River (e.g., Morris and Thompson 1985; Mantha 2009), and may indicate a general trend of the Late Intermediate Period as a time of conflict among these groups. When settlements moved from the *yunga* zone to much higher elevations, and how this pattern relates to the socio-economic transformation that became the emergence of Chupachu and other polities with major leaders that are described in the colonial documents, remains to be investigated.

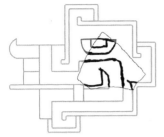

CHAPTER SIX

Problems for Future Research in the Upper Huallaga Basin

The 2001 settlement data that here ties together the available archaeological data in the Upper Huallaga Basin is still useful not only to describe a diachronic change in the cultural sequence of the Upper Huallaga Basin, but also to highlight the research problems yet to be solved.

The problems with the archaeological data of this region are caused by the uneven distribution of the data both chronologically and geographically. The relative chronology is well established only for the Late Preceramic Period, Initial Period, and Early Horizon, and the absolute chronology is defined for only a part of the Early Horizon (see Appendix A). The regional chronology after the Early Horizon is worse and almost no reference dates tied to excavation data are available. For example, it is impossible to know the location of "Middle Horizon" sites in the Upper Huallaga Basin, although I believe several sites there were occupied from AD 600–1000. Poor chronological control of material styles after the Early Intermediate Period makes this situation even more difficult. Finer chronological divisions are urgently required to understand the later sequence in this region.

In addition, because uneven distribution of both settlement pattern and excavation data prevented the description of each period with the same level of confidence, the interpretation of the cultural sequence presented in the previous chapter became an uneven interpretive patchwork of solid archaeological data and more speculative data. Most of the excavation data are concentrated in the Late Preceramic Period, Initial Period, and Early Horizon, and thus data earlier and later than these periods are stressfully scarce. The limitations of the survey area in 2001 also made it difficult to describe a comprehensive cultural sequence at a regional level. In particular, there is almost no data set to connect the Kotosh Higueras Phase society with the later period sites characterized by the multistory structures located in the high-altitude area above 3,000 masl.

In sum, both additional systematic survey in higher elevation areas and new excavations at selected sites will be required to provide clues to understanding several key issues in the archaeology of the Upper Huallaga Basin.

In my synthesis (see Chapter 5), I intended to describe a diachronic process at a regional level by focusing on intraregional interactions. In this context, I think it worth listing the examples of key issues that are tied to the broader theme of Andean archaeology that thus need to be addressed by future research.

Chronological Position of the Earliest
Public Architecture in the Highlands

The discovery of Mito-style temples in the 1960s opened a new line of research in Andean archaeology, that of Late Preceramic monumental architecture. However, in the last twenty years, the focus of this research has moved to the coastal regions. New findings at the site of Caral (e.g., Shady Solis, Haas, and Creamer 2001; Shady and Leyva 2003; Shady 2006; Shady Solis 2014) and in the Norte Chico region (e.g., Haas and Creamer 2006) on the central coast show that large-scale monumental centers appeared around 3000 BC. In the case of Caral, a room with a fire pit at its center was pointed out by some archaeologists for its similarities to the Mito-style temple (e.g., Shady 2003; Shady and Machacuay 2003; Contreras 2010). In this context, Jonathan Haas and Winfield Creamer discuss the temporal priority of monumental architecture on the coast to the Mito-style Kotosh Religious Tradition temples in the highlands. They even considered that the Late Preceramic monumental architecture of the highlands is derived from earlier coastal public centers (Haas and Creamer 2006:767). However, this argument requires a careful re-examination of the highland Kotosh Religious Tradition sites. The most serious problem is the lack of radiocarbon dates associated with Mito-style Kotosh Religious Tradition public buildings (Burger and Salazar-Burger 1980, 1985, 1986; Bonnier 1997b). Representative sites such as Kotosh in the Upper Huallaga Basin, Huaricoto in Callejón de Huaylas, and La Galgada in the Tablachaca Valley (Grieder et al. 1988) have not been explored well enough to identify the earliest occupations and thus need additional excavation to evaluate the emergence of monumental architecture in each region (see also Shimada 2006:762). Moreover, the dating of the Late Preceramic sites in the highlands generally did not receive the benefit of advances in AMS dating. In the case of Kotosh especially all the dates are affected by the technical difficulties of radiocarbon dating during the 1960s, as represented by huge error ranges (see Appendix A). Therefore, it is dangerous to assume the temporal priority of coastal monuments to those of the highlands solely on the basis of available radiocarbon dates.

Another point that needs more careful consideration is the difference in architectural patterns between the coast and the highlands. The large centers of the Late Preceramic Period on the central coast are generally composed of large plazas and platform structures. Architecture similar to that of the Kotosh Religious Tradition was a relatively marginal element in the huge architectural complex (T. Pozorski and S. Pozorski 1990, 1996; Shady 2003; Shady and Machacuay 2003). On the other hand, in the case of the highlands, Kotosh Religious Tradition temples are a central architectural element at each site (Matsuzawa 1972; Burger and Salazar-Burger 1980, 1985, 1986; Grieder et al. 1988). If the Kotosh Religious Tradition temples in the highlands are derivative of the coastal centers, it is necessary to explain why the marginal architectural element of the coast became popular in the highlands. On this point I agree with Shimada's (2006:762) commentary to Haas and Creamer's (2006:767) argument. These views seem to dismiss the possible early interactions between the central coast and central highlands by placing temporal priority on the coastal side as an obvious fact.

For the purpose of considering these problems with the Late Preceramic monumental architecture, the most crucial data are solid radiocarbon dates associated with the highland Kotosh Religious Tradition sites. Only accurate dating of the emergence of public architecture in highland area will help to evaluate coast–highland relationships. Since 2015, Eisei Tsurumi and Yoshio Onuki have been carrying out new excavations at Kotosh that focus on the Mito temples to explore the earlier subphases of the Kotosh Mito Phase (E. Tsurumi, pers. comm., 2016). The radiocarbon dates from their research will greatly contribute to our understanding of the coast–highland interactions during the Late Preceramic Period.

Socioeconomic Organization of Initial Period Societies

During the Initial Period (1800–800 BC), new public centers with monumental architecture appeared in a wide geographical area of the central Andes. This is especially true for the coastal region as represented by the Sechin Alto complex in the Casma Valley (e.g., S. Pozorski and T. Pozorski 1987, 2002), the U-shaped temples of the Manchay culture in the Lurín Valley (e.g., Burger 1987; Burger and Salazar-Burger 1991; Burger and Salazar 2008), and the centers of the Cupisnique culture on the North Coast (e.g., T. Pozorski 1976, 1983; Elera 1993, 1998; Nesbitt 2012). Although the scale of the architecture in the highlands in general is not as monumental as on the coast, highland public centers also experienced the construction of new centers or an increase in size, as seen at Pacopampa (Seki et al. 2008; Seki 2014), Huacaloma (Terada and Onuki 1985, 1988), Kuntur Wasi (Onuki 1995; Inokuchi 2008), and Chavín de Huántar (Burger 1988, 1992; Kembel 2001, 2008; Rick 2008).

Nevertheless, it seems highly probable that the situation in the Upper Huallaga Basin during the Initial Period was quite different from these examples. There is no clear evidence of monumental architecture during this period. At Kotosh, although the Kotosh Waira-jirca Phase and Kotosh Kotosh Phase stone masonry structures were built after the abandonment of the Mito-style temples, architectural quality is not as high as in the former phase and so it might be difficult to consider them public or monumental architecture (Matsuzawa 1972; Onuki 1993). At Shillacoto, where unique burials with offerings (Izumi, Cuculiza, and Kano 1972; Kano 1979) might suggest a possible change of socioeconomic organization at the site, such as the emergence of a social hierarchy, there is little evidence of monumental architecture so far.

In studies of Initial Period Andean society, socioeconomic organization is discussed largely on the basis of the evidence of monumental architecture (e.g., S. Pozorski and T. Pozorski 1987, 2002; Seki and Sakai 1998; Burger 2009a; Burger and Salazar 2014). It might be possible to expect a quite different relationship between social organization and architecture in the case of the Upper Huallaga Basin. However, the Initial Period data is simply scarce. Excavations at carefully selected sites in the Upper Huallaga Basin are needed. At Kotosh, the main obstacle for understanding this period was the destruction that occurred before the construction of public architecture in the Kotosh Chavín Phase. The 2001 survey showed that there are at least a few sites that have a Kotosh Kotosh Phase component but that do not include the Kotosh Chavín Phase component, such as at Cotopata (Site No. 29) and Warampayloma (Site No. 36). These sites are excellent candidates for future excavations to improve our understanding of the Initial Period in the Upper Huallaga Basin.

Middle Horizon and Late Intermediate Period Societies in the Upper Huallaga Basin

Both absolute chronology and relative chronology after the Kotosh Higueras Phase are extremely poorly defined (see Chapter 5). To evaluate the influence of Wari's expansion on a regional level, we need to define the later sequence of the Upper Huallaga Basin in finer slices. Although Grosboll's (1988, 1993) detailed comparison of her survey data in the higher part of this region to the colonial *visita* documents contributes greatly to our understanding of the Late Horizon, the Middle Horizon in this region is almost unknown. It is even difficult to define the correlations of material style and the Middle Horizon as a chronological block corresponding to AD 600–1000. The only point worth emphasizing is that, through excavations at Kotosh, research in the Pechitea area by Thompson (1967), Grosboll's survey in the *quechua* and *suni* zones, and our survey in the bottomlands, no typical, or even possible, typical Wari style (or its derivative pottery styles such as Chaki-pampa and Viñaque; e.g., Menzel 1964; Knobloch 1991) have been recognized. Although there is always the possibility of a future discovery that shows some kind of tie with the Wari polity, the available data seem to suggest that the Upper Huallaga was not strongly influenced by Wari and was probably isolated from it, which is, according to some archae-ologists, considered an imperial expansion (e.g., Schreiber 1999, 2001; Watanabe 2012).

Despite the long-lasting ongoing debates on the imperial character of the Wari state (e.g., Jennings 2010), the data from the North Highlands show that there are centers farther north that have architecture or pottery in the Wari style (J. Topic and T. Topic 1987; J. Topic 1991; T. Topic and J. Topic 2010; J. Topic, T. Topic, and Melly Cava 2002; Watanabe 2012). Thus, the Wari influence is recognized in the region north of the Upper Huallaga Basin, which is closer to the Wari heartland of Ayacucho. It is also important to note that survey data from the upper Mantaro and Tarma drainages, the region between the Wari heartland and the Upper Huallaga Basin, provide similar results. According to the researchers, "we can detect no immediately obvious 'influence,' in ceramics or archi-tecture or settlement pattern, from either the Lima or Wari polities" (Parsons, Hastings, and Matos Mendieta 2000:194). In this context, it seems important to consider why these regions were isolated from the "horizon" phenomenon and remained a backwater during the Middle Horizon (see Chapter 3).

The Inca Empire, its influence, and the nature of political control at a regional level has also been an important theme (e.g., Malpass 1993). The interdisciplinary research project in the 1960s led by John Murra and subsequent survey by Grosboll (1988, 1993) revealed the nature of the Inca influence on the Upper Huallaga Basin. Grosboll's ex-amination of the correlations between archaeological data and colonial *visita* documents (Ortiz de Zúñiga 1967, 1972) made it possible to evaluate this influence from multiple perspectives. She confirmed "the lack of involvement at the local level by Inca officials in most parts of the region" (Grosboll 1993:71) and showed that Inca regional administration was adapted quite flexibly, even at the regional level, in the Upper Huallaga Basin and its surrounding area.

Through her analysis of the Inca influence on material style, Grosboll (1988, 1993) points out that at many Late Horizon sites in this region the stylistic elements of the Inca as an empire are relatively scarce both in architecture and pottery. The material style of this region indicates the "Incas' lack of either interest or direct involvement" (Grosboll 1993:64). Most of the possible Inca-related architectural traits could be additions after their arrival, and thus, as Grosboll (1993:74) has discussed, the sites classified as Late Horizon sites could have a Late Intermediate Period component as well. Because colonial documents reveal the presence of multiple local leaders (*huarangas*), such as Chupachu, Yacha, Quero, Wamali, and Yaros (Ortiz de Zúñiga 1967, 1972; see also Grosboll 1993, fig. 3.3), it seems certain that multiple loosely interrelated polities were distributed in this region. As discussed earlier, these polities probably correspond to the higher elevation sites that are characterized by a multi-story building and located in an area higher than the bottomlands of the Upper Huallaga Basin. There is a "missing link" from the Kotosh Higueras Phase between the architecture of the bottomlands and Late Intermediate Period–Late Horizon architecture.

In this context, the only possible hypothesis is that a radical change occurred sometime between the Early Intermediate Period and the Late Intermediate Period. Considering the probable absence of Wari influence in the Upper Huallaga Basin, it seems problematic to accept that the Late Intermediate polities appeared as a result of the collapse of the Wari polity and the regional political reorganization associated with it. It is almost unknown how and when the local leaders of the Late Intermediate Period polities recorded in the documentary sources appeared.

Even with the new data and synthesis presented here, so many issues remain to be explored. As Onuki (1993:84) stated more than a quarter of a century ago, "innovative investigations are needed in Huánuco." This volume should be considered an opportunity for researchers to plan and carry out more systematic investigations that obtain new archaeological data.

A RECONSIDERATION OF THE RADIOCARBON CHRONOLOGY OF THE UPPER HUALLAGA BASIN

Yuichi Matsumoto

After the pioneering excavations at Kotosh in the 1960s (Izumi and Sono 1963; Izumi and Terada 1972), little archaeological research was conducted in the Upper Huallaga Basin, largely as a consequence of widespread violence in the region during the 1980s. One of the most important results of the excavations at Kotosh was the development of the first basic regional chronology from the stylistic seriation of pottery sherds and radiocarbon dating (Terada 1972:308–312; Sakai 1998). In fact, radiocarbon dating of the samples from Kotosh was one of the very early examples of the use of this technique in the history of Andean archaeology. In the half century since the excavations at Kotosh, radiocarbon dating has become quite common and techniques have advanced considerably. The usefulness of AMS (accelerator mass spectrometry) in particular, and calibrations of radiocarbon dates for better chronological control, have been shared among many archaeologists (e.g., Taylor 1987; Fiedel 1999; Lau 2004; León Canales 2006). Here I reconsider the absolute chronology of the Upper Huallaga Basin through the calibration and synthesis of available dates from Kotosh, Shillacoto, and Sajara-patac (Figure A.1).

Chronological Framework

Excavations at Kotosh produced the following chronological framework from the Late Preceramic to the Early Intermediate Period using conventional uncalibrated radiocarbon dates (Izumi and Terada 1972:307–312; see also Table A.1).

Kotosh Mito Phase	2000–1500 BC
Kotosh Waira-jirca Phase	1500–1000 BC
Kotosh Kotosh Phase	1000–800 BC
Kotosh Chavín Phase	1000–300 BC
Kotosh Sajara-patac Phase	No dates

This research at Kotosh clarified the importance of the Late Preceramic and Initial Period in the development of complex society in the Andes. Before this work, Chavín de Huántar was generally regarded as the focal point for the development of Andean civiliza-

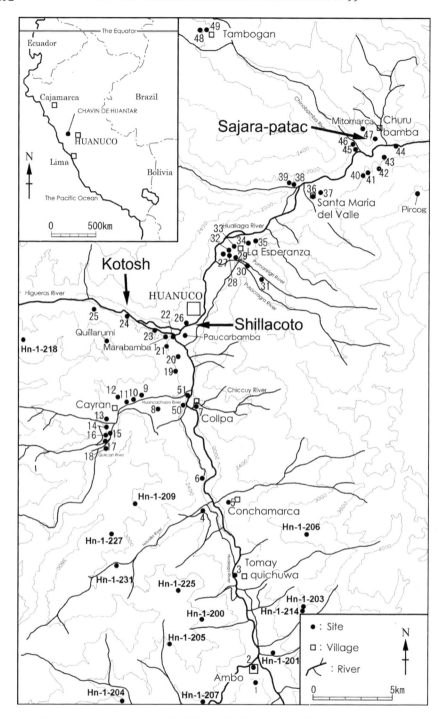

FIGURE A.1. Archaeological sites of the Upper Huallaga Basin, showing Kotosh (Site No. 24), Shillacoto (Site No. 26), and Sajara-patac (Site No. 47). Numbers are keyed to the fifty-one sites surveyed in 2001 and described in Chapter 4. Site numbers with the prefix Hn were registered by Grosboll (1988).

tion (e.g., Tello 1943, 1960). The discovery of the Kotosh Waira-jirca Phase and Kotosh Ko-tosh Phase architecture with elaborate pottery from a context that clearly predated Chavín clarified that by then pre-Chavín cultures were already highly developed. Moreover, the Late Preceramic ceremonial architecture of the Kotosh Mito Phase was an astonishing discovery at that time and created a new focus for archaeological research.

Onuki (1998:54) revised the chronology in the following way by reconsidering the Kotosh data and comparing them with other Late Preceramic, Initial Period, and Early Horizon sites beyond the Upper Huallaga Basin.

Kotosh Mito Phase	2500–1800 BC
Kotosh Waira-jirca Phase	1800–1200 BC
Kotosh Kotosh Phase	1200–600 BC
Kotosh Chavín Phase	600–250 BC
Kotosh Sajara-patac Phase	250–50 BC

Excavations at Kotosh established a fine-grained relative chronology that has provided a useful framework to describe the regional cultural context in the Upper Huallaga Basin. In the following argument, although I retain the chronological terms originally outlined by Izumi and Terada (1972) and revised by Onuki (1993, 1998), I will reevaluate the older dates from excavations in the 1960s by calibrating them and presenting them along with new radiocarbon dates from Sajara-patac. This will allow me to refine the absolute chronology of the Upper Huallaga Basin from the Late Preceramic Period to the Early Horizon.

Radiocarbon Measurements
from Excavations at Sajara-patac

Sajara-patac (Site No. 47) is located 20 km north of the city of Huánuco in the village of Pacapucro, in the Churubamba District, at an elevation of 1,898 masl (Izumi and Sono 1963:3; Onuki 1993:75; Matsumoto 2009; Matsumoto and Tsurumi 2011). This research identified four architectural phases that correspond to the Kotosh–Chavín and Kotosh Sajara-patac Phases at Kotosh and obtained five new radiocarbon dates. The following is a brief description of each architectural phase at the site of Sajara-patac and the context associated with radiocarbon samples (for more comprehensive information of the excavations at the site, see Matsumoto [2009] and Matsumoto and Tsurumi [2011]).

Sajara-patac 1 Phase

During the Sajara-patac 1 Phase, the top of the natural hill at the site of Sajara-patac was artificially terraced and red soil was used to fill hollow areas. The structures of this phase in the central part of the mound were only partly excavated to preserve the architecture of later phases. A platform with a possible plaza that had two superimposed floors extends from the north to the south on the far southern part of the structure. Large quantities of broken ceramics found on the lower floor were associated with charcoal remains (Figures A.2 and A.6). This seems to have been a feasting context associated with the construction activity before the burial of the first floor of the Sajara-patac 1 Phase architecture (Matsumoto 2007, 2009). This means that this context is close to the emergence of Sajara-patac as a ceremonial center. One charcoal sample (TKa-13677) from this context produced a date of 2525 ± 35 BP (uncalibrated).

TABLE A.1. Radiocarbon dates from the archaeological sites of Kotosh and Shillacoto in the Upper Huallaga Basin. All dates were calibrated with OxCal v. 4.3.2 (Bronk Ramsey 2017) using SHCal13, the Southern Hemisphere atmospheric curve (Hogg et al. 2013). Laboratory sample prefixes are as follows: Gak, Gakushuin University, Japan; N, Nishina Memorial Japan; Pta, Quaternary Research Dating Unit (QUADRU), c/o Enviromentek, CSIR, Pretoria, South Africa; TK, C-14 Dating Laboratory, The University Museum, The University of Tokyo, Japan.

Phase	Sample	¹⁴C age (BP)	Range (cal BC)	Probability (%) at 1σ	Range (cal BC)	Probability (%) at 2σ
Kotosh						
Kotosh Mito [a]	Gak-766b	3900 ± 100	2470–2198	66.1	2616–2610	0.2
			2163–2152	2.1	2581–2022	95.2
Kotosh Mito [a]	TK-42	3900 ± 900	3626–3596	0.7	4776–360	95.4
			3526–1371	66.1		
			1359–1298	1.4		
Kotosh Mito [a]	Gak-766a	3620 ± 100	2114–2100	2.6	2205–1659	95.4
			2037–1770	65.6		
Kotosh Mito [a]	TK-110	3470 ± 80	1876–1841	10.8	1942–1528	95.4
			1822–1796	7.4		
			1782–1636	50.0		
Kotosh Mito [a]	TK-109	3360 ± 160	1871–1845	3.3	2032–1216	95.4
			1812–1803	1.0		
			1776–1426	63.8		
Kotosh Waira–Jirca [b]	Gak-262	3800 ± 110	2344–2021	67.0	2482–1886	95.4
			1992–1984	1.2		
Kotosh Waira–Jirca [b]	Gak-765	3750 ± 90	2272–2258	2.8	2456–2418	1.8
			2208–1958	65.4	2408–2374	1.7
					2368–1882	91.9
Kotosh Waira–Jirca [b]	N-69–2	3100 ± 130	1450–1120	68.2	1612–974	94.7
					956–942	0.7
Kotosh Waira–Jirca [b]	TK-108	3000 ± 80	1282–1042	68.2	1403–973	94.0
					958–940	1.4
Kotosh Kotosh [c]	Gak-261	3070 ± 150	1431–1055	68.2	1620–896	95.4
Kotosh Kotosh [c]	N-66–a	2870 ± 230	1377–1345	2.9	1595–1588	0.2
			1304–796	65.3	1532–411	95.2
Kotosh Kotosh [c]	N-67–2	2840 ± 170	1207–1140	9.1	1430–702	89.6
			1134–804	59.1	696–540	5.8

Continued

TABLE A.1 CONTINUED.

Phase	Sample	¹⁴C age (BP)	Calibrated date				
			Range (cal BC)	Probability (%) at 1σ	Range (cal BC)	Probability (%) at 2σ
Kotosh Chavín[d]	Gak-263	3150 ± 150	1530–1188	62.7	1735–1716	0.6
			1182–1156	3.2	1694–972	94.2
			1146–1128	2.3	958–939	0.6
Kotosh Chavín[d]	N-65-2	2820 ± 120	1081–1064	3.0	1375–1350	0.6
			1058–809	65.2	1303–754	94.2
					680–670	0.3
					608–594	0.3
Kotosh Higueras[e]	Unknown	1880 ± 200	94–80	1.3	360 cal BC –cal AD 606	94.9
			71 cal BC –cal AD 426	66.9	cal AD 614–629	0.5
Shillacoto Kotosh Waira–Jirca[b]	TK-43	3200 ± 80	1514–1372	52.1	1621–1220	95.4
			1357–1300	16.1		

Source: Izumi and Terada (1972):

[a] 1972:307   [b] 1972:308   [c] 1972:309   [d] 1972:310   [e] 1972:312

Sajara-patac 2 Phase

In the Sajara-patac 2 Phase, one more terrace was constructed over the platform of the previous period, and the central plaza was built on the upper terrace (Figure A.3). Almost all the structures of the previous phase were buried and building activities carried out over them. Several rooms were constructed around the central plaza and an access to the platform from outside was built north of the mound.

Two radiocarbon dates were obtained for this phase. One sample (TKa-13675) dated to 2585 ± 35 BP (uncalibrated) was associated with fills over the floor of this phase. The other sample (TKa-13676) dated to 2490 ± 30 BP (uncalibrated) was recovered from a fire pit (Figures A.3 and A.6). Although sample TKa-13675 is not directly associated with architecture, sample TKa-13676 was obtained directly from the inside of a fire pit built into the floor during this phase.

Sajara-patac 3 Phase

During the Sajara-patac 3 Phase, the rooms of the previous phase were buried in the area east of the central plaza, and the area of the central plaza itself was reduced. In other parts of the site, the structures of the previous phase were used continuously, although a few modifications (such as refinishing floors) were done.

One radiocarbon date was obtained from this phase (Figures A.4 and A.6). This was a charcoal sample (Pta-9658) associated with a child burial located east of the central

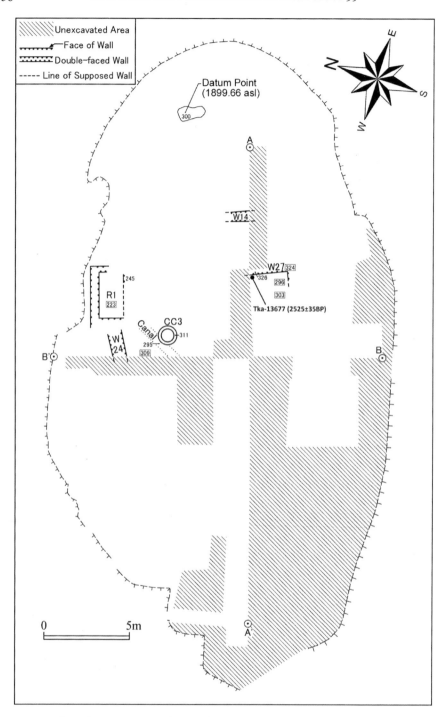

FIGURE A.2. Plan of Sajara-patac 1 Phase architecture showing the provenience of sample TKa-13677. See Figure A.6 for the profile of section A–A′. The numbers are relative values to the datum point (1,899.66 masl) set at 300 cm. The boxed numbers are floor levels. Modified from Matsumoto and Tsurumi (2011, fig. 7).

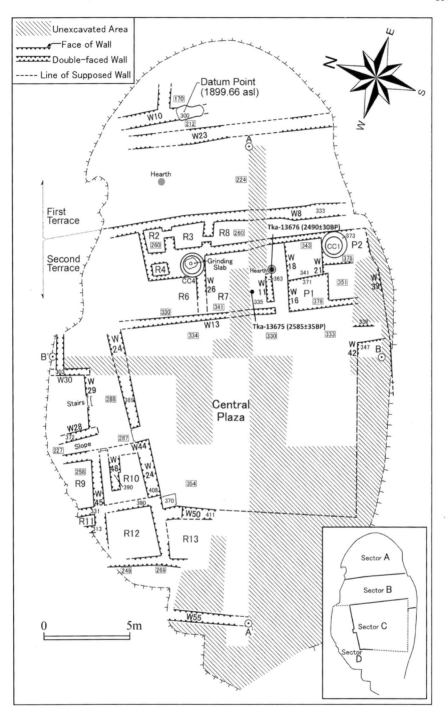

FIGURE A.3. Plan of Sajara-patac 2 Phase architecture showing the proveniences of samples TKa-13675 and TKa-13676. The numbers are relative values to the datum point (1,899.66 masl) set at 300 cm. The boxed numbers are floor levels. Modified from Matsumoto and Tsurumi (2011, fig. 13).

Table A.2. Radiocarbon dates from the archaeological site of Sajara-patac in the Upper Huallaga Basin. All dates were calibrated with OxCal v. 4.3.2 (Bronk Ramsey 2017) using SHCal13, the Southern Hemisphere atmospheric curve (Hogg et al. 2013). Laboratory sample prefixes are as follows: TKa, C-14 Dating Laboratory, The University Museum, The University of Tokyo, Japan; Pta, Quaternary Research Dating Unit (QUADRU), c/o Enviromentek, CSIR, Pretoria, South Africa.

Sample (registration no.)	Sector (stratigraphy)	Architectural phase	Context	^{14}C age (BP)	Range (cal BC)	Probability (%) at 1σ	Range (cal BC)	Probability (%) at 2σ
TKa-13677 (02SP-A-C87)	N4E1 West (3a)	Sajara-patac 1	Charcoal sample recovered on burned floor in association with a feasting context	2525 ± 35	761–727	11.6	777–430	95.4
					718–704	4.3		
					695–541	52.3		
TKa-13676 (02SP-A-C55)	S1E1 (2a)	Sajara-patac 2	Charcoal sample collected from the inside a fire pit	2490 ± 30	744–686	20.4	756–679	24.5
					665–644	7.0	671–606	15.8
					551–427	39.5	598–409	55.0
					421–416	1.3		
TKa-13675 (02SP-A-C38)	S1E1 (1a-C)	Sajara-patac 2	Charcoal sample collected from the architectural fill covering a floor	2585 ± 35	796–748	30.7	804–701	40.0
					684–667	8.6	696–540	55.4
					640–588	23.3		
					578–564	5.5		
Pta-9658 (02SP-C-33)	N1E2 (ATM-2)	Sajara-patac 3	Charcoal sample recovered from a burial associated with a floor	2270 ± 80	385–205	68.2	471–466	0.2
							450–446	0.1
							430–58	95.1
Pta-9659 (02SP-A-C76)	S3O1 (1a)	Sajara-patac 4	Charcoal sample recovered on a floor	2140 ± 70	346–321	5.6	359–270	14.7
					cal BC 208–48 –cal AD 3–10	61.1	cal BC 264 –cal AD 28	80.7

plaza. It gave a date of 2270 ± 80 BP (uncalibrated). This burial was directly over the Sajara-patac 3 Phase floor and is probably a ritual context associated with abandonment of the Sajara-patac 3 Phase architecture.

Sajara-patac 4 Phase

The Sajara-patac 4 Phase is the last architectural phase at this site. Active construction activities such as those of the previous phases were no longer carried out. The central plaza and the access to it were buried and a wall was constructed inside the plaza. This suggests that the ceremonial core of Sajara-patac was abandoned at the beginning of this phase and that Sajara-patac no longer functioned as a ceremonial center.

One sample that was collected on the floor west of the central plaza produced a date of 2140 ± 80 BP (uncalibrated). This sample was directly associated with a burned floor (Figures A.5 and A.7) and all the pottery sherds from the layer that covered the floor were Kotosh Sajara-patac Phase sherds, including Sajara-patac Chocolate Brown Plain (Onuki 1972:182–183, pl. 104).

My analysis of the pottery suggests that the first three building phases of Sajara-patac (Sajara-patac 1, 2, and 3) correspond to the Kotosh Chavín Phase and Sajara-patac 4 corresponds to the Kotosh Sajara-patac Phase at Kotosh (Inokuchi et al. 2003; Matsumoto 2007, 2009; Matsumoto and Tsurumi 2011).

Synthesizing the Radiocarbon Dates of the Upper Huallaga Basin

Izumi and Terada established a chronology using ceramic and architectural sequences and conventional uncalibrated radiocarbon dates (Terada 1972:307–312). However, overlapping dates of different phases have made it difficult to determine the end and beginning of specific phases. Although Onuki's (1998) revision fits well with the general chronology from the Late Preceramic Period to the Early Horizon in relation to other highland and coastal sites (Kato 1998:36–37), new regional data are required to confirm his revision and improve chronological accuracy at a regional level. The new radiocarbon data from Sajara-patac are important for this purpose.

In addition to the dates from Sajara-patac, all the radiocarbon data from Kotosh and Shillacoto were reconsidered using calibrated years (Tables A.1 and A.2; Figure A.8). All the dates discussed here are calibrated with OxCal v. 4.3.2 (Bronk Ramsey 2017) using SHCal13, the Southern Hemisphere atmospheric curve (Hogg et al. 2013).

The Samples from Kotosh and Shillacoto

The relatively large probability ranges, which indicate the technical difficulties of radiocarbon dating in the 1960s, were also problematic for approximating the time span of each phase. However, even with these complications, the calibrated radiocarbon dates of the Kotosh Mito Phase samples seem to show meaningful clustering (see Table A.1; Figure A.8). The earliest date, 3900 ± 100 BP (Gak-766b), which was used to place the beginning of the Kotosh Mito Phase at 2000 BC (Terada 1972:308), is now calibrated earlier: 2470–2198 cal BC at 1σ (66.1% probability) and 2581–2022 cal BC at 2σ (95.2% probability) (Table A.1; Figure A.8). Because the excavations at Kotosh suggest the possible existence of older Mito temples under the layer of the "White Temple" (*Templo Blanco*) (Izumi and Terada

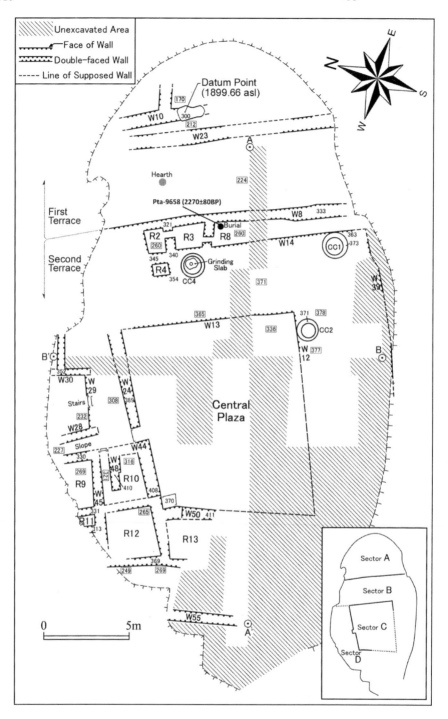

Figure A.4. Plan of Sajara-patac 3 Phase architecture showing the provenience of sample Pta-9658. The numbers are relative values to the datum point (1,899.66 masl) set at 300 cm. The boxed numbers are floor levels. Modified from Matsumoto and Tsurumi (2011, fig. 21).

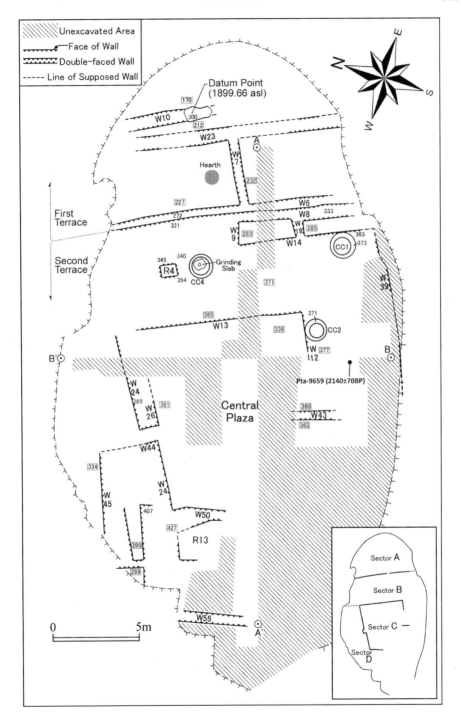

FIGURE A.5. Plan of Sajara-patac 4 Phase architecture showing the provenience of sample Pta-9659. The numbers are relative values to the datum point (1,899.66 masl) set at 300 cm. The boxed numbers are floor levels. Modified from Matsumoto and Tsurumi (2011, fig. 26).

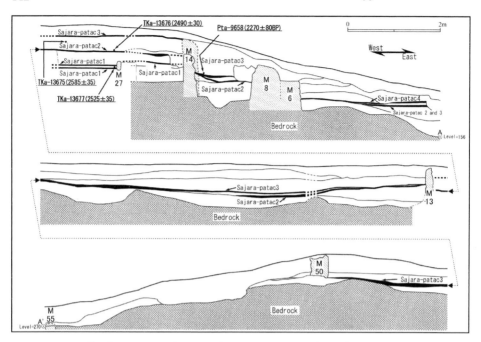

FIGURE A.6. Profile of section A–A' (east–west) at Sajara-patac. Modified from Inokuchi et al. (2003).

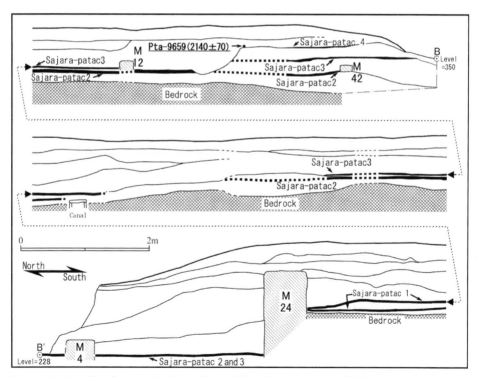

FIGURE A.7. Profile of section B–B' (north–south) at Sajara-patac. Modified from Inokuchi et al. (2003).

1972:49, 51), the beginning of the Kotosh Mito Phase could be earlier than the earliest date presented here. Therefore, considering the dates from Huaricoto (Burger and Salazar-Burger 1980, 1985) and La Galgada (Grieder and Bueno 1981, 1985; Grieder et al. 1988), I tentatively set the beginning of this phase at 2500 cal BC, as did Onuki (1998). As for the end date of the Kotosh Mito Phase, samples TK-109 and TK-110 are reasonably close, in the range of approximately 1800–1400 cal BC at 1σ. Sample TK-109 especially has a range of 1776–1426 cal BC at 1σ (63.8% probability), suggesting that the end date of the Kotosh Mito Phase could be later than 1800 BC. Taking the continuity of the Kotosh Mito Phase into the Kotosh Waira-jirca Phase (Izumi, Cuculiza, and Kano 1972; Onuki 1993, 1998) into account, the beginning date of the Kotosh Waira-jirca Phase should be considered in evaluating the date of sample TK-109.

As Terada (1972:308) noted, the Kotosh Waira-jirca Phase dates can be divided into two groups: earlier and later. The earlier two samples, Gak-262 and Gak-765, date to 3800 ± 110 BP (2482–1886 cal BC at 2σ, 95.4% probability) and to 3750 ± 90 BP (2368–1882 cal BC at 2σ, 91.9% probability), respectively. These overlap with the earlier two dates of the Kotosh Mito Phase samples (Gak-766a and Gak-766b; see Table A.1) and are quite separated from the other three dates of the Kotosh Waira-jirca Phase (samples N-69-2, TK-108, and TK-43; see Table A.1; Figure A.8). Thus, it seems reasonable to reject them as outliers. In contrast, the third earliest date, provided by sample TK-43 from Shillacoto (see Table A.1; Figure A.8), is 3200 ± 80 BP (1514–1300 cal BC at 1σ, 68.2% probability, and 1621–1220 cal BC at 2σ, 95.4% probability), which does not contradict much later dates from the Kotosh Mito Phase samples. Therefore, the end of the Kotosh Mito Phase and the beginning of the Kotosh Waira-jirca Phase should fall in the range 1700–1300 cal BC. Although the estimated range may be too large, these data suggest that it is highly probable that the beginning of the Kotosh Waira-jirca Phase is later than 1800 BC. Tentatively, I would estimate 1600 cal BC for this transition period.

The following Kotosh Kotosh Phase dates are difficult to interpret, because of the large probability ranges. However, there is not much contradiction between the latest date of the Kotosh Waira-jirca Phase (sample TK-108) and the earliest date of this period (sample Gak-261) (see Table A.1). Therefore, the end of the Kotosh Waira-jirca Phase and the beginning of the Kotosh Kotosh Phase would be around 1300–1000 cal BC and may be tentatively set at 1200 cal BC, if sample TK-108 is acceptable with a range of 1267–1024 cal BC at 1σ (68.2% probability). The end date of the Kotosh Kotosh Phase is difficult to determine, because of the early dates produced by the Kotosh Chavín Phase samples (Gak-263, N-65-2; see Table A.1; Figure A.8), therefore data for the latter phase should be evaluated first.

The Samples from Sajara-patac

The dates of the Kotosh Chavín Phase samples from Kotosh (Gak-263, N-65-2) almost completely overlap with dates of the Kotosh Kotosh Phase. Because of the superposition of the stone structures of the Kotosh Kotosh Phase and Kotosh Chavín Phase, this could be the result of an "old wood problem," or disturbed contexts. In any case, it is difficult to evaluate these dates on the basis of only samples from Kotosh. In contrast, at Sajara-patac a consistent set of four dates for the Kotosh Chavín Phase were obtained. The settlement and pottery data imply that the transition from the Kotosh Kotosh Phase to the Kotosh Chavín Phase probably occurred simultaneously in the entire Upper Huallaga Basin (see Chapter 5), so it seems reasonable to use the data from Sajara-patac instead of those of Kotosh (see Table A.2).

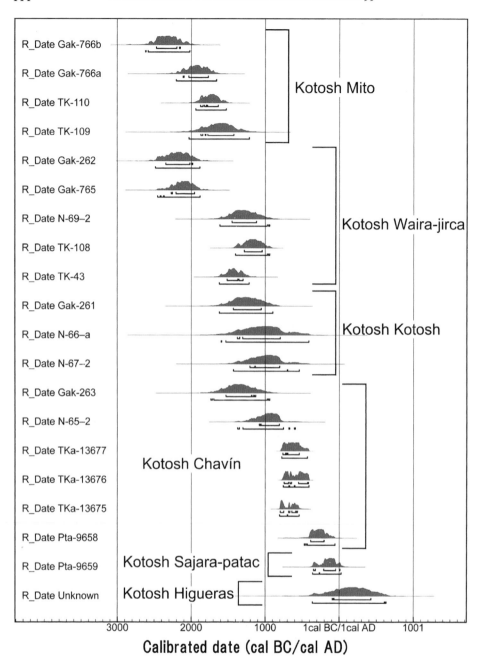

FIGURE A.8. Calibrated radiocarbon dates associated with Kotosh ceramic phases from the Upper Huallaga Basin, Peru. All dates were calibrated with OxCal v. 4.3.2 (Bronk Ramsey 2017) using SHCal04, the Southern Hemisphere atmospheric curve (Hogg et al. 2013).

Sample TKa-13677 came from the context associated with the Sajara-patac 1 Phase, the earliest architecture at Sajara-patac, and thus could be used as a date for the beginning of the Kotosh Chavín Phase. This sample dated to 2525 ± 35 BP (777–430 cal BC at 2σ, 95.4% probability).

The Sajara-patac 2 Phase produced two samples (TKa-13676 and TKa-13675). Sample TKa-13676 is from a fire pit dated to 2490 ± 30 BP (756–409 cal BC at 2σ, 95.4% probability, across three ranges). Sample TKa-13675 is from the architectural fill dated to 2585 ± 35 BP (804–540 cal BC at 2σ, 95.4% probability, across two ranges). Sample TKa-13675 produced an earlier date than sample TKa-13677, even though it was from the later building phase. Sample TKa-13675 was associated with the fill that buried the Sajara-patac 2 Phase architecture, therefore soil from an earlier phase may have been used or mixed with it.

Although the probability range is wide, because of the flat part of the calibration curve for these dates (the Hallstatt plateau), these earlier dates from Sajara-patac clearly postdate the later date of the Kotosh Chavín Phase sample (N-65-2) from Kotosh. Moreover, these data from Sajara-patac do not overlap with those of the Kotosh Kotosh Phase at Kotosh (see Figure A.8). Therefore, the two samples from Kotosh (Gak-263, N-65-2) should be eliminated from consideration. They may be materials from the Kotosh Kotosh Phase.

This argument is also supported by the change of pottery style from Sajara-patac 1 to Sajara-patac 2 (Matsumoto 2007, 2009; Matsumoto and Tsurumi 2011). Sample TKa-13677, from the earliest context at the site, was associated with a bottle rim with a black polished surface, a black polished neckless jar decorated with a circle-and-dot motif, and a red, deep bowl with graphite painting (Figure A.9). The black polished vessel (Figure A.9A, B) is common at Kotosh in the Kotosh Chavín Phase and corresponds to Paucarbamba Brilliant Plain and Paucarbamba Brilliant Decorated pottery types (Onuki 1972:186–187, pl. 110, no.19) at Kotosh. However, graphite was used to fill in the broad and shallow incisions on the red-slipped bowl (Figure A.9C). The use of graphite was popular only in the Sajara-patac 1 Phase and, at Kotosh, graphite painting as a decorative technique was restricted to the Kotosh Kotosh Phase (Onuki 1972:193). Therefore, although the pottery style of Sajara-patac 1 Phase is basically the same as that of later phases at Sajara-patac and the Kotosh Chavín Phase at Kotosh, it still includes elements of the Kotosh Kotosh Phase, which disappeared in the later phases. This suggests that in the earlier part of the Kotosh Chavín Phase at Sajara-patac the decorative technique of the former Kotosh Kotosh Phase was continued. Therefore, the date from the Sajara-patac 1 Phase is useful to define the end of the Kotosh Kotosh Phase and the beginning of Kotosh Chavín Phase.

These data suggest that the Kotosh Chavín Phase at Sajara-patac began between 750 and 400 cal BC. From the overlap among these three dates, we can assume the end of the Kotosh Kotosh Phase and the beginning of the Kotosh Chavín Phase around 700 cal BC. For the end date of the Kotosh Chavín Phase we have sample Pta-9658 (see Table A.2; Figure A.8), which was obtained from an excellent context. This sample is from with the burial located directly on the Sajara-patac 3 Phase floor and thus is probably associated with the transition from Sajara-patac 3 to Sajara-patac 4 (from the Kotosh Chavín Phase to the Kotosh Sajara-patac Phase). This burial could have been an offering made before the sealing of the ceremonial architecture at Sajara-patac. Sample Pta-9658 has been dated to 2270 ± 80 BP (385–205 cal BC at 1σ, 68.2% probability). Thus, the best guess for the end date of the Kotosh Chavín Phase would be around 300 cal BC.

For the Kotosh Sajara-patac Phase, although no radiocarbon data are available

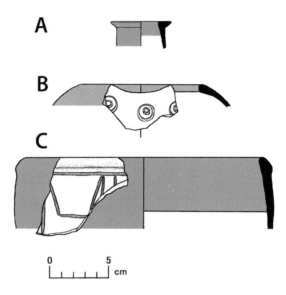

FIGURE A.9. Pottery sherds associated with sample TKa-13677. **A.** Bottle rim with a black polished surface. **B.** Black polished neckless jar decorated with a circle-and-dot motif. **C.** Deep, red-slipped bowl with graphite painting.

from Kotosh, there is a date from Sajara-patac (Pta-9659; see Table A.2; Figures A.5 and A.8). As mentioned, this sample is associated with the possible Kotosh Sajara-patac Phase floor and dates to 2140 ± 70 BP (359 cal BC to cal AD 28 at 2σ, 95.4% probability, across the two ranges). Because data for Kotosh Sajara-patac Phase architecture are scarce, it is difficult to identify whether this sample was associated with the end of the Kotosh Sajara-patac Phase. At least these dates do not contradict the dating of the end of the Kotosh Chavín Phase presented above. Considering that the context of sample Pta-9659 may not represent the end of the Kotosh Sajara-patac Phase, the date of 50 BC from Onuki's revision should be kept.

The Kotosh Higueras Phase is the most enigmatic period in the chronology of the Upper Huallaga Basin. The only available date for it, 1880 ± 200 BP, is from Kotosh (see Table A.1; Figure A.8), which barely suggests that this period at least includes the Early Intermediate Period. Given the long-term continuity of pottery styles in the Upper Huallaga Basin, as suggested by Onuki (1982) and Grosboll (1988:355), it is premature to delineate the span of this phase since it is difficult to reject the possibility that this period continued well beyond the Early Intermediate Period (see Chapters 5 and 6).

In summary, the following is a new but tentative chronology determined from these calibrated dates:

Kotosh Mito Phase	2500–1600 cal BC
Kotosh Waira-jirca Phase	1600–1200 cal BC
Kotosh Kotosh Phase	1200–700 cal BC
Kotosh Chavín Phase	700–300 cal BC
Kotosh Sajara-patac Phase	300–50 cal BC
Kotosh Higueras Phase	50 cal BC–?

Conclusions

Although this revised chronology basically confirms Onuki's revision, rather than changes the chronological framework of the Upper Huallaga Basin, each period is now associated with radiocarbon measurements that are independent of the relative chronology used for general comparisons with other regions. In particular, the new dates of the Kotosh Chavín Phase from Sajara-patac could contribute to the ongoing debate about the Chavín problem (Burger 1981, 1984, 1988, 1992, 2008, 2019; Kembel 2001, 2008; Kembel and Rick 2004; Rick 2005, 2008; Burger and Salazar 2008; Rick et al. 2010) since they are a rare set of radiocarbon measurements for an Early Horizon site south of Chavín de Huántar (for exceptions, see DeLeonardis [2005], Matsumoto and Cavero Palomino [2009], and Unkel et al. [2012]).

On the other hand, this attempt to establish a chronology of the Upper Huallaga Basin using calibrated dates highlights the need for more dates. In addition to the large probability range of the dates from Kotosh caused by technical limitations, the new dates from Sajara-patac share the same problem, because of the Hallstatt plateau. This issue makes it difficult to establish a fine-grained absolute chronology.

Therefore, I have to admit that the chronological framework presented here includes several speculative inferences and thus should be treated as a tentative, to be improved through further research. The only solution for a better chronology would be to date new samples from specified contexts through controlled excavation.

Acknowledgments. I wish to express my special thanks to Kunio Yosida of the University of Tokyo Radiocarbon Lab, who kindly collaborated with us to date the three samples from Sajara-patac. Stephan Woodborne of the Council for Scientific and Industrial Research (CSIR), Pretoria, South Africa, dated two samples from the same site. A portion of this work was funded by the Yale University Michael Coe Fieldwork Fund from the Yale University Council on Archaeological Studies.

EXCAVATIONS
AT WAIRA-JIRCA, 1966

Yoshio Onuki
and Yuichi Matsumoto

The results presented here are from the excavations conducted in 1966 at the archaeological site of Waira-jirca in the Department of Huánuco, Peru. Through a detailed examination of the field notes and photographs from that project, we will describe an architectural sequence that establishes a chronology for the site of Waira-jirca and discuss the implications for the archaeology of the Upper Huallaga Basin. The excavations at Waira-jirca revealed that the Mito-style temples of the Late Preceramic Period were included in this sequence, and thus provide a valuable data set for comparison with Kotosh and other contemporary sites in the central Andes.

Excavations at Waira-jirca

On the southern bank of the Huallaga River, along the main road connecting the modern cities of Huánuco and Tingo Maria, there are three natural hills separated by ravines (Onuki 1993:74). The site of Waira-jirca (Site No. 43; see Chapter 4) is situated on the easternmost hill close to the village called Chullqui (see Figure 1). The site is basically an artificial mound. It has an approximate diameter of 20 m and a height of 3 to 4 m. Onuki's sixteen-day investigation of the site, from July 6–21, 1966, with Hiroyasu Tomoeda, Arturo Ruiz Estrada, and Carlos Chaud Gutierrez, excavated a 4.5 by 10 m trench (Unit WJA; Figure B.1) on the top of the mound. The main objective of the project was to test the applicability of the relative chronology established at the site of Kotosh at a regional level for the Upper Huallaga Basin. All data from this project are from this excavation unit. The following detailed descriptions are based on Onuki's field notes.

Stratigraphy and Architecture

The architectural features at Waira-jirca consist of eight possible room structures recovered from Unit WJA and a perimeter wall for a terrace or platform in the northern portion of the excavation unit. Unit WJA was divided into two sectors: Sector 1, in the southern

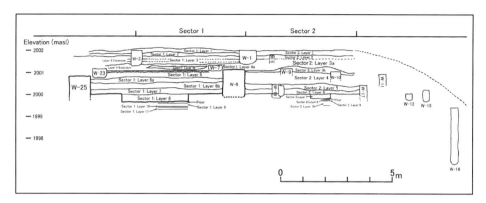

FIGURE B.1. Stratigraphy of excavation Unit WJA at the archaeological site of Waira-jirca (Site No. 43).

half of the unit, and Sector 2, in the northern half (see Figure B.1). The stratigraphy of each sector is described separately below.

The descriptions of the excavations at Waira-jirca are taken from Onuki's 1966 field notes, sketches, and photographic archives, which have been preserved at the University Museum at the University of Tokyo. The field notes have detailed information about the size of architectural elements, the soil matrix, and the stratigraphic levels, but no plan or profile drawings were found. The plans and profiles presented here (Figures B.1–B.4) should be treated as schematic reconstructions rather than documentation completed in the field. In the following descriptions, the room structures are designated with the prefix R and numbered R-1, R-2, and R-3. Walls (W) and hearths (H) are described in the same way, as W-1, W-2, W-3, and H-1, H-2, H-3, respectively. Though stratigraphy is shown with layers, these are grouped as five levels on the basis of architectural associations of the layers. These are labeled Levels A through E in descending order from the surface.

Although the chronological position of each layer and its associated architectural remains need to be defined according to both architectural styles and the pottery typology identified by the excavations at Kotosh (Matsuzawa 1972; Onuki 1972), as discussed below, the data from Waira-jirca show that the associations of architecture with pottery sherds are quite different at the two sites of Kotosh and Waira-jirca. Unfortunately, there is not enough data available to address this question, but it is an important topic for future research. In the next section we tentatively re-examine the chronological relationship between Waira-jirca and Kotosh by comparing the architectural data. Whereas the chronological identification of Waira-jirca should be determined through larger-scale stratigraphic excavations and radiocarbon dating, the available data allow us to provide a useful approximation of the site's chronology.

Level A

STRATIGRAPHY OF LEVEL A
Level A consisted of the surface layer, which may have been disturbed by modern activities, and an underlying layer associated with a hearth. This level was distinguished from other levels because the presence of Kotosh Sajara-patac Phase material was restricted to this level.

Both Sectors 1 and 2 (see Figure B.1) were covered by Layer 1, the surface layer, which was composed of dry, brown soil with a loose matrix. Pottery sherds of the Kotosh Waira-jirca Phase and the Kotosh Sajara-patac Phase were recovered from this layer.

Layer 2 in Sector 1 was composed of fine-grained dark brown soil. The pottery from this layer includes both Kotosh Waira-jirca Phase and Kotosh Sajara-patac Phase sherds.

ARCHITECTURE OF LEVEL A

Layer 2 in Sector 1 is below Layer 1. It was composed of fine-grained dark brown soil mixed in a loose matrix. A hearth with a large amount of ash was associated with it. One San Blas Red Polished sherd (Onuki 1972:180–181) was found in the ash, so it is highly probable that this layer and hearth belong to the Kotosh Sajara-patac Phase.

Although room features R-1, R-2, and R-3 were excavated in Layer 2, this layer does not correspond to the base of these room walls. All Kotosh Sajara-patac Phase materials are restricted to Layer 1 and Sector 1's Layer 2, and were mixed with Kotosh Waira-jirca Phase materials. Therefore, it is reasonable that R-1, R-2, and R-3 were reused long after their abandonment at the end of the Kotosh Waira-jirca Phase. We will return to this later in our description of Level C stratigraphy.

Level B

Level B is difficult to relate stratigraphically to other levels, because this level is defined only by a wall (W-16) and the stratigraphy associated with this single architectural feature. W-16, near the northern edge of Unit WJA on the steep slope of the mound, was difficult to connect stratigraphically to the rest of Unit WJA (see Figure B.1). There was an ash layer below W-16. Typical Kotosh Kotosh Phase pottery sherds, such as Kotosh Red Grooved, Kotosh Black Polished Incised, and Kotosh Graphited, were recovered from this ash layer and the soil that covered the north face of the wall.

Kotosh Kotosh Phase materials were recovered only in Level B. The layer directly below Level A only produced Kotosh Waira-jirca material. Considering that the Sajara-patac Phase pottery sherds were recovered only from Level A, the layers associated with wall W-16 should be placed chronologically before Level A.

Level C

Level C (Figure B.2) consists of the layers below Level A and was associated with rooms R-1, R-2, and R-3.

STRATIGRAPHY OF LEVEL C

Layer 3 in Sector 1 is below Sector 1's Layer 2, which corresponds to the floor of the Kotosh Sajara-patac Phase. The soil matrix was a very dark brown and only Kotosh Waira-jirca Phase pottery sherds were recovered from this layer.

Layer 2 in Sector 2 is below Layer 1. Layer 2 was characterized by a large amount of black ash mixed in the matrix. According to Onuki's field notes, there was a floor below this layer corresponding to R-1, R-2, and R-3. Only Kotosh Waira-jirca Phase pottery sherds were identified from this layer.

ARCHITECTURE OF LEVEL C

Room R-1 consisted of walls W-1, W-2, and W-3 (see Figure B.2). Although a wall on the western side was not uncovered, probably because of the limited scale of the excavation, it is clear that R-1 is not an independent "standalone" room, but part of a room complex.

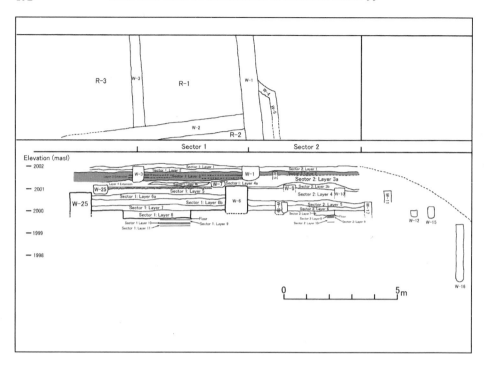

FIGURE B.2. Plan and profile of Level C of Unit WJA at Waira-jirca.

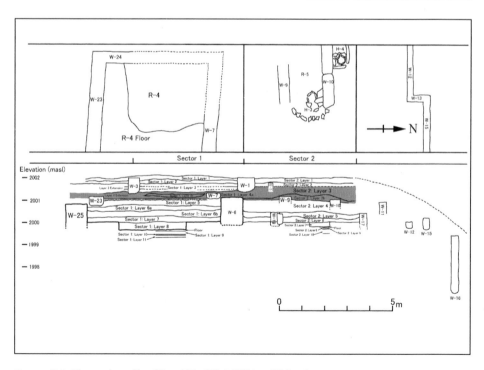

FIGURE B.3. Plan and profile of Level D of Unit WJA at Waira-jirca.

All the walls of R-1 were double-faced and were shared with R-2 to the east and R-3 to the south. R-1 and R-3 are associated with two floors. To the north of R-1, walls W-4 and W-5 outline a small room-like feature with W-1. Most of the stone used for this architectural feature is sericite schist.

Level D

All layers of Level D (Figure B.3) were associated with Kotosh Waira-jirca Phase pottery sherds.

STRATIGRAPHY OF LEVEL D

Layer 4a in Sector 1 was below walls W-1, W-2, and W-3 and made up the interior of R-4. This layer is composed of two different types of soil. The soil in the eastern part of R-4 was yellowish brown, whereas the soil of the western portion was dark brown. The dark brown soil covered the area of R-4 where there was no floor, therefore the dark brown soil may be later than the yellowish brown soil on the floor of R-4. That is, the yellowish brown soil on the floor was dug into by the dark brown soil, and so corresponds to the destruction of the floor and walls.

Layer 4b in Sector 1 was a lens layer of fine-grained white ash located in Layer 4.

Layer 3a in Sector 2 was yellowish brown soil with a large amount of fragmented sericite schist. It is highly probable that this layer corresponds to the yellowish brown soil of Sector 1's Layer 4a. Layer 3a buried a floored space placed over room R-5. The placement of Layer 3b was made, for analytical purposes, from an interpretation of the field notes. This layer buried R-5 and the two hearths associated with it (H-3, H-4).

ARCHITECTURE OF LEVEL D

In general, the architectural remains in Level D were poorly preserved, possibly because of later destruction caused by the construction of the features in Level C. Room R-4 was outlined by walls W-7, W-23, and W-24 (see Figure B.3) and was the only preserved room structure. These walls were all badly damaged, with only the bases preserved. The northwest corner was missing and the eastern wall is probably located outside of the excavation unit, but it is clear that R-4 originally was a rectangular room with a dimension of 6 by 6 m. Although most of the floor has been destroyed, the remaining portion near the western and southern edges helps us to understand the flooring process of R-4: small stones and river cobbles were spread to create a surface flat enough for a mud-plastered floor. Because the shape and size of R-4 reminds us of the Mito-style temples, it is tempting to connect R-4 with temple construction projects of the Kotosh Mito Phase at Kotosh. Unfortunately, the destruction of the central part of the floor makes it impossible to evaluate whether the split-level floors and central hearth characteristic of that architectural style were once present (e.g., Bonnier 1997b; Onuki 1999).

Another possible structure in Level D was R-5, although it is not certain that this was a room. Stone masonry walls W-9 and W-10 create a narrow space 1.5 m in length by 2 m in width. W-10 was associated with two hearths and the small stone features around them, and thus at least W-10 may have functioned as some kind of protection against wind for these hearths. Although W-12, W-13, and W-15 were associated with Kotosh Waira-jirca Phase pottery sherds and could be contemporaneous with the other architectural remains from this level, their proximity to the sloped surface makes it difficult to connect them stratigraphically with other architectural remains.

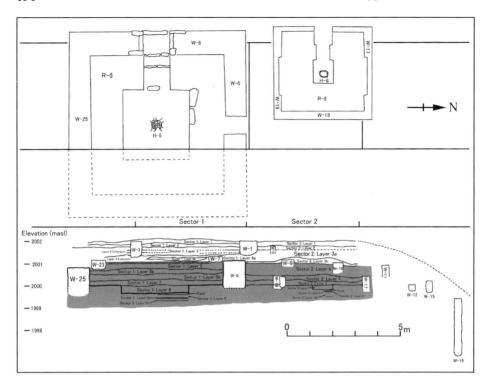

FIGURE B.4. Plan and profile of Level E of Unit WJA at Waira-jirca.

Level E

Level E (Figure B.4) corresponds to the layers that cover and fill two Mito-style temples (R-6, R-8) located on the same platform. At least, some layers of Level E were associated with Kotosh Waira-jirca Phase pottery sherds, which is notable considering that the Kotosh Mito Phase is regarded as the Preceramic Period. Although it is important to emphasize the association of the Mito temples with Waira-jirca Phase sherds here, we will return to explore this later.

STRATIGRAPHY OF LEVEL E

Layer 5 in Sector 1 filled room R-6 and probably corresponds to when R-6 was buried. There are many flat stones in this layer.

Layer 6 in Sector 1 was divided into Layers 6a and 6b. Detailed information about Layer 6a, such as color and texture, is missing, but this layer filled R-6 and was located over Sector 1's Layer 6b. Layer 6b consisted of gray ash and extended throughout R-6. According to the field notes, Sector 1's Layers 6a and 6b both covered the interior of R-6.

Layer 7 in Sector 1, located below Layer 6b, was also yellowish brown. As with Sector 1's Layers 6a and 6b, Layer 7 extended to the interior of R-6. The upper floor of R-6 was directly below Sector 1's Layer 7. Layers 6a, 6b, and 7 probably correspond to the burial of R-6 during the Kotosh Waira-jirca Phase.

Layer 8 in Sector 1 consisted of yellowish brown soil similar to Sector 1's Layer 7, but included more angular gravel. This layer was designated as a separate layer, mainly because of architectural associations. Although the soil type of Layer 8 was similar to that of Layer 7, Layer 8 corresponds to the burial of the lower level floor of R-6 and the construction of stairs that access the western wall (Figure B.5).

Part of the lower level floor was excavated in R-6. Although detailed information is not available, there was at least one layer, with a thickness of 20 to 22 cm, below the floor (Sector 1, Layer 9). A thin layer of red soil 6 cm in thickness (Sector 1, Layer 10) was below it. Below Layer 10 was a layer 15 cm in thickness with gray ash (Sector 1, Layer 11).

Layer 4 in Sector 2 was partially in the northern edge of Sector 1 and below Sector 1's Layer 4. Although this layer corresponds to Sector 1's Layer 5, it is difficult to know whether they consisted of the same soil.

Layer 5 in Sector 2 covered R-8 and thus corresponds to the time of this room's abandonment. No detailed information about this layer is available.

Layer 6 in Sector 2 was a white to dark gray ash layer that filled R-8. Its level corresponds to Sector 1's Layer 6b. Although these two layers fill different rooms independently, the proximity of the levels and the similarity of their ash layers suggests that both levels are evidence of the simultaneous filling and burying of R-6 and R-8.

Layer 7 in Sector 2 consisted of yellowish soil. No detailed information is available.

The lower portion of the split-level floor was excavated in R-8. The plastered floor, 6 cm in thickness, had a layer of red soil below it (Sector 2, Layer 8). A thin ash layer 2 to 3 cm in thickness was found underneath this red soil (Sector 2, Layer 9). Below these layers, which are related to the construction of R-8, there was a thick layer of yellowish-brown soil on possible bedrock (Sector 2, Layer 10). This suggests that this yellowish brown layer was a flat surface created on the natural hill for the Mito-style temples, rooms R-6 and R-8. A circular or semi-circular feature was excavated in this layer.

ARCHITECTURE OF LEVEL E

Two Mito-style temples (R-6, R-8) were recovered from Level E (see Figure B.5). Both were constructed on the same platform and thus are clearly contemporaneous. The following is a description of these two temple constructions.

R-6 is a square and freestanding room with a dimension of 8 by 8 m. It is characterized by its square shape, split-level floors, and a central hearth associated with the lower floor (see Figures B.4–B.6). These are typical traits of Mito-style temples found at Kotosh. On the other hand, there was a major architectural change to R-6 during its use. After the burial of the lower level floor at the center of the chamber (Layer 8), stairs leading toward the western access of the mound were built (Figure B.6). The presence of Kotosh Waira-jirca Phase pottery in Layer 8 suggests that R-6 was in use even after it ceased to be a Mito temple during the Kotosh Mito Phase.

R-8 is similar to R-6 in the sense that it is a square free-standing chamber with split-level floors (Figure B.7) associated with a central hearth, even though at 4 by 4 m it is much smaller than R-6.

It is notable that both R-6 and R-8 had red soil, which was used to create ritual spaces at other Mito-style temples, including at Kotosh (Onuki 1993:80; Bonnier 1997b:124–125). Although both R-6 and R-8 can be described as rooms, it is difficult to know whether the remaining walls retain their original height or had collapsed or been destroyed before the excavation. It is also possible that these low walls were open-air spaces or that walls of perishable materials such as adobe were placed on them.

Most of the architectural traits of R-6 and R-8 follow the typical architectural cannons of the Mito-style temple at Kotosh, yet there are a few differences. Whereas the Mito

Figure B.5. View of rooms R-6 and R-8 from the south.

temples at Kotosh are square chambers with a single access (as is the case for R-8), R-6 has two access points, one to the west and the other to the north. Furthermore, the hearth in the center of the lower floor in the Kotosh Mito temples was generally associated with a ventilation canal connected to the outside, but this was not seen in R-6. Worth mentioning also is the circular feature below the lower floor of R-8 (Figure B.8). The absence of pottery here confirms that this was constructed in the Preceramic Period. However, it is difficult to identify whether this feature was in used before R-8 was built or was part of the temple's construction. In any case, there are no similar examples at Kotosh.

Architectural Sequence at Waira-jirca

Despite the relatively small scale of the 1966 excavation, the data obtained from Waira-jirca showed that this site continued to be occupied from the Kotosh Mito Phase to the Kotosh Kotosh Phase. The presence of two Mito-style temples confirmed that this architectural

FIGURE B.6. The split-level floor of room R-6 and the stairs toward the western access.

style was shared with contemporary sites in the Upper Huallaga Basin (Onuki 1993).

The data from Level E suggest that the first construction activity at Waira-jirca was carried out during the Kotosh Mito Phase after the creation of an artificial terrace or platform on the top of the natural hill. R-6 and R-8 were built at the same time on this artificial terrace or platform, and thus were in use at the same time. Our survey in 2001 identified a possible Mito temple from a looter's pit to the north of Unit WJA (see Figure 86). This suggests that R-6 and R-8 are not the only Mito-style temples at Waira-jirca during the Kotosh Mito Phase.

As the investigators of Kotosh have argued (Izumi 1971; Izumi and Terada 1972; Onuki 1993, 1998, 1999; see also Bonnier 1997b), the split-level floors and a central hearth in a square chamber indicate the ceremonial function of Mito-style temples. However, the stratigraphic data suggest that at least R-6 was modified as a simple room by the burial of the split-level floors during the latter part of Level E, which means R-6 may have been in use even after losing its ceremonial function as a Mito temple.

In this context, the presence of Level D architecture (R-4) is enigmatic. R-4 is a rect-

FIGURE B.7. The split-level floor of room R-8 associated with a central hearth and ventilation canal, seen from the east.

angular, independent room structure associated with a carefully plastered floor. The style of R-4's stone masonry is also quite similar to that of R-6 and R-8 in the lower level: flat stones of sericite schist were selected to create wall surfaces and small stones and cobbles with mud mortar were used as interior fill. It is unfortunate that the central part of R-4 is badly destroyed. Whether split-level floors and an associated central hearth had been present could not be evaluated.

There was no clear evidence of "temple entombment" (Izumi and Terada 1972) or superposition of the Mito-style temple at Waira-jirca. If R-4 was a Mito-style temple, this superposition of R-6 and R-4 might be interpreted as an example. However, this is another problem with the site chronology. Although the excavations at Kotosh showed that so-called temple entombment ceased at the end of Kotosh Mito Phase (corresponding to the Late Preceramic Period, 2500–1600 BC), the layers that buried R-6 and R-8 and created a space for R-4 produced a certain amount of Kotosh Waira-jirca Phase (1600–1200 BC) pottery sherds. This issue needs to be examined through a more detailed comparison with the situations at Kotosh.

The architecture of Level C consisted of a series of rooms divided by double-faced walls. All three rooms (R-1, R-2, R-3) have the same architectural style. This clearly contrasts with the independent rectangular chamber in Levels D and E. At Kotosh, this type of architecture is not seen in the Kotosh Mito Phase, but is found in the Kotosh Waira-jirca Phase. According to Onuki's field notes, the Level C layers produced large amounts of pottery sherds corresponding to the Kotosh Waira-jirca Phase.

Level B is defined purely by the presence of Kotosh Kotosh Phase pottery sherds in association with wall W-16. The location of W-16 near the slope at the northern edge of the site made it impossible to connect this wall with the other levels at this site. According to Onuki's field notes, this wall is quite massive and probably functioned as a revetment, or retaining wall. Kotosh Kotosh Phase sherds were recovered from its fill and there was an ash layer underneath. It is probable that there are more Kotosh Kotosh Phase features at this site outside Unit WJA.

The layers of Level A produced typical pottery sherds of the Kotosh Sajara-patac Phase, but these were not associated with clear architectural remains. Probably there were no major construction activities during the Kotosh Sajara-patac Phase at Waira-jirca. However, as suggested by the hearth in Sector 1's Layer 2 and its association with Kotosh Sajara-patac Phase sherds, the Kotosh Waira-jirca Phase architecture was reused, perhaps during a small or ephemeral occupation.

Site Chronology of Waira-jirca

The stratigraphic associations between architecture and pottery style now allow us to evaluate the site chronology of Waira-jirca. Because no absolute dates are available, this chronology needs to be discussed in light of new radiocarbon dating (see Appendix A) and the cultural sequence at Kotosh and other excavated sites in the Upper Huallaga Basin (Izumi and Sono 1963; Izumi and Terada 1972; Onuki 1993, 1998, 1999, 2014; Matsumoto 2009; Matsumoto and Tsurumi 2011).

The architectural remains from Level E suggest that the history of Waira-jirca began in the Kotosh Mito Phase (2500–1600 BC), yet it is difficult to know the beginning date precisely. The pottery styles associated with architectural remains show that this site continued to be occupied in the Kotosh Waira-jirca Phase and the Kotosh Kotosh Phase (1600–700 BC). After the Kotosh Kotosh Phase, Waira-jirca was abandoned during the Kotosh Chavín Phase (700–300 BC) and reoccupied during the Kotosh Sajara-patac Phase in the later part of the Early Horizon.

These results basically confirm the regional chronology established at Kotosh in the 1960s and show that Kotosh can be used as a "master sequence" for the Upper Huallaga Basin. On the other hand, they also show the variations among the historical trajectories of these early sites in the region. For example, the absence of the Kotosh Chavín Phase at Waira-jirca is a clear indication that the political situation in the region affected each site in different ways.

As for the Kotosh Mito Phase at Waira-jirca, two important questions need to be evaluated by additional research. The first is about the circular feature found under R-8 and its chronological position. This structure (Figure B.8) may be related to the pre-Mito architecture discovered by Elizabeth Bonnier at the site of Piruru in the Tantamayo area, about 80 km northwest of the Upper Huallaga Basin (Bonnier 1997b). At Piruru,

FIGURE B.8. Room R-8 and a circular feature below the lower floor, seen from the west.

along with ceremonial architecture similar to that at Kotosh, Bonnier found twelve stone features that precede the Mito temple and called them "pre-Mito temples" (Bonnier 1997b:125–126). These features are characterized by small stone masonry chambers associated with a central hearth. Their architectural plans were rectangular, semi-rectangular, and circular (Bonnier 1997b, fig. 8). Although limited excavation does not allow us to evaluate whether a central hearth was present in the circular construction at Waira-jirca, the similarity of architectural plans and superposition between Waira-jirca and Piruru is noteworthy. Yet, we should be cautious about using the term pre-Mito, because no radiocarbon dates from Piruru are available. The lack of a good chronology for the Kotosh Mito Phase itself also hinders this comparison.

The second question is that of the association of pottery sherds with Mito-style temples. Whereas the Kotosh Mito Phase is defined by the presence of Mito-style temples and clearly considered to date to the Late Preceramic Period, the Mito-style temples (R-6, R-8) at Waira-jirca were associated with pottery sherds in the stratigraphy of Level E (see previous discussion). This contrasts with Kotosh, where no pottery sherds were recovered from the fill of the Mito-style temples (e.g., Izumi and Sono 1963:153; Terada 1972:303–304).

An example of pottery associated with Mito-style temples in the Upper Huallaga Basin can be seen at the site of Shillacoto (Site No. 26), where a large amount of Waira-jirca style pottery sherds was recovered from the fill layer of a Mito-style temple (Izumi, Cuculiza, and Kano 1972; Kano 1979:10–12). There a large Mito temple (SR-7) had been modified at the beginning of the Kotosh Waira-jirca Phase by the burial of the split-level floor and placement of an altar-like funerary feature on the central hearth (SR-6/Tomb No. 6). The altar (or funeral chamber) included beautiful examples of Kotosh Waira-jirca Phase pottery. This case is better interpreted as a reuse of Kotosh Mito Phase architecture during the Kotosh Waira-jirca Phase.

However, at Waira-jirca, according to Onuki's field notes, the lower floor of R-6 and the backfill of the floor (Sector 1, Layer 8) were associated with pottery sherds, suggesting that pottery was used while the Mito-style temple still functioned as a ceremonial space. In addition, if R-4 in Level D was a Mito-style temple and transition from Level E to Level D was a result of temple entombment, it could be that the ritual activities of the Late Pre-ceramic Period recognized at Kotosh were carried out at Waira-jirca in association with pottery.

Two possible scenarios need to be evaluated by additional research. The first is that the Mito-style temples at Waira-jirca continued to be used during the Kotosh Waira-jirca Phase even though this architectural style ceased to be adopted at Kotosh at that time. In this scenario, a new pottery style was accepted at Kotosh along with a new architectural style and the Mito-style architecture was abandoned, whereas Waira-jirca chose to maintain the architectural tradition of the Kotosh Mito Phase. In this case, Levels C, D, and E would date to the Kotosh Waira-jirca Phase even though R-6 and R-8 were constructed during the Kotosh Mito Phase.

In the second scenario, pottery production was introduced at Waira-jirca during the Kotosh Mito Phase, before it arrived at Kotosh. Thus, Waira-jirca began to fabricate pottery during the Kotosh Mito Phase although Kotosh did not know, or intentionally rejected, pottery production. In this case, Levels D and E belong in the Kotosh Mito Phase and only Level C corresponds to the Kotosh Waira-jirca Phase.

To evaluate these two hypotheses, radiocarbon dates with good associations with the Mito-style architecture and the diagnostic pottery at Waira-jirca are needed.

Conclusions

Although the scale of excavation in 1966 was small, it provided a valuable data set to compare Kotosh with Waira-jirca. Kotosh has been regarded as a representative site of the Upper Huallaga Basin and thus has been generally discussed in the context of inter-regional interaction, which was especially true for the Kotosh Mito Phase (e.g., Burger and Salazar-Burger 1980, 1985; Grieder et al. 1988; Bonnier 1997b; Onuki 1999, 2014) and Kotosh Chavín Phase (e.g., Izumi 1971; Burger 1988, 1992; Kaulicke 1994).

On the other hand, the data from Waira-jirca support not only the general conclusions and arguments related to Kotosh, but suggest that interactions at the intraregional level are also important. The relationships among the contemporary sites and the diachronic transitions of the Upper Huallaga Basin seem to be critical. This perspective clearly complements the arguments about interregional interactions between the Upper Huallaga Basin and other regions in the Andes.

In this context, it is interesting to focus more on the differences than the similarities between Kotosh and Waira-jirca. For example, the lack of a Kotosh Chavín Phase occupation at Waira-jirca might indicate that reactions to foreign influence differed among the sites, suggesting the political autonomy of each site at that time (see Chapter 5; see also Onuki 1993:84).

The most interesting topic for future research at Kotosh and Waira-jirca seems to be the transition from the Kotosh Mito Phase to the Kotosh Waira-jirca Phase. The relationship of Mito-style temples to the introduction of pottery production is quite different at Kotosh and Waira-jirca. The pottery associations with Mito-style temples at Waira-jirca clearly indicate that the introduction of pottery followed quite different processes at each site. Additional excavation at Waira-jirca and at other contemporary sites will provide more data on the relationship of the diachronic process of regional cultural change to the broader context of interregional interactions.

A Head Burial
from Shillacoto

Yoshio Onuki
and Yuichi Matsumoto

The data presented here are from the 1966 excavation of a head burial recovered at the archaeological site of Shillacoto in the Upper Huallaga Basin of Peru. Through an examination of the field notes and photographs from that project, we will provide a description of this unusual head burial dating to the late Initial Period.

Excavations at Shillacoto

Shillacoto (Site No. 26; see Chapter 4) is located on the northern bank of the Huallaga River near its junction with the Higueras River in the modern city of Huánuco (see Figure 1). First excavated by Onuki, Hiroyasu Tomoeda, Lorenzo Samaniego Román, and Carmen Rosa Rivera in 1966 in parallel with the excavations at Kotosh, the site had already been badly damaged by urban expansion even then (Figure C.1). Subsequent excavations were carried out by a team led by Chiaki Kano and Yasushi Miyazaki from 1967 to 1969 (Izumi, Cuculiza, and Kano 1972).

According to Kano and his colleagues, Shillacoto was composed of multiple mounds. The largest measured more than 200 by 200 m with a height of 15 m (Izumi, Cuculiza, and Kano 1972; Kano 1979). Urban growth has destroyed much of the site and today it is almost impossible to evaluate the original site size. Excavation units dug by these two projects were put on the summit of the same large mound. Unfortunately, it is now difficult to determine their precise locations. However, we do know they were relatively close to each other, but were not connected.

The project led by Onuki was primarily concerned with chronological issues related to Kotosh. Onuki showed that parts of the earlier sequence at Kotosh, the Kotosh Wairajirca Phase and Kotosh Kotosh Phase, existed at Shillacoto. Coupled with other small excavation projects at sites such as Waira-jirca (see Appendix B), Paucarbamba (Onuki 1993), Piquimina (see Appendix D), and Sajara-patac (Matsumoto and Tsurumi 2011), the investigations at Shillacoto successfully showed that the chronology established at Kotosh is applicable to the Upper Huallaga Basin in general (Onuki 1993, 1998). Larger scale later excavations produced important data, not only confirming the chronology of the former

FIGURE C.1. Excavations at the archaeological site of Shillacoto (Site No. 26) in 1966.

FIGURE C.2. Bar-shaped stones arranged as a lid of the cist in TM-3 (Tomb No. 3).

Figure C.3. A human skull in situ at the center of the excavated cist (TM-3).

FIGURE C.4. Close up view of the inverted human skull in the center of the cist in TM-3 (Tomb No. 3).

project, but also recognizing the presence of two important late Initial Period burials and a Mito-style temple larger than any found at Kotosh (Izumi, Cuculiza, and Kano 1972; Kano 1979).

An Unusual Head Burial

During their 1966 excavation, Onuki and his colleagues discovered the burial of a human head and recorded it as TM-3 (see also Onuki 1993: 84). The diagnostic artifacts associated with this burial suggested that this context dates to the later part of the Kotosh Waira-jirca Phase or the earlier part of the Kotosh Kotosh Phase at Kotosh.

The head was found in a cist (a stone-lined, covered tomb) made of quarried stones capped by bar-shaped quarried stones. The interior of the cist measured 1.6 m (north–south) by 0.5 to 0.6 m (east–west) and was 0.8 to 1.0 m in depth. The flat sides of the quarried stones were used for the interior walls. The bar-shaped stones measured 15 to 30 cm thick and were 70 to 80 cm in length. Five of these were arranged as a lid for the cist (Figure C.2). At the base of the cist there were two logs, 3 and 5 cm thick, which suggests that wood was used for this small, chamber-like cist.

There was a coarse stone wall below the cist and a finely made masonry wall on the top of the cist. The size of the excavation unit made it difficult to evaluate the relationships between these walls and the cist, but it seems probable that the cist was embedded in some kind of platform construction.

A human skull, possibly of an adult male, was found placed at the center of this cist (Figure C.3). Small stones were found arranged in a circle. The skull was placed in this circle facing to the east. The skull was intentionally placed upside down, with the lower jaw at the top (Figure C.4). Under the skull there was an organic matrix of twigs or reeds, suggesting that the skull had originally been placed on a basket, net bag, or other kind of container.

Conclusions

Although the stone cist could be contemporary with the Kotosh Kotosh Phase stratigraphic layer at the site, a few pottery sherds of the Kotosh Waira-jirca Phase were found in the interior of the cist. Therefore, all we can say is that this funerary context belongs to the later part of the Kotosh Waira-jirca Phase or the earlier part of the Kotosh Kotosh Phase. The best guess might be that burial TM-3 occurred in accordance with the transition from the Kotosh Waira-jirca to the Kotosh Kotosh Phase.

It would be interesting to compare this burial with two other important burials found from the other excavation at Shillacoto. The first is the recoded as SR-6/Tomb No. 6 in the excavations by Kano and his colleagues and belongs to the Kotosh Waira-jirca Phase. It is an altar-like structure placed on the hearth of a Mito-style temple. Human bones of possibly seven individuals were recovered in association with finely made pottery vessels and anthracite mirrors (Izumi, Cuculiza, and Kano 1972:30, 45–46). The other burial context found during the same excavation was found below the floor of the Kotosh Kotosh Phase burial chamber (SR-4/Tomb No. 4) that reused walls of the Kotosh Waira-jirca Phase. Human bones in this burial were associated with rich offerings, including complete and semi-complete vessels, projectile points, stone vessels, anthracite mirrors, marine shells, and incised bone artifacts. Interestingly, the iconography on the bone artifacts shows a clear affiliation with the artistic tradition of Chavín de Huántar (Kano 1979). The difference between these burials and the head burial of tomb TM-3 seems obvious. Whereas the former can be interpreted as burials of important individuals (Kano 1979), the latter shows rather the character of an offering that could have been a part of construction activities.

On the other hand, it seems highly probable that Tomb No. 4 found during the 1967–1969 excavations and TM-3 are contemporaneous. Both could be related to the transition from the Kotosh Waira-jirca Phase to the Kotosh Kotosh Phase. Still, it is difficult to know whether a monumental construction project was carried out at Shillacoto after the abandonment of the Kotosh Religious Tradition (e.g., Burger and Salazar-Burger 1980, 1985). However, these data seem to suggest that the architectural construction at the beginning of the Kotosh Kotosh Phase was quite important and was associated with ritual funerary events and offerings embedded in that architecture.

EXCAVATIONS
AT PIQUIMINA, 2002

Eisei Tsurumi, Kinya Inokuchi, Yoshio Onuki,
Nelly Elvira Martell Castillo, and Yuichi Matsumoto

After our 2001 survey in the bottomlands of Peru's Upper Huallaga Basin, we decided to focus in the following year on issues related to the Early Horizon, or the Chavín problem, for our next excavation project. Although Sajara-patac was chosen because of its good preservation (Inokuchi et al. 2003; Matsumoto and Tsurumi 2011), the archaeological site of Piquimina was also selected, because it had been heavily damaged and was on the verge of being completely destroyed. In addition, Piquimina's location and site type looked quite distinct when compared to Sajara-patac. Sajara-patac consists of mounds along a natural hill, but Piquimina, located much closer to the southern bank of the Huallaga River and situated on sandy terrain, does not show any mounds or architectural features. Therefore, we considered it interesting to compare these two quite different sites. For these reasons, we carried out a short excavation project at the site of Piquimina in September 2002.

Past Research at Piquimina

Seventeen kilometers northeast of the modern city of Huánuco, along the south bank of the Huallaga River, is a small village named Chullqui. The site of Piquimina (Site No. 44; see Chapter 4; see Figure 1) was identified near the riverbank during the University of Tokyo project and was excavated by Onuki, Hiroyasu Tomoeda, Fernando Chaud, and Carlos Chaud in 1966 (Onuki 1993:75). During this excavation, a burial was discovered in the sandy soil layer. It was associated with pottery from the Kotosh Chavín Phase.

We visited the site in 2001, during the survey of the Upper Huallaga Basin, thirty-five years after the earlier excavation. The site had been almost lost in the construction of a modern sports court (Figure D.1; see Chapter 2). Although we had assumed that this site had been a cemetery or domestic area of the Kotosh Chavín Period, pottery sherds of all the phases at Kotosh were identified on the surface (see Figures 89 and 90). Most of the site was gone, but we found an area along the edge of the site that was still intact. Some people in Chullqui remembered that there had been a low sand mound there. When this was destroyed, they remembered seeing stone walls and human bones associated with abundant pottery.

FIGURE D.1. The archaeological site of Piquimina in 2002.

Excavations at Piquimina

Surface remains around the sports court suggest that the original extent of the site was probably about 40 by 50 m. Four 2 by 5 m excavation units were placed around the sports court and designated Units A through D, in the order of excavation. Because most of the site had been damaged, these excavation units were arranged in an L-shape to salvage as much archaeological data as possible (Figures D.2–D.4).

Stratigraphy

As Onuki (1993:75) previously observed, Piquimina is composed of sandy soil. Although the stratigraphy was difficult to discern, we identified four layers in Unit A. The detail of each layer is as follows (Figure D.5).

Layer 1 was a surface layer composed of light brown sand. Pottery sherds of all the periods recognized at Kotosh were found in this layer mixed with modern garbage. Much of the soil of this layer could have been moved when the sports court was built.

Layer 2 was identified in all the excavation units below Layer 1. Layer 2 was composed of fine-grained yellowish brown sand. This layer had a thickness of 20 to 40 cm and was difficult to subdivide. Pottery sherds of the Kotosh Waira-jirca Phase, Kotosh Kotosh Phase, and Kotosh Chavín Phase were found in this layer.

Layer 3 was seen only in Units A and C. It was characterized by a grayish brown sandy matrix in which white grains were mixed. This layer had a thickness of 20 to 60 cm and the lower part was subdivided as Layer 3b. Pottery sherds of the Kotosh Waira-jirca Phase, Kotosh Kotosh Phase, and Kotosh Chavín Phase were found in this layer.

During our excavation, Layer 3b was treated as a part of Layer 3, but we now think it more reasonable to consider it a separate layer. It was different from Layer 3 in being

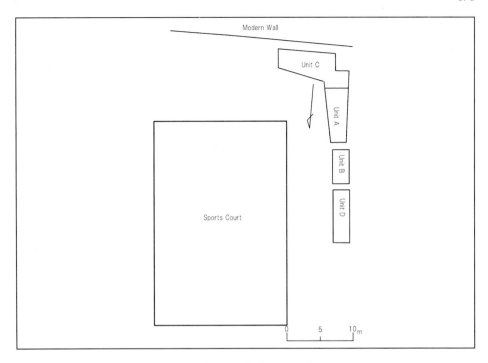

FIGURE D.2. Plan of the Piquimina site showing the location of excavations units.

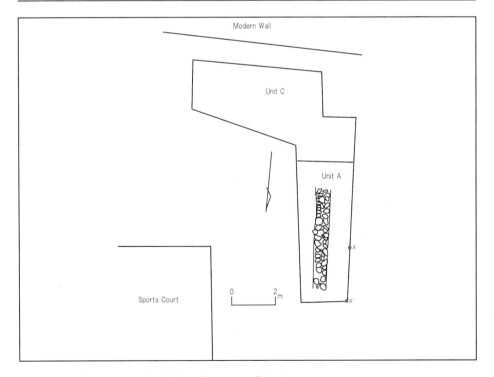

FIGURE D.3. Plan of Units A and C, and a stone wall in Unit A.

FIGURE D.4. View of excavation Unit A at Piquimina from the north.

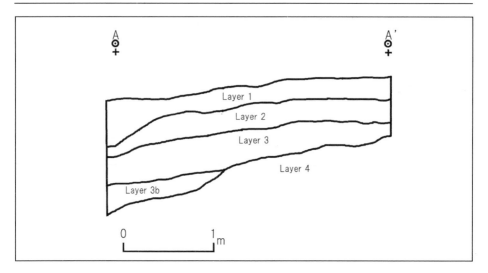

FIGURE D.5. Stratigraphy of excavation Unit A at Piquimina.

darker and its matrix did not include white grains, as did Layer 3. Only the pottery sherds of the Kotosh Waira-jirca Phase and the Kotosh Kotosh Phase were recovered.

Layer 4 was a sterile layer characterized by a greenish brown sandy matrix. The matrix was more compact and finer than in Layers 1 through 3b and did not have any artifacts.

As described here, all the layers produced pottery sherds from multiple phases and were composed of a sandy matrix. Because of the site's nearness to the Huallaga River, it seems probable that all the layers had been affected by high water or minor changes in the river's flow. Flooding or changes in river flow probably occasionally reached the site's surface in the Initial Period and Early Horizon, causing stratigraphic mixing, but the pottery sherds recovered suggest that the site continued to be used after these events.

Architectural Remains

The only architectural feature found in this excavation was a double-faced stone wall uncovered in Unit A. It measured 50 to 60 cm in width and 4.7 m in length, and consisted of two courses of flat field stones (Figures D.3, D.6, and D.7). The base of this wall was in Layer 2 (Figure D.5), therefore this wall could have been constructed during the Kotosh Chavín Phase. Because no other architectural remains were recovered from this excavation, it is impossible to know the original shape of the stone construction. Residents living around the site remembered that when the site was destroyed by heavy machinery other stone walls forming some kind of building were uncovered.

Pottery from Piquimina

General Overview

Pottery sherds from Piquimina suggest that this site was in use throughout the Initial Period and Early Horizon, from the Kotosh Waira-jirca Phase to the Kotosh Sajara-patac Phase. However, the stratigraphy is difficult to interpret, because pottery sherds from multiple periods were recovered from a single layer. On the other hand, it is difficult to say that all the layers are completely disturbed. The lower layer (Layer 3b) only produced sherds from earlier phases, the Kotosh Waira-jirca Phase and Kotosh Kotosh Phase. This confusion might be attributable to the sandy loose matrix rather than to recent disturbance of the site. The following is the brief description of the diagnostic sherds from each phase in the chronology of Kotosh.

KOTOSH WAIRA-JIRCA PHASE
Neckless jars characteristic of the Kotosh Waira-jirca Phase were identified. Rim forms are characterized by interior thickening and tapering, which corresponds to Waira-jirca Red Plain Form 2 and Kotosh Plain Form 3 (Figure D.8A, B) in the typology of Kotosh (Onuki 1972). Two specimens show surface decorations. One has a rim form similar to Kotosh Plain Form 3 and a line of punctations applied with sharply pointed implements (Figure D.8C). The other is decorated with a line of punctations below the rim like the other one, but also has a circle-and-dot motif on and below the rim made with incisions and punctations (Figure D.8D). The rim form is characterized by a ridge on the exterior just below the top of the rim. Although these decorations are rare in the Kotosh Waira-jirca Phase, this rim form is similar to Waira-jirca Red Plain Form 3 (Onuki 1972:194).

KOTOSH KOTOSH PHASE
In addition to neckless jars similar to Kotosh Plain Form 2 (Figure D.8E), a few decorated pieces typical of the Kotosh Kotosh Phase were identified. The rim of an open bowl decorated with geometric motifs and broad line incisions (Figures D.8F and D.9). The combination of flaring rim and broad shallow line is characteristic of Kotosh Grooved A (Onuki 1972:191, pl. 115, 13–16). Pottery sherds with graphite painting were also identified

FIGURE D.6. The Kotosh Chavín Phase stone wall seen from the north.

FIGURE D.7. The Kotosh Chavín Phase stone wall seen from the south.

(Figures D.8G and D.9). This decoration is characteristic of the Kotosh Graphited pottery type and restricted to the Kotosh Kotosh Phase at Kotosh (Onuki 1972:192–193).

KOTOSH CHAVÍN PHASE
Neckless jars characteristic of the Kotosh Chavín Phase are represented by examples corresponding to Kotosh Plain Form 1 (Figure D.10A, B). There is an example of a decorated sherd that is part of a bottle chamber (Figures D.10C and D.11). Appliqué, broad-line incisions, and punctations are used, yet it is difficult to know the original design of the iconography. The surface is highly polished to a metallic luster characteristic of the Paucarbamba Brilliant Plain and Paucarbamba Brilliant Decorated types (Onuki 1972:186–187).

KOTOSH SAJARA-PATAC PHASE
A rim sherd from a short-necked jar with a red-slipped surface was identified (Figure D.10D). This sherd has the brick red color typical of Sajara-patac Red. The are below the rim is decorated with broad-line incisions and punctations applied with blunt implements, also typical of the Sajara-patac Red Decorated and Sajara-patac Chocolate Brown Decorated types. This rim form corresponds to Sajara-patac Chocolate Brown Decorated Form 2 in that it has a beveled rim and the neck is short enough to interpret as a kind of everted rim.

Cupisnique Pottery from Piquimina
A fragment of Cupisnique-style pottery was recovered from Layer 2 of Unit C (Figure D.12). This sherd most probably came from the chamber of a bottle that was brought from the North Coast of Peru. The iconography on this fragment was part of a larger image of a side view of the head of a stylized feline (see Figure D.13). The surface is dark gray

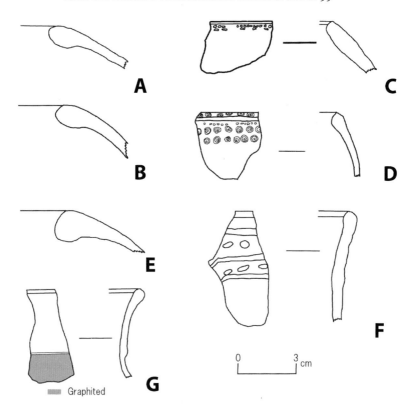

FIGURE D.8. Examples of Kotosh Waira-jirca Phase (A–D) and Kotosh Kotosh Phase (E–G) pottery.

FIGURE D.9. Examples of Kotosh Kotosh Phase pottery.

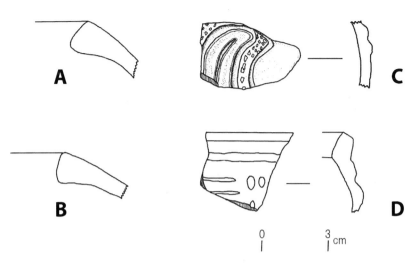

FIGURE D.10. Examples of Kotosh Chavín Phase (A–C) and Kotosh Sajara-patac Phase (D) pottery.

FIGURE D.11. Examples of Kotosh Chavín Phase pottery.

and highly polished to a metallic luster. The paste is characterized by a very compact and fine-grained matrix. This characteristic color, surface finish, and paste reasonably makes it a fine gray ware. In general, many similar examples are seen almost exclusively among artifacts classified as Cupisnique-style (Larco Hoyle 1941; T. Pozorski 1983; Elera 1993, 1998) recognized from excavated and looted pieces from the North Coast (e.g., Alva 1986; Nesbitt, Gutiérrez, and Vásquez 2010; Sakai and Martínez 2010). Although we do not know the original shapes of the rim and neck of this Cupisnique-style bottle from Piquimina, similar examples from the North Coast suggest that this was a stirrup-spout bottle.

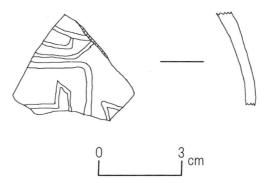

0   3 cm

FIGURE D.12. Cupisnique-style sherd (*below*) and its drawing (*above*).

Whereas the Initial Period and Early Horizon pottery style in the Upper Huallaga Basin shows strong ties with the eastern slope of the Andes and north-central highlands in its vessel forms and decoration (Lathrap 1962, 1970, 1971; Onuki 1993; Deboer 2003), it generally does not include any coastal stylistic elements. In this context, this Cupisnique-style sherd from Piquimina is a rare example. It is thus necessary to consider its chronological position and how it reached the Upper Huallaga Basin.

Unfortunately, the stratigraphy does not help much. Layer 2 produced sherds from the Kotosh Waira-jirca, Kotosh Kotosh, and the Kotosh Chavín Phases (see Appendix A). However, this Cupisnique-style sherd belongs to the late Initial Period for two reasons. First, the incisions used are characteristic of the late Initial Period according to stylistic and chronological studies of North Coast pottery. These narrow and sharp incisions were applied with sharp, pointed implements when the paste was dry and leather-hard, but before firing. This technique is characteristic of the late Initial Period and contrasts with the deep and broad incisions used during the Early Horizon (Elera 1986:221–241; Burger 1992:90, 213–255). Second, this type of fine gray ware is recognized not only at North Coast sites, but is distributed across a wider geographical area of the central Andes. Be-

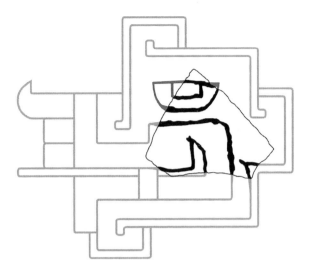

Figure D.13. Hypothetical reconstruction of Cupisnique-style pottery motif from Piquimina.

cause in most cases the proveniences of stirrup-spout bottles in museum collections are unknown, these have limited value in chronological studies. Moreover, because most are in museum or private collections it is difficult to use them for detailed analyses of paste and surface finish. However, we were able to examine in detail stirrup-spout bottles excavated from good archaeological contexts and found several with the same paste, decorative technique, and surface treatment.

In the upper Jequetepeque Valley, the Idolo Phase at Kuntur Wasi corresponds to the late Initial Period. Among the pottery types of this phase, ID Gris Fino (Fine Gray pottery of the Idolo Phase at Kuntur Wasi) corresponds to fine gray ware and is very similar to the sherd from Piquimina both in paste and surface finish (Inokuchi 2006:70–71). Although at Kuntur Wasi the same type of paste and surface treatment is seen in the Early Horizon, in the Kuntur Wasi Phase (KW Gris Fino), this differs from ID Gris Fino in its rim forms and the techniques used for incisions (Inokuchi 1998:165, 2006:71). Bottles of fine gray ware are also known from Las Huacas in the middle Jequetepeque Valley (Tsurumi 2008, note 5) and Limoncarro in the lower Jequetepeque Valley (Sakai and Martínez 2010:173, fig. 3d), both belonging to the late Initial Period. Farther south, in the Nepeña Valley of the north-central coast examples of fine gray ware were unearthed from a trash context associated with feasting activities (Ikehara and Shibata 2005). A bottle from Ancón (Rosas La Noire 2007, pl. XIV-6) probably is of this type, because of its trapezoidal stirrup and representation of the side view of a feline head. In the highlands, Raku A from the Ofrendas Gallery at Chavín de Huántar clearly corresponds to fine gray ware (Lumbreras 1993, 2007:543, fig. 503a; see also Burger 1984:350, fig. 100). A Cupisnique-style stirrup-spout bottle of this type is reported from even farther south in the south-central highlands by Matsumoto and Nesbitt, who described an example from Campanayuq Rumi (Matsumoto 2010b, figs. 7.9 and 7.10; Nesbitt and Matsumoto 2014), which is probably the southern limit of the distribution of fine gray ware. This indicates that fine gray ware was distributed quite widely in the central Andes. The bottle sherd from Piquimina needs to be understood in this broad geographical context of interregional interactions.

Conclusions

Although the site of Piquimina has been badly damaged and has almost vanished, our excavations salvaged some useful information relating to the Initial Period and Early Horizon of the Upper Huallaga Basin.

First, it is notable that all Initial Period and Early Horizon phases identified at Kotosh are confirmed at Piquimina, which suggests the long-term use of this site, for about 1,600 years (see Appendix A). In addition to our excavation, Onuki's work in 1966 and information from local residents suggest that this site was quite different from public centers such as Kotosh and Sajara-patac. In this context, the foreign Cupisnique bottle sherd from Piquimina is important. This type of vessel tends to be found in funerary contexts and was probably an exotic good imported to this area. This agrees with Onuki's 1966 finding of a funerary context in the Kotosh Chavín Period at the same site. It is possible that this site was used as a cemetery throughout the Initial Period and Early Horizon.

On the other hand, a double-faced wall discovered by our excavation and a square structure that existed before being lost to modern construction activities imply the presence of room features, suggesting another function of the site. In light of the absence of domestic areas around mound sites and public centers of the Upper Huallaga Basin, Piquimina may have been a site with domestic or residential components. Piquimina seems to have been a type of site different from ceremonial centers with public architecture.

The long-term use of Piquimina suggests that the two nearby sites, Waira-jirca and Sajara-patac, are chronologically complementary. Waira-jirca was in use from the Kotosh Mito Phase to the Kotosh Kotosh Phase. Sajara-patac functioned as a ceremonial center during the Kotosh Chavín Phase and continued to be occupied during the Kotosh Sajara-patac Phase (Onuki 1993; Inokuchi et al. 2003; Matsumoto 2009; Matsumoto and Tsurumi 2011). We can assume that although the ceremonial center was moved at the beginning of the Kotosh Chavín Period, people continued to use Piquimina for other purposes, such as a cemetery or for domestic occupation.

Archaeological Research in the Upper Huallaga Basin in Retrospect

Yoshio Onuki

In 1954, a new center for research and education in cultural anthropology was established in the Faculty of Arts and Sciences at the University of Tokyo. This center was independent from, but closely related to, both what was then the Department of Anthropology in the Faculty of Natural Sciences and the Department of Archaeology in the Faculty of Letters. The center was headed by Eiichiro Ishida (general anthropology), along with Seiichi Izumi (social anthropology), Toshihiko Sono (archaeology), Taryo Obayashi (ethnology), Kazuo Terada (physical anthropology), and Chie Nakane (social anthropology).

In 1952, and again in 1956, Izumi traveled to Brazil to lead a sociological project organized by UNESCO (United Nations Educational, Scientific, and Cultural Organization) and the Japanese government for the purpose of researching Japanese immigrants in Brazil. During his return trip to Japan in 1956 through Bolivia Izumi stopped in Peru. In Lima, he met a Japanese entrepreneur, Yoshitaro Amano, who invited Izumi for dinner at his home and fervently told him about the prehistoric Andean civilization. Amano was collecting archaeological objects, which had been discarded by looters, from ancient cemeteries on the coast, especially those in the Chancay Valley. The story told by Amano and his enthusiasm for the Andean past so fascinated Izumi that he decided to switch his main research from the social anthropology of Korea and northeastern Asia to Andean prehistory.

After a period at Harvard University attending Gordon R. Willey's seminar there, Izumi traveled again to Peru. On his return to Japan he organized the University of Tokyo Scientific Expedition to the Andes in 1958 and invited Eiichiro Ishida to be its director. Ishida wrote:

> The plan of an Andean expedition materialized soon after the Iraq–Iran Archaeological Expedition of the University of Tokyo started in 1956. As the Iraq–Iran project began with the excavation of Neolithic village site in search of the origin of the most ancient civilization of the Old World, we also became very interested in the birth and formation of the New World civilizations, and consequently in the comparative study of the origins of two civilizations. (Ishida 1960:407)

The University of Tokyo Excavations at Kotosh

This first University of Tokyo expedition covered the coastal region from the Department of Tumbes in northern Peru to the area near Arica in Chile, and from the Department of Cajamarca and the Callejón de Huaylas in the north-central and southern highlands to Bolivia. Ishida, Izumi, and Terada visited Chavín de Huántar and then Izumi traveled to Huánuco to see the two sites, Shillacoto and Kotosh, made known by Julio C. Tello, but scarcely visited by other archaeologists after him (Onuki 1998). Izumi was particularly impressed by the site of Kotosh and several pottery pieces exhibited in a small museum at the Leoncio Prado high school in the city of Huánuco, where there were also some Chavín-style sherds. Convinced that Kotosh should be excavated to search for the origin of Chavín culture, he thought that the next expedition should focus on excavation there. In each of three seasons of excavations at Kotosh, in 1960, 1963, and 1966, the expedition had members that specialized in archaeology and anthropology as well as specialists in other fields, such as physical anthropology, botany, geology, and geography. Only the members who participated directly in the archaeological excavations are presented here.

The 1960 Field Season
Members of the 1960 University of Tokyo field season included Seiichi Izumi, Toshihiko Sono, Naotsune Watanabe, Kazuo Terada, Takaji Sadasue, Chikasato Ogyu, and Yoshio Onuki. Pedro Rojas Ponce from the Museo Nacional de Arqueología, Antropología e Historia del Perú in Lima worked with us from the beginning. His fluent English promoted mutual understanding and provided us with guidance on Peruvian culture in general. Cirilo Huapaya Manco, also from the Museo Nacional, worked with Terada and Watanabe at Garbanzal and other sites around Tumbes. We also received encouraging visits from Luis E. Valcárcel, Manuel Chavez Ballon, and Arturo Jiméz Borja.

The 1963 Field Season
Members of the 1963 University of Tokyo field season included Seiichi Izumi, Toshihiko Sono, Kazuo Terada, Chiaki Kano, Tsugio Matsuzawa, Hiroyasu Tomoeda, Yasushi Miyazaki, and Yoshio Onuki. Three anthropology students from the Universidad Nacional de San Cristóbal de Huamanga in Ayacucho—Mario Benavides, Enrique González Carré, and Augusto Cruzat—participated in excavations for about one month. We received visits from Luis G. Lumbreras, Emilio Choy, Jorge C. Muelle, Toribio Mejía Xesspe, Jose Casafranca, and others.

The 1966 Field Season
Members of the 1966 University of Tokyo field season included Seiichi Izumi, Chiaki Kano, Tsugio Matsuzawa, Hiroyasu Tomoeda, Yasushi Miyazaki, Tatsuhiko Fujii, Takeshi Ueno, Hiroyoshi Yamamoto, and Yoshio Onuki. Also very welcomed was the participation of Arturo Ruiz Estrada, Lorenzo Samaniego Román, Carmen Rosa Rivera from the Universidad Nacional Mayor de San Marcos in Lima, and Fernando Chaud and Carlos Chaud from the Universidad Nacional de San Cristóbal de Huamanga in Ayacucho.

In 1966, small-scale excavations were conducted at four other sites around Huánuco: Shillacoto (Appendix C; see also Onuki 1993), Paucarbamba (Onuki 1993), Waira-jirca (Appendix B; see also Onuki 1993), and Sajara-patac (Onuki 1993; see also Matsumoto 2009; Matsumoto and Tsurumi 2011).

Important results of the research from the 1960, 1963, and 1966 seasons are summarized here. For the detailed descriptions of the stratigraphy, architecture, and artifacts, see the two volumes of the Kotosh reports (Izumi and Sono 1963; Izumi and Terada 1972).

Chronology

The archaeological investigations at Kotosh in 1960 (Izumi and Sono 1963) began with trench excavations, as almost all archaeology in Japan had been done according to the European methodology. The first trench ran from the top of the mound down to the flat area at its foot. Designated KTB, the excavated unit was 2 m wide and sectored every 5 m along its length of 47 m. Walls and corresponding floors were identified as architectural sets. Other small structures and features were related to the architecture, and finally to the artifact assemblages, to identify the cultural phases. After setting up these procedures, radiocarbon dating was used to establish the site chronology. Each phase was then given its own name.

At the beginning of the 1960s there were only two institutes in Japan that provided radiocarbon measurements. There were often problems with the accuracy of the technique at that time. After almost fifty years and many radiocarbon dates for the Formative Period, in this volume Matsumoto has revised this chronology (see Appendix A). To avoid confusion, I will use this revised chronology.

The Kotosh Mito Phase is preceramic and recognized at three sites: Kotosh, Shillacoto (Izumi, Cuculiza, and Kano 1972), and Waira-jirca (see Appendix B). In the most popular chronological framework of Andean prehistory, this phase has been considered to belong to the Archaic Period. In recent discussions, however, it is argued that the final phase of the Archaic Period should be considered the beginning of the Formative Period. Consequently, the term "Initial Formative" is proposed for before the Early Formative (Onuki 1999; Fux 2013). When applied to the chronology for the Upper Huallaga Basin, this scheme of five subdivisions for the Formative Period is as follows, in order from the earliest to the latest:

The Kotosh Mito Phase	2500(?)–1600 BC	Initial Formative Period
The Kotosh Waira-jirca Phase	1600–1200 BC	Early Formative Period
The Kotosh Kotosh Phase	1200–700 BC	Middle Formative Period
The Kotosh Chavín Phase	700–250 BC	Late Formative Period
The Kotosh Sajara-patac Phase	250–50 BC	Final Formative Period
The Kotosh Higueras Phase	50 BC–AD(?)	Regional Development

As described below, small-scale excavations at four other sites around the city of Huánuco firmly corroborated this chronology.

The Discovery of Pre-Chavín Phases with Pottery

The 1960 excavations discovered a Kotosh Chavín Phase room with a niche. An elaborate burial of a child was found under the room's wall and there was a subterranean canal below the floor. The pottery fragments had the typical characteristics of so-called Chavín pottery, such as a well-polished surface, broad-line curvilinear incision, rocker-stamping, stirrup-spout bottle forms, and so on.

After documenting the room, we removed the Kotosh Chavín Phase level and found that there were more layers and architectural features below. The associated ceramics were quite different from the previous level in surface treatment, forms, and decorative technique. The ceramic surfaces were smoothed or even lightly polished, but lacking in the kind of brilliance of Chavín pottery. The forms were also different, such as flanged bowls, triangular bowls, and bowls with flaring walls or composite silhouette sides and with convex bases. Decoration was done with broad-line incisions and the lines and dots were filled with post-fired painting in red, white, and yellow in many cases. This was not the so-called Chavín style and should have been considered non-Chavín as well as pre-Chavín. Furthermore, although less elaborate, rooms were constructed with stone walls. All these architectural and pottery styles were considered to mark a pre-Chavín phase named the Kotosh Kotosh Phase.

Below the layers of this phase another construction level was identified. It was associated with yet another and different pottery assemblage. Its incised lines were very narrow and sharp, and the decoration of zoned hachure with red post-fired painting was very characteristic. Although not elaborate, several rooms were uncovered. This was named as the Kotosh Waira-jirca Phase, because the ceramics resembled several fragments collected from the surface of Waira-jirca, a site about 35 km to the east of Kotosh in the same Upper Huallaga Basin (see also Appendix B).

As Tello had predicted (Tello 1943; Onuki 1993:69), the earlier pre-Chavín pottery styles found at Kotosh were in definitely clear stratigraphic and architectural contexts. Furthermore, the pottery was not one style, but two clearly distinguishable styles in form and decoration as well as stratigraphic position. We believed they must be a key to providing a new perspective for understanding the origin of Chavín culture, and of pottery itself, in the central Andes.

The principal characteristics of these pottery styles are the lack of a brilliantly polished surface, the stirrup-spout bottle form, and curvilinear broad-line incision; that is, the representative traits of Chavín-style pottery. Instead, they are characterized by bowls with out-flaring sides, triangular bowls, neckless jars with comma-shaped rims, and incised geometric designs with post-fired inlays of red, yellow, and white pigments, and so on. Although these examples are definitely earlier than Chavín, it is difficult to assume that they would have given birth to the Chavín style pottery.

Discovery of the "Oldest Temple in the Americas"

A much bigger surprise awaited us below the pre-Chavín levels at Kotosh when a corner of a building with stone walls in very good condition was discovered. The inside was filled with river cobbles to the height of the roof. The floor and the inner face of the walls were neatly plastered with fine cream-colored soil. Large and small niches were set in the walls and part of the wall below one of those niches was covered with sand instead of stones. Removing the sand revealed a clay relief of crossed hands. The size of the building, the neatly plastered surface, the wall niches, and the relief of crossed hands were enough to convince us that this was a building used for certain special purposes, probably ritual ones. Almost immediately, Izumi named it the "Temple of the Crossed Hands" (*Templo de las Manos*

Cruzadas). Toshihiko Sono, who was cleaning the sand off the relief with a brush and bamboo spatula, said that he could hardly control his trembling hands.

No pottery fragments were found either inside or outside the temple. It was possible that we had reached the preceramic level. There were two phases with pottery earlier than the Chavín level, and the temple was below even these. In 1960, the only radiocarbon date for Chavín was said to be around 800 BC. These pottery phases should then be earlier than 800 BC. We thought that the lower level, the Kotosh Waira-jirca Phase, must go back at least six hundred years, and that the temple level must be much earlier. As a consequence, the temple must date to at least 2000 BC, to the Preceramic Period. In 1960, there was no example of such an early temple structure anywhere in Peru or in the Americas, so the Temple of the Crossed Hands was therefore the oldest temple in the Americas. On his way home, Izumi dropped by Harvard University to inform Willey of this finding. Later, Willey devoted four full pages to Kotosh in his next book (Willey and Tulloch 1971:102–105).

In 1963 and 1966, during the second and third seasons at Kotosh, the excavation of the temple was expanded. With the results from these field seasons the site chronology and pottery typology were revised. Among the most important results may be the data about the Temple of the Crossed Hands and other contemporary buildings of the Kotosh Mito Phase (Izumi and Terada 1972). Although Izumi presented a brief summary at the 1968 Dumbarton Oaks conference on Chavín, the details of the architecture were not available until published (Izumi 1971). Therefore, the discovery and definition of the Kotosh Mito temples occurred from 1960 to 1966.

Characteristics of Early Temples

The early period is generally called the Archaic Period, or the final or Late Archaic, and recently the Initial Formative Period. There are some main characteristics common to the temples of this period.

First, the Kotosh temple is not simply a one-room construction, but a group of rooms with independent entrances. These entrances were built on three stepped terraces separated by fairly high retaining walls, but connected by stairs. Although by 1960 the top terrace had been lost to looting, the original height could have reached about 15 m. Just above the Temple of the Crossed Hands was the "Temple of the Small Niches" (*Templo de los Nichitos*) of almost the same size. Although later activity during the Kotosh Chavín Phase destroyed half of this temple, this feature provided information about the construction process.

A second characteristic of these early temples was revealed by the excavation of the overlying temples on the lowest terrace. Temples were repeatedly reconstructed in a ritualized process in which a temple was built, demolished, and buried with soil and stones, and then a new temple was built on top of it. Izumi's term for this process, "temple entombment" (Izumi and Matsuzawa 1967), began to be used more frequently in the literature of Andean archaeology, and the name of the proposer was blurred (Onuki 2002:65). Much later, during the 1985 excavation at Huacaloma in Cajamarca, I was convinced the term "temple renewal" would be better and use it to this day (Onuki 1993, 2002). During the Kotosh Mito Phase, such large-scale temple renewal was repeated at least three times. The first was the "White Temple" (*Templo Blanco*), then the Temple of the Crossed Hands, and finally the Temple of the Small Niches.

A third feature of these early temple groups was that each new temple was built on a prepared layer of ashes. The old temple was buried or covered with a thick layer of earth (red soil in many cases) on which a hearth with underground flues was set. The principal parts of the temple were built after the preparation of the floor above an ash layer. This was not typically how houses were built, so clearly it was a ritual process.

Another characteristic is that the floor inside the temple was split into two levels, named by Elizabeth Bonnier (1997b) the *epicausto* (lower) and the *pericausto* (upper), with a hearth in the center of the lower floor and generally two ventilation flues under the floor and walls running from the hearth to the outside.

A fifth characteristic is that the floor and the surface of the walls were elaborately plastered with fine cream-white clay. And although the outside of the walls of the Temple of the Crossed Hands was painted red, no trace of red paint or relief decoration was seen in any other temples at Kotosh.

This new information about the earliest sophisticated public architecture (temples) in the Late Archaic Period was obtained mostly during the early half of the 1960s. The use of radiocarbon dating was still in its initial stage of application in archaeology, and many techniques, such as the analysis of starch crystals or collagen, were yet unknown. Looking back, much has been left undone. Most needed are data on subsistence, such as food production, and the discovery of burials from the Kotosh Mito Phase, for skeletal and DNA analyses that may make it possible to pinpoint the origin of the temple builders.

Further Research in the Upper Huallaga Basin

In 1966 and 1969, I carried out small-scale excavations around Huánuco at the sites of Shillacoto, Paucarbamba, Waira-jirca, Sajara-patac, and Piquimina with Hiroyasu Tomoeda, Carmen Rosa Rivera, Lorenzo Samaniego, Arturo Ruiz, Mario Benavides, Fernando Chaud, and Carlos Chaud. Shillacoto was excavated again later in 1969 and a temple of the Kotosh Mito Phase and two special stone masonry tombs of the Kotosh Waira-jirca Phase and Kotosh Kotosh Phase were unearthed almost completely (Izumi, Cuculiza, and Kano 1972; Kano 1979). The excavations of small trenches at other sites corroborated very well the chronology established at Kotosh, although at Piquimina we dug only a burial with scattered fragments of the Kotosh Chavín Phase (for more recent excavation at Piquimina, see Appendix D). Also interesting were the chronological differences in the occupations of each site. I have summarized this site distribution (Onuki 1993) and a Japanese team later conducted a more extensive survey of distribution (Inokuchi et al. 2002; this volume).

These investigations provided clues to the patterns of site distribution in the Formative Period (see also Chapter 5). First, at sites with Kotosh Waira-jirca Phase and Kotosh Kotosh Phase occupations, it is very possible that there are Kotosh Mito Phase structures below them. So, although there is some discontinuity between the Kotosh Mito Phase and the Kotosh Waira-jirca Phase, the same location was preferred for a new settlement, which may suggest continuous occupation by the same group of people. Second, the distance between sites is approximately 5 km, so that these were visible from the immediate neighboring sites; that is, Shillacoto is almost visible from Kotosh, Jancao is visible from Shillacoto, and Warampayloma is visible from Jancao, and so on, all about 5 km apart.

Third, it seems that the people of the Kotosh Chavín Phase preferred to construct a new temple or settlement on virgin soil. At both Paucarbamba and Sajara-patac there was no preceding occupation below the Kotosh Chavín Phase. At Shillacoto and Waira-jirca there was no sign of Kotosh Chavín Phase occupation and a survey of the surface indicated the same pattern at Warampayloma. Fourth, the Kotosh Sajara-patac Phase is found above the Kotosh Chavín Phase and the number of sites in this period notably increased, suggesting population growth after the Kotosh Chavín Phase.

I think many of these results from the research of the 1960s are confirmed by the newer data set for the Upper Huallaga Basin presented in this volume.

Concluding Remarks: A General Perspective and the Need for More Research

Although the data available are still relatively scarce, a general perspective of the cultural processes of the Formative Period in the Upper Huallaga Basin will define the tasks yet to be done in the study of the Formative Period for this region.

The area of the Upper Huallaga Basin considered here is basically the valley bottom extending from Ambo to Chullqui, and the lower part of the Higueras River where it joins the Huallaga River. It is only in this bottom area that we find the well-developed alluvial lowlands and terraces suitable for agricultural activities. Past an elevation of about 2,000 masl the terraces change to a steep slope where crop cultivation is difficult or almost impossible. These lowlands and terraces belong to the *yunga* zone (Pulgar Vidal 1987) or to the area that includes Tosi's ee-MB, bs-MB, and bh-MS zones (Tosi 1960). Almost all archaeological sites are found in this area of the valley bottom. Some sites are on the tops of the ridges or mountains surrounding the valley, generally at around 3,000 masl.

There is no trace of sedentary occupation before the earliest phase of the Formative Period, the Kotosh Mito Phase. However, earlier than this the neighboring high elevation area, the *puna* zone of Pulgar Vidal's classification, has abundant evidence of the early hunter-gatherers around the lakes of Junín and Lauricocha (e.g., Cardich 1964; Rick 1980; Lavallee et al. 1995). These people are known by their willow-leaf type stone points and petroglyphs in rock shelters and caves. A large rock on the very steep slope above the Kotosh site, called Quillarumi, is highly conspicuous when seen from the site of Kotosh (see also Chapter 4). This rock offers a wide space for shelter at its base and has several paintings that resemble the petroglyphs in the adjacent *puna* zone. Quillarumi has been used by local herders of cows and goats, and thus no material evidence is left on the surface. Therefore, even without dating, such resemblance may suggest the valley bottom was visited in some way, sporadically or seasonally, by the hunter-gatherers of the *puna* zone. The willow-leaf type chipped stone points were fairly common during the Kotosh Mito Phase, which suggests that there was certain relationship between the people of the valley and the *puna* hunter-gatherers.

The first sedentary occupations were on the terraces rather close to the valley bottom. For some ritual or public purpose they constructed special stone masonry buildings, which we may call temples in the widest sense. These temples were built according to a complex plan, as seen in the temples at Kotosh and Shillacoto. Although no domestic structures have survived to be excavated, we can suppose that they had been located around or near the temples, forming temple-centered communities. Each community had its own temple or several temple buildings, and those communities were distributed about

5 km from each other. The difference in size and complexity of temples among these communities is noticeable and may reflect certain aspects of the social organization, but here we refrain from going further.

We do not have good data about their subsistence economy. If the Kotosh Mito Phase is partly contemporaneous with Caral and other sites on the central coast, it is possible that the Mito Phase people had crops such as potato, sweet potato, maize, beans, and avocado. Although direct evidence has yet to be found, it is highly probable that manioc played an important role in these communities. We know that manioc cultivation began before 3000 BC in Colombia (Castillo Espitia and Aceituno Bocanegra 2006) and that the earliest pottery in the Jequetepeque Valley was associated with manioc starch (Tsurumi 2008:163, 167), therefore it is likely that manioc had spread across the central coast by the third millennium BC. As the site locations of the Kotosh Mito Phase suggest, they were situated in a zone favorable for the cultivation of manioc and other plants.

Pottery was introduced at the end of the Kotosh Mito Phase, probably from the central coast. Pottery fragments were found in the fill of a small temple at Waira-jirca (see Appendix B for the stratigraphy at Waira-jirca). These were part of a thin-walled neckless jar with a rim that was not thickened, resembling the neckless olla found at Las Haldas near Casma (e.g., Fung Pineda 1969). Then, rather suddenly, all the temples were abandoned or destroyed and overlaid by a new series of buildings that were much less elaborate and did not have special ritual or public characteristics (see Appendix B).

Although the temple-centered community disappeared, in the Kotosh Waira-jirca Phase a new kind of settlement developed in the same places. The Kotosh Kotosh Phase followed the Waira-jirca Phase in these localities. These two phases did not continue the temple ritual of the Mito Phase that every community had used to compete for its architectural elaboration enthusiastically. The most notable change from the Mito Phase is this abandonment of temple construction and the adoption of well-made pottery. We do not know, even fifty after years its discovery, where this pottery came from and why it was not diffused beyond the Upper Huallaga Basin.

A really drastic change came with the Kotosh Chavín Phase. Shillacoto and Waira-jirca were abandoned. Kotosh suffered from large-scale changes that led to the destruction of half of the Temple of the Small Niches. A new sturdy platform, built to support a series of small rooms, had below the floor a subterranean canal. A new style of decorated pottery was introduced, yet existing pottery types in general did not change. It seems that during this phase people preferred new terrain for new construction projects. New sites were constructed at Paucarbamba and Sajara-patac. The 2001 survey carried out by Inokuchi, Tsurumi, and Matsumoto (this volume) revealed a few more sites in this Kotosh Chavín Phase, but the characteristics of these sites will not be known until excavations are done. The data from Kotosh show that camelid bones markedly increased and deer bones decreased in the Kotosh Chavín Phase. In the lithic assemblage, willow-leaf-shaped chipped stone points disappeared or drastically decreased and instead polished stone points made of slate appeared for the first time, along with chipped points of obsidian.

The Kotosh Chavín Phase was succeeded by the Kotosh Sajara-patac Phase, when new settlements were built on top of the Kotosh Chavín Phase architecture. However, the number of sites markedly increased. These sites were distributed from Ambo to Churubamba along the Huallaga River. It is not yet clear whether or not Kotosh Chavín Phase occupations will be found below features of the Kotosh Sajara-patac Phase, therefore we cannot say with certainty in which phase this expansion of the Kotosh Sajara-patac Phase settlements started. In the analysis of mammal bones from the Kotosh excavations, camelid bones were predominant. This means that the population was familiar with domesticated camelids, even if not engaged in keeping animals themselves.

After this somewhat affluent lifestyle, a new culture arrived in the Upper Huallaga Basin and the settlements of the Kotosh Sajara-patac Phase were totally abandoned. This new phase, the Kotosh Higueras Phase, probably came from the higher elevation upper Marañón area. There is no trace of continuity from the preceding phase, which makes us wonder about the fate of the people of the Kotosh Sajara-patac Phase.

The excavations at Kotosh, Shillacoto, Paucarbamba, Waira-jirca, and Sajara-patac were conducted during the 1960s, more than a half century ago. Although there has been some research since, as presented in this volume, more work is necessary to obtain a detailed perspective of the Formative Period in the Upper Huallaga Basin, which will undoubtedly contribute substantially to our understanding of the Formative Period in the central Andes in general.

REFERENCES

ALVA, WALTER. 1986. *Frühe Keramik aus dem Jequetepeque-Tal, Nordperu* [*Cerámica Temprana en el Valle de Jequetepeque, Norte del Perú*]. Munich: C.H. Beck. 194 pp. (Materialien zur Allgemeinen und Vergleichenden Archäologie 32.)

BILLMAN, BRIAN R. 1996. "The Evolution of Prehistoric Political Organizations in the Moche Valley, Peru" [dissertation]. Santa Barbara: University of California, Santa Barbara. 385 pp. Order No. 9708060, ProQuest Dissertations & Theses Global. https://search.proquest.com/docview /304232703?accountid=15172.

—1999. Reconstructing prehistoric political economies and cycles of political power in the Moche Valley, Peru. In: Brian R. Billman and Gary M. Feinman, eds. *Settlement Pattern Studies in the Americas: Fifty Years Since Virú*. Washington, DC: Smithsonian Institution Press. pp. 131–159. (Smithsonian Series in Archaeological Inquiry.)

BIRD, ROBERT M. 1970. "Maize and Its Cultural and Natural Environment in the Sierra of Huánuco, Peru" [dissertation]. Berkeley: University of California, Berkeley. 240 pp. Order No. 7109767, ProQuest Dissertations & Theses Global. https://search.proquest.com/docview /302517552?accountid=15172.

—1984. The Chupachu/Serrano cultural boundary: multifaceted and stable. In: David L. Browman, Richard L. Burger, and Mario A. Rivera, eds. *Social and Economic Organization in the Prehispanic Andes*. Proceedings of the 44th International Congress of Americanists, Manchester, 1982. Oxford: BAR Publishing. pp. 79–95. (British Archaeological Reports, International Series 194.)

BISCHOF, HENNING. 2008. Context and contents of early Chavín art. In: William J. Conklin and Jeffrey Quilter, eds. *Chavín: Art, Architecture and Culture*. Los Angeles: Cotsen Institute of Archaeology Press at UCLA. pp. 107–142. (Monograph 61.) https://www.jstor.org/stable /j.ctvdmwx21.10.

BONNIER, ELISABETH. 1997a. Morfología del Espacio Aldeano y su Expresión Cultural en los Andes Centrales. In: Elisabeth Bonnier and Henning Bischof, eds. *Arquitectura y Civilización en los Andes Prehispánicos*. Mannheim: Sociedad Arqueológica Peruano-Alemana, Reiss-Museum Mannheim. pp. 29–41. (Archaeologica Peruana 2.)

—1997b. Preceramic architecture in the Andes: the Mito tradition. In: Elisabeth Bonnier and Henning Bischof, eds. *Arquitectura y Civilización en los Andes Prehispánicos*. Mannheim: Sociedad Arqueológica Peruano-Alemana, Reiss-Museum Mannheim. pp. 120–144. (Archaeologica Peruana 2.)

BRONK RAMSEY, CHRISTOPHER. 2017. Methods for summarizing radiocarbon datasets. *Radiocarbon* 59(6):1809–1833. https://doi.org/10.1017/RDC.2017.108.

Burger, Richard L. 1980. Trace-element analysis of obsidian artifacts from Pachamachay, Junín. In: John W. Rick, ed. *Prehistoric Hunters of the High Andes*. New York: Academic Press. pp. 257–261.

—1981. The radiocarbon evidence for the temporal priority of Chavín de Huántar. *American Antiquity* 46(3):592–602. https://doi.org/10.2307/280603.

—1984. *The Prehistoric Occupation of Chavín de Huántar, Peru*. Berkeley: University of California Press. 403 pp. (University of California Publications in Anthropology 14.)

—1987. The U-shaped pyramid complex, Cardal, Peru. *National Geographic Research* 3(3):363–375.

—1988. Unity and heterogeneity within the Chavín Horizon. In: Richard Keatinge, ed. *Peruvian Prehistory*. Cambridge: Cambridge University Press. pp. 99–144.

—1992. *Chavín and the Origins of Andean Civilization*. New York: Thames and Hudson. 248 pp.

—1993. The Chavín Horizon: stylistic chimera or socioeconomic metamorphosis? In: Donald S. Rice, ed. *Latin American Horizons*. Washington, DC: Dumbarton Oaks Research Library and Collection. pp. 41–82.

—2008. Chavín de Huántar and its sphere of influence. In: Helaine Silverman and William H. Isbell, eds. *Handbook of South American Archaeology*. New York: Springer. pp. 681–703.

—2009a. Los Fundamentos sociales de la arquitectura monumental del Período Inicial en el valle de Lurín. In: Richard L. Burger and Krysztof Makowski, eds. *Arqueología del Período Formativo en la Cuenca Baja de Lurín*, Volume 1. Lima: Fondo Editorial de la Pontificia Universidad Católica del Perú. pp. 17–36.

—2009b. ed. *The Life and Writings of Julio C. Tello: America's First Indigenous Archaeologist*. Iowa City: University of Iowa Press. 364 pp.

—2019. Understanding the socioeconomic trajectory of Chavín de Huántar: A new radiocarbon sequence and its wider implications. *Latin American Antiquity* 31(2):373–392. https://doi.org/10.1017/laq.2019.17.

Burger, Richard L., and Lucy C. Salazar. 2008. The Manchay culture and the coastal inspiration for highland Chavín civilization. In: William J. Conklin and Jeffrey Quilter, eds. *Chavín: Art, Architecture and Culture*. Los Angeles: Cotsen Institute of Archaeology Press at UCLA. pp. 85–106. (Monograph 61.) https://doi.org/10.2307/j.ctvdmwx21.9.

—2014. ¿Centro de qué? Los sitios con arquitectura pública de la cultura Manchay en la costa central del Perú. In: Yuji Seki, ed. *El Centro Ceremonial Andino: Nuevas Perspectivas para los Períodos Arcaico y Formativo*. Osaka: National Museum of Ethnology. pp. 291–313. (Senri Ethnological Studies 89.) http://hdl.handle.net/10502/5396.

Burger, Richard L., and Lucy C. Salazar-Burger. 1980. Ritual and religion at Huaricoto. *Archaeology* 33(6):26–32. https://www.jstor.org/stable/41726522.

—1985. The early ceremonial center of Huaricoto. In: Christopher B. Donnan, ed. *Early Ceremonial Architecture in the Andes: A Conference at Dumbarton Oaks, 8th to 10th October 1982*. Washington, DC: Dumbarton Oaks Research Library and Collection. pp. 111–138.

—1986. Early Organizational Diversity in the Peruvian Highlands: Huaricoto and Kotosh. In: Ramiro Matos M., Solveig A. Turpin, and Herbert H. Eling Jr., eds. *Andean Archaeology: Papers in Memory of Clifford Evans*. Los Angeles: Institute of Archaeology, University of California, Los Angeles. pp. 65–82. (Monograph 27.)

—1991. The second season of investigations at the Initial Period center of Cardal, Peru. *Journal of Field Archaeology* 18(3):275–296. https://doi.org/10.2307/529934.

—1993. The place of dual organization in early Andean ceremonialism: A comparative review. In: Luis Millones and Yoshio Onuki, eds. *El Mundo Ceremonial Andino*. Osaka: National Museum of Ethnology. pp. 97–116. (Senri Ethnological Studies 37.) https://doi.org/10.15021/00003035.

Cardich, Augusto. 1958. *Los Yacimientos de Lauricocha: Nuevas Interpretaciones de la Prehistoria Peruana*. Buenos Aires: Centro Argentino de Estudios Prehistóricos. 65 pp. (Studia Praehistorica 1.)

—1964. *Lauricocha: Fundamentos para una Prehistoria de los Andes Centrales*. Buenos Aires: Centro Argentino de Estudios Prehistóricos. 171 pp. (Studia Praehistorica 3.)

Carrión Cachot, Rebeca. 1948. La cultura Chavín. Dos nuevas colonias: Kuntur Wasi y Ancón. *Revista del Museo Nacional de Antropología y Arqueología* 2(1):99–172.

Castillo Espitia, Neyla, and Francisco J. Aceituno Bocanegra. 2006. El bosque domesticado, el bosque cultivado: Un proceso milenario en el Valle Medio del Río Porce en el noroccidente colombiano. *Latin American Antiquity* 17(4):561–578. https://doi.org/10.2307/25063072.

Contreras, Daniel A. 2010. A Mito-style structure at Chavín de Huántar: Dating and implications. *Latin American Antiquity* 21(1):3–21. https://www.jstor.org/stable/25766976.

—2011. How far to Conchucos? A GIS approach to assessing the implications of exotic materials at Chavín de Huántar. *World Archaeology* 43(3):380–397. https://doi.org/10.1080/00438243.2011.605841.

Daggett, Richard E. 1984. "The Early Horizon Occupation of Nepeña Valley, North Central Coast of Peru" [dissertation]. Amherst: University of Massachusetts, Department of Anthropology. 506 pp. Order No. 8410275, ProQuest Dissertations & Theses Global. https://search.proquest.com/docview/303307959?accountid=15172.

DeBoer, Warren R. 2003. Ceramic assemblage variability in the Formative of Ecuador and Peru. In: J. Scott Raymond and Richard L. Burger, eds. *Archaeology of Formative Ecuador: A Symposium at Dumbarton Oaks, 7 and 8 October 1995*. Washington, DC: Dumbarton Oaks Research Library and Collection. pp. 465–486. https://www.doaks.org/resources/publications/books/archaeology-of-formative-ecuador.

DeLeonardis, Lisa. 2005. Early Paracas cultural contexts: New evidence from Callango. *Andean Past* 7(Art. 7):27–55. https://digitalcommons.library.umaine.edu/andean_past/vol7/iss1/7.

Elera, Carlos G. 1986. "Investigaciones sobre Patrones Funerarios en el Sitio Formativo del Morro de Eten, Valle de Lambayeque, Costa Norte del Perú" [bachelor's thesis]. Lima: Pontificia Universidad Católica del Perú. 310 pp.

—1993. El complejo cultural Cupisnique: Antecedentes y desarrollo de su ideología religiosa. In: Luis Millones and Yoshio Onuki, eds. *El Mundo Ceremonial Andino*. Osaka: National Museum of Ethnology. pp. 229–257. (Senri Ethnological Studies 37.) http://doi.org/10.15021/00003040.

—1997. Cupisnique y salinar: Algunas reflexiones preliminares. In: Elisabeth Bonnier and Henning Bischof, eds. *Arquitectura y Civilización en los Andes Prehispánicos*. Mannheim: Sociedad Arqueológica Peruano-Alemana; Reiss-Museum Mannheim. pp. 177–201. (Archaeologica Peruana 2.)

—1998. "The Puemape Site and the Cupisnique Culture: A Case Study on the Origins and Development of Complex Society in the Central Andes, Peru" [dissertation]. Calgary, Alberta, Canada: University of Calgary, Department of Anthropology. 679 pp. Order No. NQ38464, ProQuest Dissertations & Theses Global. https://search.proquest.com/docview/304495437?accountid=15172.

Fiedel, Stuart J. 1999. Older than we thought: Implications of corrected dates for Paleoindians. *American Antiquity* 64(1):95–115. https://doi.org/10.2307/2694348.

Fujii, Tatsuhiko. 1972. Stone artifacts. In: Seiichi Izumi and Kazuo Terada, eds. *Andes 4: Excavations at Kotosh, Peru, 1963 and 1966*. Tokyo: University of Tokyo Press. pp. 249–260.

Fung Pineda, Rosa. 1969. Las Aldas: Su ubicación dentro del proceso histórico del Perú antiguo. Dédalo. *Revista de Arte y Arqueología* 9–10:5–208.

Fux, Peter. 2013. *Chavín: Peru's Enigmatic Temple in the Andes*. Zurich: Scheidegger and Spiess. 405 pp.

Ghezzi, Ivan. 2006. Religious warfare at Chankillo. In: William H. Isbell and Helaine Silverman, eds. *Andean Archaeology III: North and South*. New York: Springer. pp. 67–84. https://doi.org/10.1007/0-387-28940-2_4.

Girault, Louis. 1981. Fouilles Sur le Site de Piruru en 1968 et 1970. *Bulletín de l'Institut Français d'Études Andines* 10(1–2):101–112.

Grieder, Terence, and Alberto Bueno Mendoza. 1981. La Galgada: Perú before pottery. *Archaeology* 34(2):44–51. https://www.jstor.org/stable/41727123.

—1985. Ceremonial architecture at La Galgada. In: Christopher B. Donnan, ed. *Early Ceremonial Architecture in the Andes: A Conference at Dumbarton Oaks, 8th to 10th October 1982.* Washington, DC: Dumbarton Oaks Research Library and Collection. pp. 93–109.

GRIEDER, TERENCE, ALBERTO BUENO MENDOZA, C. EARLE SMITH JR., AND ROBERT M. MALINA. 1988. *La Galgada, Peru: A Preceramic Culture in Transition.* 1st ed. Austin: University of Texas Press. 282 pp.

GROSBOLL, SUE. 1988. "An Archaeological Approach to the Demography of Prehispanic Andean Communities" [dissertation]. Madison: University of Wisconsin, Department of Anthropology. 794 pp. Order No. 8813134, ProQuest Dissertations & Theses Global. https://search.proquest.com /docview/303576756?accountid=15172.

—1993. And he said in the time of the Yunga, they paid tribute and served the Yunga. In: Michael A. Malpass, ed. *Provincial Inca: Archaeological and Ethnohistorical Assessment of the Impact of the Inca State.* Iowa City: University of Iowa Press. pp. 44–76.

HAAS, JONATHAN, AND WINIFRED CREAMER. 2006. Crucible of Andean civilization. *Current Anthropology* 47(5):745–775. https://doi.org/10.1086/506281.

IKEHARA, HUGO, AND KOICHIRO SHIBATA. 2005 [2008]. Festines e integración social en el Período Formativo: Nuevas evidencias de Cerro Blanco, valle bajo de Nepeña. In: Peter Kaulicke and Tom D. Dillehay, eds. Encuentros: Identidad, poder y manejo de espacios públicos. *Boletín de Arqueología PUCP* 9(2005):123–159. http://revistas.pucp.edu.pe/index.php/boletindearqueologia /article/view/1709/1649.

INOKUCHI, KINYA. 1998. La cerámica de Kuntur Wasi y el problema Chavín. In: Peter Kaulicke, ed. Perspectivas Regionales del Período Formativo en el Perú. *Boletín de Arqueología PUCP* 2(1998):161–180. http://revistas.pucp.edu.pe/index.php/boletindearqueologia/article /view/746.

—2006. Pottery from Kuntur Wasi site. In: Yasutake Kato, ed. *Studies of the Process for the Formation of Ancient Andean Civilization.* Report of Grants-in-Aid for Scientific Research (S) 2002–2006. Project no. 14101003. Saitama University. pp. 59–90. [In Japanese.]

—2008 [2010]. La arquitectura de Kuntur Wasi: Secuencia constructiva y cronología de un centro ceremonial del Período Formativo. In: Peter Kaulicke and Yoshio Onuki, eds. El Período Formativo: Enfoques y evidencias recientes. Cincuenta años de la Misión Arqueológica Japonesa y su vigencia. *Boletín de Arqueología PUCP* 12(2008):219–247. http://revistas.pucp.edu.pe /index.php/boletindearqueologia/article/view/968.

INOKUCHI, KINYA, YOSHIO ONUKI, EISEI TSURUMI, YUICHI MATSUMOTO, AND NELLY MARTELL CASTILLO. 2003. Excavations at the site of Sajara-patac in Peru. *Kodai America [America Antigua]* 6:35–52. [In Japanese.]

INOKUCHI, KINYA, YOSHIO ONUKI, EISEI TSURUMI, YUICHI MATSUMOTO, AND ALVARO RUIZ RUBIO. 2002. Preliminary Report of the General Survey in Huánuco, Peru. *Kodai America [America Antigua]* 5:69–88. [In Japanese.]

ISBELL, WILLIAM H. 1974. Ecología de la expansión de los Quechua-hablantes. *Revista del Museo Nacional* 40:139–155.

ISBELL, WILLIAM H., AND KATHARINA J. SCHREIBER. 1978. Was Huari a state? *American Antiquity* 43(3):372–389. https://doi.org/10.2307/279393.

ISHIDA, EIICHIRO, KOICHI AKI, TAIJI YAZAWA, SEIICHI IZUMI, HISASHI SATO, IWAO KOBORI, KAZUO TERADA, AND TARYO OBAYASHI. 1960. *Andes 1: The Report of the University of Tokyo Scientific Expedition to the Andes in 1958.* Tokyo: Bijutsu-Shuppansha. 528 pp. [In Japanese with English summary.]

IWATSUKA, SHUKO. 1963. Natural environment (I). In: Seiichi Izumi and Toshihiko Sono. *Andes 2: Excavations at Kotosh, Peru, 1960.* Tokyo: Kadokawa Publishing Co. pp. 15–21.

IZUMI, SEIICHI. 1971. The development of the formative culture in the Ceja de Montana. In: Elizabeth P. Benson, ed. *Dumbarton Oaks Conference on Chavín, October 26th and 27th, 1968.* Washington, DC: Dumbarton Oaks Research Library and Collection, Trustees for Harvard University. pp. 49–72.

IZUMI, SEIICHI, PEDRO J. CUCULIZA, AND CHIAKI KANO. 1972. *Excavations at Shillacoto, Huánuco, Peru*. Tokyo: University of Tokyo Press. 82 pp. (University Museum Bulletin 3.)

IZUMI, SEIICHI, AND TSUGIO MATSUZAWA. 1967. Chuuou Andes ni okeru mudoki shinden bunka: Kotosh Mito ki wo chuushin to site [Early pre-ceramic cultist culture of the central Andes: On the Kotosh Mito Phase]. *Latin America kenkyuu* [*Latin American Studies*] 8:39–69.

IZUMI, SEIICHI, AND TOSHIHIKO SONO. 1963. *Andes 2: Excavations at Kotosh, Peru, 1960*. Tokyo: Kadokawa Publishing Co. 210 pp.

IZUMI, SEIICHI, AND KAZUO TERADA, EDS. 1972. *Andes 4: Excavations at Kotosh, Peru, 1963 and 1966*. Tokyo: University of Tokyo Press. 375 pp.

JENNINGS, JUSTIN, ED. 2010. *Beyond Wari Walls: Regional Perspectives on Middle Horizon Peru*. Albuquerque: University of New Mexico Press. 278 pp.

KANO, CHIAKI. 1979. *The Origins of the Chavín Culture*. Washington, DC: Dumbarton Oaks, Trustees for Harvard University. 87 pp. (Studies in Pre-Columbian Art and Archaeology 22.) https://www.jstor.org/stable/i40056976.

KATO, YASUTAKE. 1998. Andes Bunmei no Kigen wo Motomete ([On the pursuit of the origin of the Andean civilization]. In: Yasutake Kato and Yuji Seki, eds. *Bunmei no Souzouryoku: Koodai andes no shinden to shakai* [*Creativity of Civilization: Temples and Societies in the Ancient Andes*]. Tokyo: Kadokawa Shoten. pp. 7–42. [In Japanese.]

KATO, YASUTAKE, AND YUJI SEKI, EDS. 1998. *Bunmei no Souzouryoku: Koodai andes no shinden to shakai* [*Creativity of Civilization: Temples and Societies in the Ancient Andes*]. Tokyo: Kadokawa Shoten. 350 pp. [In Japanese.]

KAULICKE, PETER. 1994. *Los Orígenes de la Civilización Andina: Arqueología del Perú*. Lima: Editorial Brasa. 606 pp. (Historia General del Perú 1.)

—2008 [2010]. Espacio y tiempo en el Periodo Formativo: Una introducción. In: Peter Kaulicke and Yoshio Onuki, eds. El Período Formativo: Enfoques y evidencias recientes. Cincuenta años de la Misión Arqueológica Japonesa y su vigencia. *Boletín de Arqueología PUCP* 12(2008):9–23. http://revistas.pucp.edu.pe/index.php/boletindearqueologia/article/view/824.

—2010. *Las Cronologías del Formativo: 50 Años de Investigaciones Japonesas en Perspectiva*. Lima: Fondo Editorial de la Pontificia Universidad Católica del Perú. 438 pp.

KEMBEL, SILVIA RODRIGUEZ. 2001. "Architectural Sequence and Chronology at Chavín de Huántar, Perú" [dissertation]. Stanford: Stanford University, Department of Anthropological Sciences. 317 pp. Order No. 3026846, ProQuest Dissertations & Theses Global. https://search.proquest.com/docview/304727155?accountid=15172.

—2008. The architecture at the monumental center of Chavín de Huántar: Sequence, transformations, and chronology. In: William J. Conklin and Jeffrey Quilter, eds. *Chavín: Art, Architecture and Culture*. Los Angeles: Cotsen Institute of Archaeology Press at UCLA. pp. 35–82. (Monograph 61.) https://doi.org/10.2307/j.ctvdmwx21.8.

KEMBEL, SILVIA RODRIGUEZ, AND JOHN W. RICK. 2004. Building authority at Chavín de Huántar: Models of social organization and development in the Initial Period and Early Horizon. In: Helaine Silverman, ed. *Andean Archaeology*. Malden, MA: Blackwell. pp 51–75.

KNOBLOCH, PATRICIA J. 1991. Stylistic date of ceramics from the Huari centers. In: William H. Isbell and Gordon F. McEwan, eds. *Huari Administrative Structure: Prehistoric Monumental Architecture and State Government*. Washington, DC: Dumbarton Oaks Research Library and Collection. pp. 247–258.

LARCO HOYLE, RAFAEL. 1941. *Los Cupisniques: Trabajo presentado al Congreso Internacional de Americanistas de Lima XXVII Sesion*. Lima: Casa editora "La Crónica" y "Variedades" S. A. 259 pp.

LATHRAP, DONALD W. 1962. "Yarinacocha: Stratigraphic Excavations in the Peruvian Montaña" [dissertation]. Cambridge: Harvard University. 1,032 pp. Order no. 025843, ProQuest Dissertations & Theses Global. https://search.proquest.com/docview/302095256?accountid=15172.

—1970. *The Upper Amazon*. London: Thames and Hudson. 256 pp.

—1971. The tropical forest and the cultural context of Chavín. In: Elizabeth. P. Benson, ed. *Dumbarton Oaks Conference on Chavín, October 26th and 27th, 1968.* Washington, DC: Dumbarton Oaks Research Library, Trustees for Harvard University. pp. 73–100.

Lathrap, Donald W., and Lawrence Roys. 1963. The archaeology of the Cave of the Owls in the Upper Montaña of Peru. *American Antiquity* 29(1):27–38. https://doi.org/10.2307/278628.

Lau, George F. 2004. The Recuay culture of Peru's north-central highlands: A reappraisal of chronology and its implications. *Journal of Field Archaeology* 29(1/2):177–202. https://doi.org /10.2307/3181492.

Lavallée, Daniele, Michèle Julien, Jane Wheeler, and Claudine Karlin. 1995. *Telarmachay. Cazadores y pastores prehistóricos de los Andes.* Lima: l'Institut Français d'Études Andines. 445 pp. (Travaux de l'Institut Français d'Études Andines 88.)

León Canales, Elmo. 2006 [2007]. Radiocarbono y calibración: Potencialidades para la arqueología andina. *Arqueología y Sociedad* 17(2006):67–89. https://revistasinvestigacion.unmsm .edu.pe/index.php/Arqueo/article/view/13136/11670.

Lumbreras, Luis G. 1989. *Chavín de Huántar en el nacimiento de la Civilización Andina.* Lima: Instituto Andino de Estudios Arqueológicos. 245 pp.

—1993. *Chavín de Huántar. Excavaciones en la Galería de las Ofrendas.* Mainz am Rhein: Philipp von Zabern. 461 pp. (Materialien zur Allgemeinen und Vergleichenden Archäologie 51.)

—2007. *Chavín: Excavaciones Arqueológicas.* 1st ed. Lima: Universidad Alas Peruanas. 2 volumes.

MacNeish, Richard S., Angel G. Cook, Luis G. Lumbreras, Robert Vierra, and Antoinette Nelkin-Terner. 1981. *Prehistory of the Ayacucho Basin, Peru.* Volume 2, Excavations and Chronology. Ann Arbor: University of Michigan Press. 279 pp.

Maekawa, Fumio. 1963. Natural environment (II). In: Seiichi Izumi and Toshihiko Sono. *Andes 2: Excavations at Kotosh, Peru, 1960.* Tokyo: Kadokawa Publishing Co. pp. 23–36.

Makowski, Krzysztof. 2009. Poder y estatus social a fines del Periodo Formativo: Los cementerios del valle bajo de Lurín. In: Richard L. Burger and Krzysztof Makowski, eds. *Arqueología del Período Formativo en la Cuenca Baja de Lurín.* Lima: Fondo Editorial, Pontificia Universidad Católica del Perú. pp. 237–282. (Colección Valle de Pachacamac 1.)

Malpass, Michael A., ed. 1993. *Provincial Inca: Archaeological and Ethnohistorical Assessment of the Impact of the Inca State.* Iowa City: University of Iowa Press. 290 pp. https://www.jstor.org /stable/j.ctt20h6sfb.

Mantha, Alexis. 2009. Territoriality, social boundaries and ancestor veneration in the central Andes of Peru. *Journal of Anthropological Archaeology* 28(2):158–176. https://doi.org/10.1016 /j.jaa.2009.02.002.

Matsumoto, Yuichi. 2007. "Use of Ritual Space in the Site of Sajarapatac, Huanuco, Peru"; paper presented at the 47th Annual Meeting of the Institute of Andean Studies; 2007 January 12–13; Berkeley, California.

—2009 [2010]. El manejo del espacio ritual en el sitio de Sajara-patac y sus implicancias para el "fenómeno Chavín." In: Peter Kaulicke and Yoshio Onuki, eds. El Período Formativo: Enfoques y evidencias recientes. Cincuenta años de la Misión Arqueológica Japonesa y su vigencia. *Boletín de Arqueología PUCP* 13(2009):133–158. http://revistas.pucp.edu.pe/index.php /boletindearqueologia/article/view/998.

—2010a. Huallaga gawa jyouryuuiki ni okeru keiseiki no saikentou [Reconsidering the Formative Period in the Upper Huallaga Basin]. *Kodai America [America Antigua]* 13:1–31. [In Japanese.]

—2010b. "The Prehistoric Ceremonial Center of Campanayuq Rumi: Interregional Interactions in the Peruvian South-central Highlands of Peru" [dissertation]. New Haven: Yale University, Department of Anthropology. 602 pp. Order no. 3440573, Dissertations & Theses @ Yale University, ProQuest Dissertations & Theses Global. https://search.proquest.com/docview /847555915?accountid=15172.

Matsumoto, Yuichi, and Yuri Cavero. 2009 [2010]. Una aproximación cronológica del centro ceremonial de Campanayuq Rumi, Ayacucho. In: Peter Kaulicke and Yoshio Onuki, eds. El Período Formativo: Enfoques y evidencias recientes. Cincuenta años de la Misión Arqueológica

Japonesa y su vigencia. *Boletín de Arqueología PUCP* 13(2009):323–346. http://revistas.pucp
.edu.pe/index.php/boletindearqueologia/article/view/1020.

MATSUMOTO, YUICHI, JASON S. NESBITT, AND DENESY PALACIOS JIMÉNEZ. 2012. Mitomarca: A
possible fortification in the Upper Huallaga Basin. Research Reports Andean Past 10. *Andean Past*
10(art. 14):274–279. https://digitalcommons.library.umaine.edu/andean_past/vol10/iss1/14.

MATSUMOTO, YUICHI, AND EISEI TSURUMI. 2011. Archaeological investigations at Sajara-patac
in the Upper Huallaga Basin, Peru. *Ñawpa Pacha* 31(1):55–100. https://doi.org/10.1179
/naw.2011.31.1.55.

MATSUZAWA, TSUGIO. 1972. Constructions. In: Seiichi Izumi and Kazuo Terada, eds. *Andes 4:
Excavations at Kotosh, Peru, 1963 and 1966.* Tokyo: University of Tokyo Press. pp. 55–176.

McCORMAC, F. GERRY, ALLAN G. HOGG, PAUL G. BLACKWELL, CAITLIN E. BUCK, THOMAS F.
G. HIGHAM, AND PAULA J. REIMER. 2004. ShCal04 Southern Hemisphere Calibration, 0-11.0 Cal
Kyr BP. *Radiocarbon* 46(3):1087–1092. https://doi.org/10.1017/S0033822200033014.

MENZEL, DOROTHY. 1964. Style and time in the Middle Horizon. *Ñawpa Pacha* 2(1):1–105.
https://doi.org/10.1179/naw.1964.2.1.001.

MILLER, GEORGE R., AND RICHARD L. BURGER. 1995. Our father the cayman, our dinner the
llama: Animal utilization at Chavín de Huántar, Peru. *American Antiquity* 60(3):421–458.
https://doi.org/10.2307/282258.

MOORE, JERRY D. 2005. *Cultural Landscapes in the Ancient Andes: Archaeologies of Place.*
Gainesville: University Press of Florida. 270 pp.

MORALES, DANIEL C. 1977. "Investigaciones arqueológicas en las Salinas de San Blas (Junín) y
sus implicaciones en el Período Formativo en la Sierra Central del Perú" [bachelor's thesis]. Lima:
Universidad Nacional Mayor de San Marcos. 207 pp.

—1984. Algunos sitios arqueológicos del reino de Guanuco. *Boletín de Lima* 33:87–95.

—1998. Importancia de las Salinas de San Blas durante el Periodo Formativo en la Sierra Central del
Perú. In: Peter Kaulicke, ed. Perspectivas Regionales del Período Formativo en el Perú. *Boletín de
Arqueología PUCP* 2(1998):273–288. http://revistas.pucp.edu.pe/index.php/boletindearqueologia
/article/view/783.

MORRIS, CRAIG, AND DONALD E. THOMPSON. 1985. *Huánuco Pampa: An Inca City and Its
Hinterland.* New York: Thames and Hudson. 288 pp.

MURRA, JOHN V. 1967. La visita de los Chupauchu como fuente etnológica. In: John V. Murra,
ed. *Visita de la Provincia de León de Huánuco en 1562*, Volume 1. Huánuco, Peru: Universidad
Nacional Hermilio Valdizan. pp. 381–406. (Documentos para la Historia y Etnológia Huánuco y
la Selva Central.)

NESBITT, JASON. 2012. "Excavations at Caballo Muerto: An Investigation into the Origins of
the Cupisnique Culture" [dissertation]. New Haven: Yale University, Department of
Anthropology. 461 pp. Order no. 3525307, Dissertations & Theses @ Yale University; ProQuest
Dissertations & Theses Global. https://search.proquest.com/docview/1039318323?account
id=15172.

NESBITT, JASON, BELKYS GUTIÉRREZ, AND SEGUNDO VÁSQUEZ. 2008 [2010]. Excavaciones
en Huaca Cortada, complejo de Caballo Muerto, valle de Moche: un informe preliminar. In:
Peter Kaulicke and Yoshio Onuki, eds. El Período Formativo: Enfoques y evidencias recientes.
Cincuenta años de la Misión Arqueológica Japonesa y su vigencia. *Boletín de Arqueología
PUCP* 12(2008):261–286. http://revistas.pucp.edu.pe/index.php/boletindearqueologia/article/
view/970.

NESBITT, JASON, AND YUICHI MATSUMOTO. 2014. Cupisnique pottery at the south highland site
of Campanayuq Rumi: Implications for late Initial Period interaction. *Peruvian Archaeology*
1:47–58.

NOMLAND, GLADYS AYER. 1939. New archaeological site at San Blas, Junín, Peru. *Revista del
Museo Nacional* 8(1):61–66.

ONUKI, YOSHIO. 1972. Pottery and clay artifacts. In: Seiichi Izumi and Kazuo Terada, eds. *Andes
4: Excavations at Kotosh, Peru, 1963 and 1966.* Tokyo: University of Tokyo Press. pp. 177–248.

—1982. Una perspectiva prehistórica de la utilización ambiental en la Sierra Nor-Central de los Andes centrales. In: Luis Millones and Hiroyasu Tomoeda, eds. *El Hombre y su Ambiente en los Andes Centrales*. Osaka: National Museum of Ethnology. pp. 211–228. (Senri Ethnological Studies 10.) http://doi.org/10.15021/00003385.

—1993. Las actividades ceremoniales tempranas en la Cuenca del Alto Huallaga y algunos problemas generales. In: Luis Millones and Yoshio Onuki, eds. *El Mundo Ceremonial Andino*. Osaka: National Museum of Ethnology. pp. 69–96. (Senri Ethnological Studies 37.)

—1995. ED. *Kuntur Wasi y Cerro Blanco. Dos Sitios del Formativo en el Norte del Perú*. Tokyo: Hakusen-sha. 217 pp.

—1998. Kousa sita te no shinden [Temple of the crossed hands]. In: Yasutake Kato and Yuji Seki, eds. *Bunmei no Souzouryoku: Koodai andes no shinden to shakai* [*Creativity of Civilization: Temples and Societies in the Ancient Andes*]. Tokyo: Kadokawa Shoten. pp. 43–94. [In Japanese.]

—1999 [2000]. El Periodo Arcaico en Huánuco y el concepto del Arcaico. In: Peter Kaulicke, ed. El Periodo Arcaico en el Perú: Hacia una definición de los orígenes. *Boletín de Arqueología PUCP* 3(1999):325–333. http://revistas.pucp.edu.pe/index.php/boletindearqueologia/article/view/2280.

—2002. Japanese research on Andean prehistory. *Japanese Review of Cultural Anthropology* 3(2002):57–78. https://doi.org/10.14890/jrca.3.0_57.

—2014. Una reconsideración de la fase Kotosh Mito. In: Yuji Seki, ed. *El Centro Ceremonial Andino: Nuevas Perspectivas para los Períodos Arcaico y Formativo*. Osaka: National Museum of Ethnology. pp. 105–122. (Senri Ethnological Studies 89.) http://doi.org/10.15021/00002370.

ORTIZ DE ZUÑIGA, IÑIGO. 1967. *Visita de la Provincia de León de Huánuco en 1562*, Volume 1. John V. Murra, ed. Huánuco, Peru: Universidad Nacional Hermilio Valdizan. 436 pp. (Documentos para la Historia y Etnológia Huánuco y la Selva Central.)

—1972. *Visita de la Provincia de León de Huánuco en 1562*, Volume 2. John V. Murra, ed. Huánuco, Peru: Universidad Nacional Hermilio Valdizan. 494 pp. (Documentos para la Historia y Etnológia Huánuco y la Selva Central.)

PALACIOS JIMÉNEZ, DENESY. 1988. Los Kotosh de Huánuco. *Revista Kotosh* 13:32–36.

PARSONS, JEFFREY R., CARLES M. HASTINGS, AND RAMIRO MATOS MENDIETA. 2000. *Prehispanic Settlement Patterns in the Upper Mantaro and Tarma Drainages, Junín, Peru*. Volume 1, The Tarma-Chinchaycocha Region. Ann Arbor: University of Michigan. 537 pp. (Memories of the Museum of Anthropology 34.)

—2013. *Prehispanic Settlement Patterns in the Upper Mantaro, Junín, Peru*. Volume 2, The Wanka Region. Ann Arbor: University of Michigan. 374 pp. (Memoirs of the Museum of Anthropology 53.)

PHILLIPS, PHILIP, AND GORDON R. WILLEY. 1953. Method and theory in American archeology: An operational basis for culture–historical integration. *American Anthropologist* 55(5, pt. 1):615–631. https://www.jstor.org/stable/664720.

POZORSKI, SHELIA, AND THOMAS POZORSKI. 1987. *Early Settlement and Subsistence in the Casma Valley, Peru*. 1st ed. Iowa City: University of Iowa Press. 149 pp.

—2002. The Sechín Alto Complex and its place within Casma Valley Initial Period development. In: William H. Isbell and Helaine Silverman, eds. *Andean Archaeology I: Variations in Sociopolitical Organization*. New York: Kluwer Academic/Plenum Publishers. pp. 21–51. https://doi.org/10.1007/978-1-4615-0639-3_2.

POZORSKI, THOMAS G. 1976. "Caballo Muerto: A Complex of Early Ceramic Sites in the Moche Valley, Peru" [dissertation]. Austin: University of Texas at Austin. 473 pp. Order no. 7626687, ProQuest Dissertations & Theses Global. https://search.proquest.com/docview/288269644?accountid=15172.

—1983. *The Caballo Muerto Complex and Its Place in the Andean Chronological Sequence*. Pittsburgh: Carnegie Museum of Natural History. 40 pp. (Annals of the Carnegie Museum of Natural History 52, art. 1.)

POZORSKI, THOMAS, AND SHELIA POZORSKI. 1990. Huaynuná, a Late Cotton preceramic site on the North Coast of Peru. *Journal of Field Archaeology* 17(1):17–26. https://doi.org/10.1179/009346990791548501.

—1996. Ventilated hearth structures in the Casma Valley, Peru. *Latin American Antiquity* 7(4): 341–353. https://doi.org/10.2307/972263.

PULGAR VIDAL, JAVIER. 1987. *Geografía del Perú: Las Ocho Regiones Naturales del Perú.* 9th ed. Lima: Peisa. 244 pp.

RAVINES, ROGER, JUAN OSSIO, AND HERNANDO NÚÑEZ C. 1964. Busquedas arqueológicas en la Cuenca del Huallaga. *Cuadernos de Antropología* 2(2):31–38.

RENFREW, COLIN. 1982. Polity and power: Interaction, intensification, and exploitation. In: Colin Renfrew and Malcolm Wagstaff, eds. *An Island Polity.* Cambridge: Cambridge University Press. pp. 264–290.

—1986. Introduction: Peer polity interaction and socio-political change. In: Colin Renfrew and John. F. Cherry, eds. *Peer Polity Interaction and Socio-political Change.* Cambridge: Cambridge University Press. pp. 1–18.

RICK, JOHN W., ED. 1980. *Prehistoric Hunters of the High Andes.* New York: Academic Press. 360 pp.

—2005. The evolution of authority and power at Chavín de Huántar, Peru. In: Kevin J. Vaughn, Dennis Ogburn, and Christina A. Conlee, eds. *Foundations of Power in the Prehispanic Andes.* Arlington, VA: American Anthropological Association. pp. 71–89. Imprint date 2004. (Archaeological Papers of the American Anthropological Association 14.) https://doi.org/10.1525 /ap3a.2004.14.071.

—2006 [2008]. Un análisis de los centros ceremoniales del Periodo Formativo a partir de los estudios en Chavín de Huántar. In: Peter Kaulicke and Tom D. Dillehay, eds. Procesos y expresiones de poder, identidad y orden tempranos en Sudamérica. Primera parte. *Boletín de Arqueología PUCP* 10(2006):201–214. http://revistas.pucp.edu.pe/index.php/boletindearqueologia/article /view/1653.

—2008. Context, construction, and ritual in the development of authority at Chavín de Huántar. In: William J. Conklin and Jeffrey Quilter, eds. *Chavín: Art, Architecture and Culture.* Los Angeles: Cotsen Institute of Archaeology Press at UCLA. pp. 3–34. (Monograph 61.) https://doi.org /10.2307/j.ctvdmwx21.7.

RICK, JOHN W., CHRISTIAN MESIA, DANIEL CONTRERAS, SILVIA R. KEMBEL, ROSA M. RICK, MATTHEW SAYRE, AND JOHN WOLF. 2009 [2010]. La cronología de Chavín de Huántar y sus implicancias para el Período Formativo. In: Peter Kaulicke and Yoshio Onuki, eds. El Período Formativo: Enfoques y evidencias recientes. Cincuenta años de la Misión Arqueológica Japonesa y su vigencia. *Boletín de Arqueología PUCP* 13(2009):87–132. http://revistas.pucp.edu.pe/index.php /boletindearqueologia/article/view/984.

ROSAS LA NOIRE, HERMILIO. 2007. *La Secuencia Cultural del Periodo Formativo en Ancón.* Lima: Avqi Ediciones. 384 pp. (Tesis 3.)

ROWE, JOHN HOWLAND. 1957. Archaeological dating and cultural process. *Southwestern Journal of Anthropology* 15(4):317–324. https://doi.org/10.1086/soutjanth.15.4.3628895.

—1962. Stages and periods in archaeological interpretation. *Southwestern Journal of Anthropology* 18(1):40–54. https://www.jstor.org/stable/3629122.

ROZENBERG, CATHERINE. 1982. La Materiel Archeologique de Piruru II: La Collection Louis Girault Universite Hermilio Valtizán-Huánuco-Perú. *Bulletín de l'Institut Français d'Études Andines* 11(3–4):115–141.

SAKAI, MASATO. 1998. Nendaisokuteihou to jiki no kettei [Dating and determination of period]. In: Yasutake Kato and Yuji Seki, eds. *Bummei no Souzouryoku: Koodai andes no shinden to shakai* [*Creativity of Civilization: Temples and Societies in the Ancient Andes*]. Tokyo: Kadokawa Shoten. pp. 316–324. [In Japanese.]

SAKAI, MASATO, AND JUAN J. MARTÍNEZ. 2008 [2010]. Excavaciones en el Templete de Limon-carro, valle bajo de Jequetepeque. In: Peter Kaulicke and Yoshio Onuki, eds. El Período Formativo: Enfoques y evidencias recientes. Cincuenta años de la Misión Arqueológica Japonesa y su vigencia. *Boletín de Arqueología PUCP* 12(2008):171–201. http://revistas.pucp.edu.pe/index.php /boletindearqueologia/article/view/965.

Salcedo Camacho, Luis E., Enrique Molina, Luis E. Cáceres, L. Patricia Habetler, Víctor H. Curay, and Juan Rofes. 2000. Trabajos de puesta en valor en el Complejo Arqueológico Garu. *Revista Desafíos* 1:60–74.

Sánchez Murrugarra, Ricardo, and Denesy Palacios Jiménez. 1988. Garu: Un complejo urbano preincaico. In: Víctor Rangel Flores, ed. *Arquitectura y Arqueología: Pasado y Futuro de la Construcción en el Perú*. Chiclayo, Peru: Universidad de Chiclayo, Museo Brüning. pp. 153–162.

Schreiber, Katharina J. 1999. Regional approaches to the study of prehistoric empires: Examples from Ayacucho and Nasca, Peru. In: Brian R. Billman and Gary M. Feinman, eds. *Settlement Pattern Studies in the Americas: Fifty Years Since Virú*. Washington, DC: Smithsonian Institution Press. pp. 160–171.

—2001. The Wari empire of Middle Horizon Peru: The epistemological challenge of documenting an empire without documentary evidence. In: Susan E. Alcock, Terrence N. D'Altroy, Kathleen D. Morrison, and Carla M. Sinopoli, eds. *Empires: Perspectives from Archaeology and History*. 1st ed. New York: Cambridge University Press. pp. 70–72.

Seki, Yuji. 2014. La diversidad del poder en la sociedad del Periodo Formativo: Una perspectiva desde la sierra norte. In: Yuji Seki, ed. *El Centro Ceremonial Andino: Nuevas Perspectivas para los Períodos Arcaico y Formativo*. Osaka: National Museum of Ethnology. pp. 175–200. (Senri Ethnological Studies 89.) http://doi.org/10.15021/00002373.

Seki, Yuji, and Masato Sakai. 1998. Sei naru Oka [Sacred hill]. In: Yasukata Kato and Yuji Seki, eds. *Bunmei no Souzouryoku: Koodai andes no shinden to shakai* [*Creativity of Civilization: Temples and Societies in the Ancient Andes*]. Tokyo: Kadokawa Shoten. pp. 95–162. [In Japanese.]

Seki, Yuji, Juan Pablo Villanueva, Masato Sakai, Diana Alemán, Mauro Ordóñez, Walter Tosso, Araceli Espinoza, Kinya Inokuchi, and Daniel Morales. 2008 [2010]. Nuevas evidencias del sitio arqueológico de Pacopampa, en la sierra norte del Perú. In: Peter Kaulicke and Yoshio Onuki, eds. El Período Formativo: Enfoques y evidencias recientes. Cincuenta años de la Misión Arqueológica Japonesa y su vigencia. *Boletín de Arqueología PUCP* 12(2008):69–95. http://revistas.pucp.edu.pe/index.php/boletindearqueologia/article/view/851.

Shady, Ruth. 2003. Caral-Supe y la Costa Norcentral del Perú: La cuna de la civilización andina y formación del estado prístino. In: Ruth Shady and Carlos Leyva, eds. *La Ciudad Sagrada del Caral-Supe: Los Orígenes de la Civilización Andina y la Formación del Estado Pristino en el Antiguo Perú*. Lima: Instituto Nacional de Cultura. pp. 139–46.

—2006 [2008]. La civilización Caral: Sistema social y manejo del territorio y sus recursos: Su trascendencia en el proceso cultural andino. In: Peter Kaulicke and Tom D. Dillehay, eds. Procesos y expresiones de poder, identidad y orden tempranos en Sudamérica. Primera parte. *Boletín de Arqueología PUCP* 10(2006):59–89. http://revistas.pucp.edu.pe/index.php/boletindearqueologia/article/view/1642.

Shady, Ruth, and Carlos Leyva, eds. 2003. *La Ciudad Sagrada de Caral-Supe: Los Orígenes de la Civilización Andina y la Formación del Estado Prístino en el Antiguo Perú*. Lima: Instituto Nacional de Cultura. 342 pp.

Shady, Ruth, and Marco Machacuay. 2003. El altar del fuego sagrado del templo mayor de la ciudad sagrada de Caral-Supe. In: Ruth Shady and Carlos Leyva, eds. *La Ciudad Sagrada del Caral-Supe: Los Orígenes de la Civilización Andina y la Formación del Estado Prístino en el Antiguo Perú*. Lima: Instituto Nacional de Cultura, Proyecto Especial Arqueológico Caral-Supe. pp. 169–185.

Shady Solis, Ruth. 2014. La civilización Caral: Paisaje cultural y sistema social. In: Yuji Seki, ed. *El Centro Ceremonial Andino: Nuevas Perspectivas para los Períodos Arcaico y Formativo*. Osaka: National Museum of Ethnology. pp. 51–103. (Senri Ethnological Studies 89.) http://doi.org/10.15021/00002369.

Shady Solis, Ruth, Jonathan Haas, and Winifred Creamer. 2001. Dating Caral, a preceramic site in the Supe Valley on the central coast of Peru. *Science* 292(5517):723–726. http://www.jstor.org/stable/3083548.

Shimada, Izumi. 2006. Comments on "Crucible of Andean civilization: The Peruvian coast from 3000 to 1800 BC" by Jonathan Haas and Winifred Creamer. *Current Anthropology* 47(5):761–762. http://doi.org/10.1086/506281.

SILVA, JORGE E. 1996. "Prehistoric Settlement Patterns in the Chillón River Valley, Peru" [dissertation]. Ann Arbor: University of Michigan, Department of Anthropology. 1,256 pp. Order No. 9635611, ProQuest Dissertations & Theses Global. https://search.proquest.com/docview /304247207?accountid=15172.

SILVERMAN, HELAINE. 2002. *Ancient Nasca Settlement and Society.* Iowa City: University of Iowa Press. 224 pp.

TAYLOR, ROYAL E. 1987. *Radiocarbon Dating: An Archaeological Perspective.* 1st ed. Orlando, FL: Academic Press. 212 pp.

TELLO, JULIO C. 1943. Discovery of the Chavín culture in Peru. *American Antiquity* 9(1):135–160. https://doi.org/10.2307/275457.

—1960. *Chavín, cultura matriz de la civilización andina (primera parte).* Lima: Universidad Nacional Mayor de San Marcos. 425 pp. (Publicación Antropológica del Archivo Julio C. Tello 2.)

TERADA, KAZUO. 1972. Conclusions. In: Seiichi Izumi and Kazuo Terada, eds. *Andes 4: Excavations at Kotosh, Peru, 1963 and 1966.* Tokyo: University of Tokyo Press. pp. 303–312.

TERADA, KAZUO, AND YOSHIO ONUKI. 1982. *Excavations at Huacaloma in the Cajamarca Valley, Peru, 1979.* Tokyo: University of Tokyo Press. 351 pp. (Report 2 of the Japanese Scientific Expedition to Nuclear America.)

—1988. *Las excavaciones en Cerro Blanco y Huacaloma, Cajamarca, Perú, 1985.* Tokyo: Andes Chosashitsu, Departamento de Antropología Cultural, Universidad de Tokio. 47 pp.

—1985. *The Formative Period in the Cajamarca Basin, Peru: Excavations at Huacaloma and Layzón, 1982.* Tokyo: University of Tokyo Press. 345 pp. (Report 3 of the Japanese Scientific Expedition to Nuclear America.)

THOMAS, R. BROOKE. 1973. *Human Adaptation to a High Andean Energy Flow System.* University Park, PA: Pennsylvania State University. 181 pp. (Occasional Papers in Anthropology 7.)

—1976. Energy flow at high altitude. In: Paul T. Baker and Michael A. Little, eds. *Man in the Andes: A Multidisciplinary Study of High-Altitude Quechua.* Stroudsburg: Dowden, Hutchinson and Ross. pp. 379–404. (US/IBP Synthesis Series 1.)

THOMPSON, DONALD E. 1967. Investigaciones arqueológicas en las Aldeas Chupachu de Ichu y Auquimarca. In: John V. Murra, ed. *Visita de la Provincia de León de Huánuco en 1562.* Volume 1. Huánuco, Peru: Universidad Nacional Hermilio Valdizan. pp. 357–367. (Documentos para la Historia y Etnológia Huánuco y la Selva Central.)

TOPIC, JOHN R. 1991. Huari and Huamachuco. In: William H. Isbell and Gordon F. McEwan, eds. *Huari Administrative Structure: Prehistoric Monumental Architecture and State Government.* Washington, DC: Dumbarton Oaks Research Library and Collection. pp. 141–164.

TOPIC, JOHN, AND THERESA LANGE TOPIC. 1987. The archaeological investigation of Andean militarism: Some cautionary observations. In: Jonathan Haas, Shelia Pozorski, and Thomas Pozorski, eds. *The Origins and Development of the Andean State.* pp. 47–55. Cambridge: Cambridge University Press. (New Directions in Archaeology.)

TOPIC, JOHN R., THERESA TOPIC, AND ALFREDO MELLY CAVA. 2002. Catequil: The archaeology, ethnohistory, and ethnography of a major provincial Huaca. In: William H. Isbell and Helaine Silverman, eds. *Andean Archaeology I: Variations in Sociopolitical Organization.* New York: Kluwer Academic/Plenum. pp. 303–336. https://doi.org/10.1007/978-1-4615-0639-3_11.

TOPIC, THERESA LANGE, AND JOHN R. TOPIC. 2010. Contextualizing the Wari-Huamachuco relationship. In: Justin Jennings, ed. *Beyond Wari Walls: Regional Perspectives on Middle Horizon Peru.* Albuquerque: University of New Mexico Press. pp. 188–212.

TOSI JR., JOSEPH A. 1960. *Zonas de Vida Natural en el Perú: Memoria Explicativa Sobre El Mapa Ecológico del Perú.* Lima: Instituto Interamericano de Ciencias Agrícolas de la OEA, Zona Andina. 271 pp.

TSURUMI, EISEI. 2008 [2010]. La secuencia cronológica de los centros ceremoniales de la Pampa de las Hamacas y Tembladera, valle medio de Jequetepeque. In: Peter Kaulicke and Yoshio Onuki, eds. El Período Formativo: Enfoques y evidencias recientes. Cincuenta años de la Misión

Arqueológica Japonesa y su vigencia. *Boletín de Arqueología PUCP* 12(2008):141–169. http://revistas.pucp.edu.pe/index.php/boletindearqueologia/article/view/964.

UNKEL, INGMAR, MARKUS REINDEL, HERMANN GORBAHN, JOHNY A. ISLA CUADRADO, BERND KROMER, AND VOLKER SOSSNA. 2012. A comprehensive numerical chronology for the pre-Columbian cultures of the Palpa valleys, south coast of Peru. *Journal of Archaeological Science* 39(7):2294–2303. https://doi.org/10.1016/j.jas.2012.02.021.

WATANABE, SHINYA. 2012 [2014]. Sociopolitical dynamics and cultural continuity in the Peruvian northern highlands: A case study from Middle Horizon Cajamarca. In: Los rostros de Wari: Perspectivas interregionales sobre el horizonte medio. *Boletín de Arqueología PUCP* 16(2012):105–129. http://revistas.pucp.edu.pe/index.php/boletindearqueologia/article/view/9166.

WILLEY, GORDON R. 1945. Horizon styles and pottery traditions in Peruvian archaeology. *American Antiquity* 11(1):49–56. https://doi.org/10.2307/275530.

—1953. *Prehistoric Settlement Patterns in the Virú Valley, Peru.* Washington, DC: US Government Printing Office. 453 pp. (Bureau of American Ethnology Bulletin 155.)

WILLEY, GORDON R., AND PHILIP PHILLIPS. 1958. *Method and Theory in American Archaeology.* Chicago: University of Chicago Press. 269 pp.

WILLEY, GORDON R., AND AVIS TULLOCH. 1971. *An Introduction to American Archaeology.* Volume 2, South America. Englewood Cliffs, NJ: Prentice-Hall. 559 pp.

WILSON, DAVID J. 1988. *Prehispanic Settlement Patterns in the Lower Santa Valley, Peru: A Regional Perspective on the Origins and Development of Complex North Coast Society.* Washington, DC: Smithsonian Institution Press. 590 pp.

WING, ELIZABETH S. 1972. Appendix 4, Utilization of animal resources in the Peruvian Andes. In: Seiichi Izumi and Kazuo Terada, eds. *Andes 4: Excavations at Kotosh, Peru, 1963 and 1966.* Tokyo: University of Tokyo Press. pp. 327–352.

ZIÓŁKOWSKI MARIUSZ S., MIECZYSŁAW F. PAZDUR, ANDRZEJ KRZANOWSKI, AND ADAM MICHCZYŃSKI. 1994. *Andes: Radiocarbon Database for Bolivia, Ecuador and Peru.* Warszawa: Andean Archaeological Mission of the Institute of Archaeology, Warsaw University. 604 pp.

INDEX